# FOUNDING FATHERS

# FOUNDING FATHERS
## BRIEF LIVES OF THE FRAMERS OF THE UNITED STATES CONSTITUTION

*Second Edition, Revised*

## M. E. BRADFORD

FOREWORD BY RUSSELL KIRK

UNIVERSITY PRESS OF KANSAS

Originally published in 1982 under the title *A Worthy Company* by the Plymouth Rock Foundation, these biographical sketches of the Framers were revised and reprinted in Volume 2 of *Jonathan Elliot's Debates in the Several State Conventions on the Adoption of the Federal Constitution*, edited by James McClellan and M. E. Bradford and published by James River Press. This newly revised and enlarged edition of the sketches is published by arrangement with the author and Plymouth Rock Foundation.

Published by the University Press of Kansas (Lawrence, Kansas 66049), which was organized by the Kansas Board of Regents and is operated and funded by Emporia State University, Fort Hays State University, Kansas State University, Pittsburg State University, the University of Kansas, and Wichita State University

Library of Congress Cataloging-in-Publication Data

Bradford, M. E. (Melvin E.), 1934–1993
    Founding Fathers : brief lives of the framers of the United States
Constitution / M. E. Bradford ; foreword by Russell Kirk.—2d ed.,
rev.
        p.    cm.
    Originally published in 1982 under the title A Worthy Company by
the Plymouth Rock Foundation, Inc.
    Includes bibliographical references and index.
    ISBN 0-7006-0656-4—ISBN 0-7006-0657-2 (pbk.)
    1. Statesmen—United States—Biography.   2. United States—
Politics and government—1783–1789.   3. United States—
Constitutional history.   4. United States—Constitution—Signers—
Biography.   I. Title.   II. Title: Worthy company.
E302.5.B74   1994
973.3'092'2—dc20                                              93-20982
    [B]

Printed in the United States of America
10 9 8 7 6 5 4 3
The paper used in this publication meets the minimum requirements of the American National Standard for Permanence of Paper for Printed Library Materials Z39.48-1984.

In Memory of John P. East
Late United States Senator
from North Carolina

# CONTENTS

# FOREWORD

During little more than a decade, the late M. E. Bradford published seven volumes, consisting chiefly of his essays, from *A Better Guide Than Reason: Studies in the American Revolution* to *Original Intentions: On the Making and Ratification of the United States Constitution,* published after his death in 1993. Also, he wrote a number of important pamphlets during the same period, engaged in much scholarly editing, and reviewed several significant books. In the midst of these chores, he took a hand in Texas politics and lectured widely. His work, together with that of Forrest McDonald, James McClellan, Ellis Sandoz, and a few other recent scholars, has much improved our understanding of the formative era of the republic and of America's political and cultural history down to the present.

Dr. Bradford died at the age of fifty-eight. He was a wise, good-natured, life-loving man, so impressive as to be almost overwhelming in height and bulk, as much at home in the discipline of humane letters as in that of American history. His books will endure a great while.

He was very much a southerner, which caused him to be detested by various of the denizens of New York City. His mentor was Donald Davidson, whose biography Bradford had been writing for some years but which remains unfinished now. Clyde Wilson, editor of Calhoun's papers, writes:

> Those who hoped that the Southern tradition was moribund have received a stunning setback in the career of Bradford. No scholar of our time has affirmed the positive value of that bond with greater energy, regularity, and persistence. Bradford's deliberate confrontation of the modern "vision of mind as the proper model of society," by a defense of the traditional ground of the South, has been carried out for three decades now with great skill on the unfriendly terrain of modern academic discourse. . . . The measure of Bradford's achievement is the headway he has made against impossible odds— an unexpected feat of intellectual virtuosity that has guaranteed the survival of the intellectual defense of Southern tradition into the twenty-first century.

Bradford's national reputation is founded upon his painstaking and accurate scholarship—and upon his rhetorical skill as well. In this present volume, *Founding Fathers,* he has delved deeply into the abundant correspondence of the fifty-five Framers at Philadelphia and into the letters of many of the delegates to state ratifying conventions, too. In general, American historians have been daunted by the tremendous task of fighting their way through antique printed collections of politicians' letters and through thousands of holograph letters, uncollected, in dusty archives and private hands, but Mel Bradford was possessed of fortitude and a desire to write *real* history. He knew that there is no better way to ascertain the much-debated "original intent" of the Framers than to pass beyond the somewhat meager journals of the Convention, and beyond *The Federalist Papers,* to the labyrinthine treasury of letters the Framers wrote home or to one another.

His brief lives of the Founding Fathers, free of ideological prejudices, tell us the sort of delegates those fifty-five were: gentlemen, with few exceptions, attached to precedent and custom, prescription and "ancient constitutions." Those colonial gentlemen, so very British, were not in the least inclined to destroy the prevailing pattern of American society. More fully than most commentators upon those Framers, Bradford has carefully examined their several religious persuasions or affiliations, discovering few Deists or unchurched.

His studies led him to respect particularly John Dickinson, "penman of the Revolution," an American disciple of Burke's school, neglected by biographers and political theorists almost until the present. Bradford held in lowest esteem the clever James Wilson, canny Scot, egalitarian Federalist. It seems curious that it has been a great while since any comparable examination of the lives and opinions of the Framers has been published. *Founding Fathers* presumably will remain the basic manual, in succinct compass, for decades to come. He makes it clear that in general the Framers, most conspicuously Dickinson, repudiating coffeehouse abstractions, followed a better guide than the Enlightenment's Reason. As Patrick Henry (an especial hero of Bradford's) had put it, "I have but one lamp by which my feet are guided, and that is the lamp of experience."

Mel and I corresponded frequently and contrived to meet at least once a year. At our last meeting, near Dallas, he told my wife that maintaining his physical existence had become a considerable burden for him. He had fought the good fight, had been much loved, and will not soon be forgotten.

Professor Bradford was no *Neo*conservative; that breed, indeed, did him as much mischief as they could in Washington circles. Rather, he was a guardian of what T. S. Eliot called the Permanent Things. In November 1992, speaking at the University of the South (founded by champions of what became the Lost Cause), he sketched the true conservative's duties:

> Because man is a fallen, contingent creature of a certain constant
> nature, and because he does not always agree to such simple proposi-

tions concerning himself, the work of the conservative in any civilized society (one that does premise the aforementioned truths) is like that of the groundskeeper of any good property: keeping the grass cut, the hedges trimmed, the staff trained and all of the holdings under observation, including the plants and animals to be found there. Or if not a groundskeeper, then a steward who serves an absent master—a steward who has a share in the patrimony which will derive from the estate now in his keeping. Something is thus *conserved*. And some art is required in such preservation—husbandry, in statecraft, in trade, in finance, in priestcraft and in teaching: those ends for the sake of which the conservative practices politics in the first place.

Endowed with a powerful sense of humor and a keen perception of reality, Bradford was so good an expositor of the views and lives of the Founding Fathers because he looked and thought much like a Founder himself. In literature as in politics, he spoke as one having authority. In this age of anxiety, many students at the University of Dallas found in Professor Bradford the kindly sage they had vaguely sought: a man of learning who was no mere sophist and certainly no ideologue; not one who adhered confidently to truths not yet discovered yesterday. To converse with him, some of them found, was rather like walking with Confucius in Lu; for as did Confucius, so M. E. Bradford, never a neoterist or an egoist, repeatedly appealed to immemorial wisdom and the long-filtered experience of a people—better guides than Reason.

This volume is no polemic: it is a sober and painstaking examination of the background, the mentality, and the interests of the fifty-five practical statesmen of the Philadelphia Convention, judiciously regarded. Amid present ferment about deconstruction, multiculturalism, and other fads and foibles of the academy, this study by a "groundskeeper" of the American intellectual and social order will wake some minds and hearts of the rising generation.

How much perceptive learning Bradford compresses into these sketches! Although John Adams and Thomas Jefferson—the two most eminent Americans in political thought that year—were abroad at the time of the Constitutional Convention, nevertheless there gathered at Philadelphia in 1787 such men of mark as could not well be assembled in any convention near the end of the twentieth century. Bradford conjures up men too seldom mentioned in college textbooks—I think especially of his portrait of Roger Sherman, "shoemaker, surveyor, jurist, lay theologian, and statesman"—and describes their strong influence at the Great Convention and later. Bradford's evocative power puts flesh again upon what many young people of our day had taken for mere dry constitutional bones.

RUSSELL KIRK

# INTRODUCTION

The following biographical sketches are of the lives of the Framers of the U.S. Constitution who were present in Philadelphia during some part of the Great Convention. They are arranged in the sequence observed in the signing of the instrument they produced there: from North to South, New Hampshire to Georgia.

Insofar as available information has made it possible, the emphasis in each of the sketches is upon the individual Framer's constitutional theory, on the variety of Union he hoped to see created, and his reasons for favoring or disapproving particular components of the draft under consideration. I have also attempted to see each man against a backdrop of the community he represented and to view his life in the round, working from a general evaluative statement to a description of his career prior to 1787 to a gloss on his role in the Great Convention and then to final observations on his post-Convention experience. In this way I touch upon the professional, personal, economic, and intellectual lives of this "company of notables." An effort has been made to represent these men in their own language where important questions are at stake and to give the reader some indication of the special coloring or flavor of their distinctive personalities—in a limited way to follow the example of Plutarch, the favorite classical author of early Americans. The bibliographical notes at the end of each sketch are selective but should assist the reader in learning more about the life of the subject and especially about his politics in the late spring and summer of 1787.

The members of the Constitutional Convention were men of the eighteenth century, but of the English and Scottish Enlightenment, not the French. They acted within corporate bonds, out of the momentum of a civilization already more than a thousand years old when the United States achieved independence. It is easy to forget how homogeneous a nation this was in the beginning, apart from the slaves. Despite differences of region and religion, of wealth and class, Americans were even more united in culture than in blood. True enough, the great divisions that had riven English society since the 1640s and the period of the Commonwealth continued, and because of them Americans were brought eventually to fight a civil war. But Americans had not struggled through the Revolution to cut themselves off from their inherited cultural identity as a distinctive offshoot of English history, nor had they come to Philadelphia to drive such a wedge between their present and their past. Their task, rather, was one of preservation and of such innovations as were necessary if a known and cherished world was to be handed on intact to their posterity. They were not men who were speculative in their politics. With the possible exceptions of Madison, Hamilton, Wilson, and young Charles Pinckney III, they were prescriptive Whigs who had made a revolution on the model of the Glorious Revolution of 1688—in order to continue as they were.

The majority of the Framers were for their time well-educated men. Their discourse was of history (British, Roman, American, biblical, and to a lesser extent, European), of law, and of the recent unhappy experience of their countrymen under the Articles of Confederation. Their purpose in revising the government was, not to invent the "best city" of the philosophers, but to raise a revenue, retire the public debt, establish a sound currency, remove trade barriers among the states, secure domestic order, and provide for the common defense. As many as thirty-five of the fifty-five Framers were slaveholders. Most were either wealthy or comfortably situated, though many were weighed down by the damage done to their holdings by the war, by speculation, and by an uncertain economy. Several had great plantations, and most had considerable property. Nine or ten had large-scale commercial experience, and others were successful merchants. More than half of them had had some experience in the legal profession, either as attorney or as judge. And although only five or six could be called aristocrats, most held a place in the gentry of their own states and were present in the Convention because their neighbors recognized that they were the kind of "natural aristocrats" who were most properly trusted with the responsibilities of government.

In addition, with no more than five exceptions, they were orthodox members of one of the established Christian communions. An internal transformation of American society in the direction of a secularized egalitarian state was the furthest thing from the minds of these men. The majority of them were committed to representative government, to the continued existence of the sovereign states, and to a dependence upon the virtue of the people acting as independent political, economic, and moral agents as the best security for the hope of a common future. But they also believed in the imperfection of human nature and had no patience with the notion that men were essentially good or that institutions were the culprit in the darker chapters of history. Those among the Framers who nodded conventionally toward the theory of natural rights belonging to some aboriginal presocial state would in most cases have agreed that such a hypothetical condition would have been an unpleasant experience, "nasty, brutish, and short." They were closer to Hobbes than to Rousseau. Man, they recognized, was made to live in society and under government, out of providential necessity.

In the place of a prince and an arbitrary Parliament, which had denied them the rights of Englishmen, they worked to establish a federal system of checks and balances under a sovereign law. Yet they were wise enough to realize that if a government tried to enforce laws to cover every situation, that government would eventually become a tyranny more dreadful than anything attempted by George III. Hence, they were careful to limit the fundamental scope of the law itself, leaving what they called "internal police" and many of the great questions concerning value and faith to the regulation of state and local governments and to the operation of society itself. The world of eighteenth-century America was a realm including many social, political, and religious establishments. The neutrality of government with respect to their interactions was not the neutrality of indifference that would permit the destruction of society.

With regard to the public experience of the members of the Philadelphia Convention in the course of their political careers, we can make some useful generalizations. For one thing, there was no anomaly in the selection of this particular group to serve as delegates. Thirty-six of the fifty-five had been members of the Continental or Confederation Congresses. Most of them had been or were to be called upon repeatedly by their neighbors and peers to fill other offices of trust. Twenty were at one time governors of states; twenty were to become U.S. senators; thirteen, members of the House of Representatives; eight, federal judges. Washington and Madison would become president of the United States, and Elbridge Gerry, vice-president. Several would serve as diplomats representing the republic overseas. Others would hold cabinet posts. Their total political experience at the state and national levels is so great as to suggest that as a company they are a dependable barometer of American attitudes and beliefs at the close of the eighteenth century: in the important things resembling most of their countrymen but more capable of making the necessary political discriminations that would "preserve, protect, and defend" the common good.

The differences of opinion that separated the Framers (and there were some) had to do with such questions as the proper method for counting the census and determining taxes and proportions of strength in the Congress, and the possibilities of a tariff and a navigation act, the development of western lands, regulations concerning impeachment and the executive veto, enforcing the sanctity of contracts and (as opposed to the future existence of slavery as an institution) the extension of the slave trade. With reference to most of these concerns, they *expected* to make compromises, working out of a good will for one another fostered in the common experience of winning their national independence. On the other hand, concerning the future of the several states as in some ways still sovereign entities, there was a hard fight. The extreme nationalists, represented by Madison, Hamilton, George Read, James Wilson, and Gouverneur Morris, wished to reduce the states as far as possible, to deny them equal representation in both houses of the Congress, and to give the general government a right to review and veto all state legislation. They were forestalled by the middle group in the Convention who acted in concert with a few

Antifederalists who were not certain they wished to go beyond the revision of the Articles of Confederation, the official mandate that had brought them together. The little drama began with the initiative of the nationalists as embodied in a Virginia Plan. After some debate an adversary entered the lists in the person of the canny William Paterson and his "small state" or New Jersey Plan. Complication ensued, followed by stasis, hot weather, and some very hot tempers. At this point there was a recess for the Fourth of July, and with the report from the Great Committee (made up of one member from each of the states represented), the sensible center of the Convention took control: such men as Roger Sherman and Oliver Ellsworth, John Rutledge, William Richardson Davie, and William Samuel Johnson. From that time onward, the drama moved steadily toward resolution.

Once the Constitution had been signed, many members of the Convention continued to worry about the scope of the powers granted to the new federal government and the way in which those powers might be expanded to benefit one part of the Union at the expense of another, one class of citizens in power at the cost of the liberty and property of their less organized countrymen. Finally, the Antifederalists emerged as two varieties of confirmed opponents of ratification of the proposed Constitution: old-fashioned Whigs who thought that the Revolution had been fought to preserve the autonomy of local communities from the designs of a remote and arbitrary power; and those who wanted fiat money, a moratorium on the payment of debt, and direct democracy. Both types of Antifederalists demanded that a bill of rights be included or added to the Constitution to replace the guarantees of liberty and property they had enjoyed under English law.

In contrast there were at least four kinds of Federalists. One group was separated in politics from the Antifederalists only in that they saw in the Constitution, or in the Constitution *with* a bill of rights, none of the perils at which their antagonists took alarm. They were simply sanguine men who had, amid the fires of revolution, developed a confidence in certain American leaders and their view of republicanism based on service rendered during the Revolutionary War. They trusted George Washington and did not look beyond him. By 1798 many of them were ready for Thomas Jefferson.

A second species of commitment to the new enterprise of a "more perfect union" can be thought of as a federalism of fear. It had three branches or subspecies. The first is best defined by reaction to Shays' Rebellion in Massachusetts and to related but lesser upheavals in several of the other states. This federalism issued from a horror of anarchy and the leveling mob. Confusion about property rights, laxness in law enforcement, resistance to tax policy, and violations of the minimum standards of civility drove many Americans (not all of them wealthy) who saw in New England the growing shadow of radicalism to look to a national power, an "energetic" government, for a negative on the forces of disruption. However, no national commitment to civil liberties or equal rights was a part of their concern, but instead a preservation of things as they were. Indeed, the same basically localist, status quo position was maintained by most of the frightened Federalists, including the members of the two other subspecies: the numerous military Federalists who feared the incapacity of the states to resist external threats; and the Federalists who were already concerned about the dangers of an American civil war should the chance of forging lasting bonds pass by forfeit.

The third group of Federalists I think of as the "wealth and power" men, though I have generally used the phraseology "commercial Federalists." Robert Morris was often their spokesman, or Nathaniel Gorham of Massachusetts. Many were merchants and speculators. They saw in the federal system a vehicle for what the English political philosopher Michael Oakeshott called the "enterprise association" theory of the state—and saw also for themselves a good place in the business. In the ratifying conventions James Wilson of Pennsylvania put their case. With the glamour of wealth, he began the great address, which is almost all we have from that state's proceedings, and from that theme he rarely strayed:

> For my own part, I have been often lost in astonishment at the vastness of the prospect before us. To open the navigation of a single river was lately thought, in Europe, an enterprise equal to imperial glory. But could the commercial scenes of the Scheldt be compared with those that, under a good government, will be exhibited on the Hudson, the Delaware, the Potomac, and the numerous other rivers, that water and are intended to enrich the dominions of the United States?

To the same effect Oliver Ellsworth of Connecticut described grants of authority and money to the central power as an "investment" whose value was to be calculated with a view to "returns." In the eyes of these Federalists the purpose of the state was commercial. Its job was to build canals, promote industry, and ensure the fulfillment of contracts—to assist in accumulating wealth.

The fourth group of Federalists as defined by circumstance was the "everlasting glory" men. Hamilton was the leader of these bolder spirits. His interest in the economic well-being of the country had its referent in the purpose he expected such prosperity to serve. These Federalists looked to the mark the new republic would make in the pages of history. They were the would-be favorites of fortune, the servants of the Zeitgeist. Their preferred idiom was military and imperial and their patriotism Bonapartist. Though they might encourage science, education, immigration, business, or agriculture, it was always with the larger "manifest destiny" of Americans as a unified force in mind that they defined these private enterprises as worthwhile.

The fifty-five Americans who had a share in drafting the U.S. Constitution and who then communicated it to the people of the states for rejection or approval were aware of the momentous implications of their task. The responsibilities of citizenship were, they recognized, part of their moral obligation. Even more serious were the duties of the ruler and magistrate, who would be held accountable to a higher authority for the use they made of their special powers. Yet on the whole they enjoyed the work and found in it the kind of high adventure that belongs to the lawgiver as opposed to the warrior, the poet, and the saint. Out of this complex of motives for and against the Constitution, we can construct a key to the subsequent course of American history. They regarded the Union as conditional, an "experiment" in George Washington's terms, and knew that it would require work and minor revision if the fundamental law was to operate as they hoped—but not too much revision or too often. Nevertheless, they meant for their form of government to last, and most of them were confident that it would, so long as it was not manipulated out of shape by ideology or human selfishness. They were not demigods and they did not "invent" their country. But assuredly the passage of time has earned for them the right to be called a worthy company, a term of praise they would have clearly understood.

A few caveats and words of explanation seem called for. The fifty-five men who took part in the deliberations at Philadelphia in 1787 were not, in a strict sense, the "authors" of the Constitution: they wrote it, but it was the delegates to the state ratification conventions who, in their capacity as representatives of the people of each state considered separately, put the stamp of authority upon it. Their work had as much to do with the meaning of the entire process of making the Constitution as did that of the statesmen treated here, but they are best examined elsewhere, in the setting where they gave our fundamental law their imprimatur.

Not only have I restricted myself to the fifty-five Framers, I have devoted many more words to some of them than to others. The principles of allocation were two: importance and the availability of information. James Madison, for instance, obviously had a far greater impact upon the framing than did, say, Jacob Broom of Delaware. Obviously, too, Madison left a huge corpus of correspondence and other writing to posterity, whereas we have of Broom only occasional scraps. To have given the two men equal time, as it were, would be a distortion. On a related matter, I have included tangential materials only when, in my judgment, they were relevant or necessary to an understanding of my subjects. For example, two of the delegates were Roman Catholics, and in several colonies that would earlier have precluded their taking part in government. But it would scarcely be appropriate to discuss here the history of colonial religious laws.

I have included no documentary annotation. Confirmation of what I have written, however, is to be found in the documents and studies cited in the bibliographies following each sketch. On a few occasions the sources conflict with one another in regard to dates of birth. When the sources disagree, I have usually followed the dates given in the *Dictionary of American Biography.*

This book was first published in 1982 by the Plymouth Rock Foundation. I have since updated and revised both text and bibliography and purged it of such errors that I found (or were called to my attention by others) in the original. The present University Press of Kansas edition is aimed at keeping in print a reference book which, for whatever flaws it may have, is the only work of its kind.

One final comment. I have tried to be objective both in tone and in substance. I know I have not entirely succeeded. Some of the Framers appeal to me more than others; the ideas of some are more akin to mine than others. But on the whole, I think I can fairly say that there is less of me in this book than in anything else I have written. I have striven to make it disinterested, so as to serve those who want to understand who the Founding Fathers were.

I wish to thank especially Ellen McDonald and Forrest McDonald for their considerable help in making this edition possible. For encouragement, advice, and support I am indebted also to Russell Kirk, James McClellan, Rus Walton, Clyde Wilson, Kenneth Cribb, Boyd Cathey, Eileen Gregory, and my wife, Marie. I appreciate very much the generous assistance of Megan Schoeck, production editor of the University Press of Kansas; and that of Karen Webb and Deanna Norwood, who helped in the preparation of the revised manuscript. I also acknowledge, with gratitude, financial support from the Kemper Educational and Charitable Fund, the Earhart Foundation, the Marguerite Eyer Wilbur Foundation, Liberty Fund, and the Henry Salvatori Foundation.

# NEW HAMPSHIRE

## JOHN LANGDON

June 26, 1741–September 18, 1819
Merchant, soldier, and political leader

*One of the two most important figures of his state at the time of the Constitutional Convention. A moderate commercial Federalist with a genuine popular touch. Greatly loved by the people of his state, of whose values he was an epitome. A local-minded Federalist with no vision of the magical benefits of an energetic national government and no loyalty to a union that did not derive from his loyalty to a state and a particular community. Son of John and Mary Hall Langdon, great-grandson of Tobias Langdon of Portsmouth. Educated in the grammar schools of that community, on Yankee merchant ships, and as a clerk in one of the great mercantile houses in the West Indian trade. Soon in business on his own. A man of considerable property when the Revolution broke out. One of the first of the established members of his community to act against British authority and to risk his wealth in the struggle for liberty.*

John Langdon sat on the New Hampshire Committee of Correspondence and on another committee responsible for enforcing regulations against importations. In 1774, he led his neighbors in the seizure and confiscation of munitions from the British fort in their harbor. He was elected to the New Hampshire Assembly in 1775 and was made speaker of that body. The General Court in 1775 and 1776 appointed Langdon as a delegate to the Continental Congress. In 1776 he was elected colonel of the New Hampshire militia and in the following year served in the campaign against Gen. John Burgoyne that resulted in the British surrender at Saratoga, New York. Because of his zeal in the patriot cause, his investment of his person and his means in the struggle for independence, and his work in building ships for an American navy and as an agent for British prizes captured at sea, he became a popular man in his state.

From 1777 to 1781, he was speaker of the New Hampshire legislature. In

1784, he was elected for another term in the Congress, but he declined to serve. In 1784, he was state senator, and in 1785, he became the president of his state. In 1786–1787, he was again chosen speaker of the legislature while New Hampshire's most famous soldier and patriot, Gen. John Sullivan, served two terms as the state's chief executive. During General Sullivan's administration, while the legislature was in session at Exeter in September 1786, New Hampshire experienced its version of Shays' Rebellion, a riot by a mob of disaffected men who surrounded the meeting of the General Court and Senate, demanded an "emission of paper money, an equal distribution of property, and release from debts." President Sullivan, with the militia at his back, dispersed these insurgents in an almost bloodless battle. But it was against the backdrop of their uprising that the New Hampshire legislature dispatched John Langdon and young Nicholas Gilman (a supporter of General Sullivan) to sit with the Constitutional Convention in Philadelphia and to continue from there to the next session of the Confederation Congress, bearing tidings in both assemblies that there was evidence in New Hampshire of "an infidel age" in which the "indolent, extravagant and wicked may divide the blessings of life with the industrious, the prudent and the virtuous." Or at least were likely to do so unless prevented.

Langdon and Gilman (traveling at Langdon's expense) did not take their seats in the Great Convention until late July. But once there, they acted in concert and were steady in their support of the moderate Federalist position. They voted to give the government adequate powers for the regulation of commerce, the support of a military establishment, and taxation. The merchants of New Hampshire were convinced that only a stronger central government could restore to them the trading opportunities they had lost by leaving the British Empire.

John Langdon was a member of the committee that hammered out compromises which made the Constitution possible. He spoke at least twenty times during the debates and was a vigorous proponent of provisions restricting interstate tariffs. Langdon announced as his opinion that there should be no necessary hostility between state and national governments. Because of his experience with the parsimony of his neighbors in New Hampshire, he was opposed to having members of Congress compensated by the states and also opposed to a federal power to issue paper money. Altogether, his position during the Convention placed him somewhere near the center of the spectrum of opinions represented there. His only surprising act while in Philadelphia was to maintain that the national government might require the authority (by a two-third's vote) to veto state laws hurtful to the general interest and harmony of the Union. And even here what he had in mind was the unruly democracy of the state legislatures with respect to debts, paper money, and egalitarian fancies. Within a decade he had changed his mind about giving such powers to the central government.

Langdon was an active member of both of New Hampshire's ratifying conventions, the first in February and the second in June 1788. With Nicholas Gilman he had assisted other advocates of the new Constitution in securing its referral to the several commonwealths by the Confederation Congress. And he led the fight for ratification in New Hampshire, first arranging for the adjournment of the February convention, thus preventing an Antifederalist victory, and then bringing in the committee report that persuaded the second convention to approve the document as written. His letter of June 21, 1788, reporting these results to General Washington gave to his state its cherished description as the "Key Stone in the Great Arch."

John Langdon was once more elected president of New Hampshire in 1788, but he resigned to enter the U.S. Senate upon the organization of the new Congress. There he represented New Hampshire until 1801. He was for a time a leading Federalist and was the first president pro tem of the upper house. A great holder of Continental securities, he supported Hamilton's funding system and the creation of the United States Bank. But he opposed the assumption of state debts and refused to support Jay's Treaty, reacting in the latter case to the interests of the West Indian trade. It is, however, unjust to attribute personal motives to every position Langdon assumed in the Confederation Congress, the Constitutional Convention, or the Congress of the United States. By 1800, he had become disenchanted with the policies of the Federalist leadership and their plans for a powerful central government, and he had aligned himself with the followers of Thomas Jefferson.

On his return to New Hampshire, he served again in the state legislature and was on two additional occasions elected speaker. In 1805, he became New Hampshire's first Democratic-Republican governor, and he continued in that office until 1811, excepting one year's hiatus during the Embargo. In 1812, he refused the vice-presidential nomination of his party, as he had earlier refused the post as secretary of the navy, and he retired to private life, to the comforts of his family, and to his beloved Portsmouth. In his last decades John Langdon was a patriarchal presence in the public life of his state, almost an institution in himself, personifying both in office and out the will of the Granite State that every man should be left unhindered in the execution of his own business—and New Hampshire left free to be itself. (See Lawrence Shaw Mayo, *John Langdon of New Hampshire* [Port Washington, N.Y.: Kennikat Press, 1970]; Jere R. Daniell, *Experiment in Republicanism: New Hampshire Politics and the American Revolution, 1741–1794* [Cambridge, Mass.: Harvard University Press, 1970]; Lynn W. Turner, *William Plumer of New Hampshire, 1759–1850* [Chapel Hill: University of North Carolina Press, 1962]; John Langdon Elwyn, "Some Account of John Langdon," in *Early State Papers of New Hampshire*, ed. Albert S. Batchellor, vol. 20 [Manchester, N.H., 1892], pp. 850–880; William Plumer, "John Langdon," in *Early State Papers of New Hampshire*, ed. Albert S. Batchellor, vol. 21 [Manchester, N.H., 1892], pp. 804–812; Forrest McDonald, *E Pluribus Unum: The Formation of the American Republic, 1776–1790* [Indianapolis: Liberty Press, 1979], pp. 194–204, 348–350, and passim; Lynn Warren Turner, *The Ninth State: New Hampshire's Formative Years* [Chapel Hill: University of North

Carolina Press, 1983]; Nancy Elaine Briggs Oliver, "Keystone of the Federal Arch: New Hampshire's Ratification of the United States Constitution" [Ph.D. dissertation, University of California, Santa Barbara, 1972]; Margaret C. S. Christman, *The First Federal Congress, 1789–1791* [Washington, D.C.: Smithsonian, 1989], pp. 282–285.)

# NICHOLAS GILMAN
August 3, 1755–May 2, 1814
Merchant, soldier, and political leader

*The quintessential silent New Englander, who through a long career in public life said little and followed the lead of more decisive men. Son of Nicholas and Ann Taylor Gilman of Exeter. Brother of John Taylor Gilman, several times governor of their state. Linked, with his brother, to Gen. John Sullivan and the high Federalist faction in the state but supportive of John Langdon (who was paying his expenses) once they reached the Convention. Educated in the public schools and employed early in helping to run his father's general store. Enlisted in the Continental army upon the outbreak of the Revolution, and was a captain in the regular service at the conclusion of the war. Employed again in the family business until his election to the Confederation Congress for the period 1786–1788. A handsome man. Described by a French diplomat as one of the proudest men in America.*

Nicholas Gilman was one of the first of the experienced soldiers to answer President Sullivan's call for the militia to suppress the 1786 insurrection at Exeter. He was by this service and by a general reputation for sound opinions propelled into a place of confidence among the leaders of New Hampshire and therefore elected one of the state's four delegates to the Great Convention (two of them, John Pickering and Benjamin West, declined to attend). But as John Langdon had suspected and as later events confirmed, he was not so obdurate a nationalist as to offend against the residual attachment to local things and the local independence of his wealthy associate. Gilman voted the moderate Federalist position throughout the Great Convention, and, though inconspicuous there, the young man (he was thirty-two at the time) was very helpful to his older colleague in getting the Constitution transmitted to the states by the Confederation Congress. Later, though not a member of the New Hampshire ratifying convention, he vigorously supported the Constitution in his home state. He was elected by his neighbors to the first Congress convened under the new system, where he served in the House of Representatives until 1797.

At some point between 1797 and 1800, he began to have serious doubts about the Federalist commitment to strong central government. Though in conflict with the politics of his more famous brother, he joined the Democratic-Republicans. In 1802, President Thomas Jefferson appointed him as bankruptcy commissioner, and in 1804 he was elected by the New Hampshire legislature (where he often served, even while holding national office) to the U.S. Senate. Gilman spent the rest of his life in that post. Though wealthy, he retained the confidence of the small farmers and plain people of the New Hampshire backcountry. He was a man well liked and well trusted in his corner of America. (See Forrest McDonald, *We the People: The Economic Origins of the Constitution* [Chicago: University of Chicago Press, 1958], pp. 39–41, and his *E Pluribus Unum: The Formation of the American Republic, 1776–1790* [Indianapolis: Liberty Press, 1979], pp. 194–204, 348–350, and passim; Jere R. Daniell, *Experiment in Republicanism: New Hampshire Politics and the American Revolution, 1741–1794* [Cambridge, Mass.: Harvard University Press, 1970]; Lawrence Shaw Mayo, *John Langdon of New Hampshire* [Port Washington, N.Y.: Kennikat Press, 1970]; Robert G. Ferris, ed., *Signers of the Constitution* [Washington, D.C.: National Park Service, 1976], pp. 169–170; William Plumer, "Nicholas Gilman," in *Early State Papers of New Hampshire,* ed. Albert S. Batchellor, vol. 21 [Manchester, N.H., 1892], pp. 802–804; Lynn Warren Turner, *The Ninth State: New Hampshire's Formative Years* [Chapel Hill: University of North Carolina Press, 1983]; Nancy Elaine Briggs Oliver, "Keystone of the Federal Arch: New Hampshire's Ratification of the United States Constitution" [Ph.D. dissertation, University of California, Santa Barbara, 1972]; Margaret C. S. Christman, *The First Federal Congress, 1789–1791* [Washington, D.C.: Smithsonian, 1989], pp. 263–265.)

# MASSACHUSETTS

# ELBRIDGE GERRY

July 17, 1744–November 23, 1814
Statesman, signer of the Declaration of Independence
and the Articles of Confederation, leader of the
Revolution in Massachusetts, merchant, and vice-
president of the United States

*Antifederalist. The Framer of the Constitution most frequently opposed to its general tenor and to many of its particulars. With George Mason, the formal adversary in the debates of the Convention. Decidedly an Old Republican and a protector of the Massachusetts lares and penates. But no democrat. Drawn to participate in the Great Convention by the shock of Shays' Rebellion and the economic insecurity of the government under the Articles of Confederation. Born and raised in Marblehead, Massachusetts. The third of twelve children of Thomas and Elizabeth Greenleaf Gerry. Father from Devonshire, England, but before 1735 one of the leading merchants in Massachusetts' second largest town and a sober Puritan, who through foreign trade became a part of Marblehead's "codfish aristocracy." Educated by the local clergy and at Harvard College, from which he graduated in 1762. Then joined his father and older brothers in the family business of shipping dried fish to Europe and the West Indies. Entered public life in May 1772, when he was elected a representative from his rocky native peninsula to the General Court of Massachusetts. Propelled into the political arena by his alarm at innovations in the colonial policy of the British government.*

From the time of the Sugar Act and the Stamp Act in 1764–1765, the Gerry family had led the way in Marblehead in organizing popular resistance to energetic regulation by the English of the political and economic life of their North American colonies. Marblehead, as a seafaring community, was particularly affected by these policies. In 1770 Gerry and his brother Thomas Jr. were elected members of a local committee to enforce a boycott on tea. Numerous public meetings, some of them chaired by Elbridge's father, prepared the way for stronger measures. Furthermore, once in the legislature, young Gerry fell under the influence of Samuel Adams. In May 1773 Gerry was reelected to the General Court; and when local self-government was interrupted in Massachusetts in 1774–1775, he was elected to the first Provincial Congress, which the citizens of the state assembled in defiance of the new royal military governor, Gen. Thomas Gage. He was by that body appointed to the Executive Committee of Safety and reappointed upon his reelection to the Provincial Congress in 1775.

As a member of Marblehead's Committee of Correspondence and of the equivalent committee of the state legislature, Gerry came to know the leading men throughout Massachusetts. With Adams and John Hancock, he was responsible for the military preparations that led to the fighting at Lexington and Concord, and he faced great danger in the months before hostilities broke out. He also made use of his pen in drafting the Essex Resolves and in preparing an atrocity narrative of the beginning of the war designed to stimulate American recruitment and patriotic fervor. In the months when Massachusetts fought almost alone, Gerry was also chairman of the state's Committee of Supply, some of the business of which was handled directly by the family firm in Marblehead.

In January 1776, Gerry was elected representative from Massachusetts to the Second Continental Congress. Once seated there, he was quick to urge separation from the "prostituted government of Great Britain." He was a member of the congressional Committee on the Commissary and was much involved in the administration of American military forces. Uneasy about alliance with France, he joined those who sought the recall of Benjamin Franklin. He continued to do government business through his brothers and the family firm in Marblehead but frowned on profiteering and helped to arrange a convention among the New England states fixing the prices of many important items. He showed a keen interest in the soundness of the currency, in naval affairs, and in privateering—in which he had been profitably involved since late 1775. Gerry was an influential and effective member of the Congress, but in late 1779 and early 1780 he took offense at criticism of his conduct in the press and at the refusal of his colleagues to reduce Massachusetts' quota of supplies. He insisted that prices be measured according to the schedule agreed on in New Haven in 1778 and, when refused, withdrew to Boston to seek vindication before the state legislature. For three years he remained nominally a member of Congress, though absent in protest at what he perceived as its misconduct. While in Massachusetts, he served in the lower house of the legislature and prospered in trade and privateering.

Shortly after his return to Congress and the conclusion of the Revolutionary War, Gerry was active in schemes for the development of the Northwest Territory, in the effort to reduce the standing army, and in the movement to abolish the Society of the Cincinnati. But as a member of the merchant class, he was most concerned with the credit and financial responsibility of the United States. He asserted that the nation's commerce required that all outstanding obligations of the national government be retired. He left Congress in November 1785 and in the following year was reelected to the Massachusetts legislature. In 1786 he purchased a fine house in Cambridge, a confiscated Tory property; retired from business with a comfortable fortune in real estate and securities; and married a wealthy young woman from New York.

Elbridge Gerry brought to the Constitutional Convention in Philadelphia precisely those qualities that had drawn him into the American Revolution and then made it difficult for him to cooperate with his countrymen in that endeavor. As he made clear in 119 speeches and in many motions and secondings of motions, he had not come to Philadelphia to vote Massachusetts out of existence or to compromise its political and cultural integrity. A revision of the Articles of Confederation that would provide for the commercial needs of the member commonwealths, raise a revenue, retire the debt (a goodly share of which he held), and discourage the raucous spirit of democracy abroad in the land would be quite enough. Some kind of viable federal government was necessary if Massachusetts were to have its share of western lands and if commercial treaties with foreign nations were to be negotiated and enforced. Furthermore, a special court to hear legal disputes among the states or between citizens of different states might prove useful. Machinery was necessary for dealing with certain maritime claims and for raising an army out of a militia, but nothing that smacked of the kind of power over local government and local concerns against which the Revolution had been fought, nor any measure that might bring into being the kind of artificial aristocracy or ministerial party of placemen living off the special favors of a sovereign government that had plagued Great Britain since Sir Robert Walpole's administration. Gerry did not withdraw from the Great Convention when it moved against his kind of particularistic republicanism. He was successful in his attempts to modify many provisions of the original Virginia Plan, and his objections to other provisions finally retained helped to establish the universe of discourse within which the ratification debates in the states occurred.

The theory of American politics entertained by Gerry is among the most difficult and complicated of the positions brought into the Great Convention by the Framers. Its mainsprings, fear of remote, tyrannical authority and of the "danger of the leveling spirit" in local populations, were, as Samuel Eliot Morison has observed, in conflict with each other. And the efforts of Gerry's more recent biographers to reduce his political practice and announced beliefs to a unified system have not been altogether successful. Gerry's reaction to energetic government from Whitehall, to the occupation of Boston, and to the Coercive Acts was in keeping with conventional Old Whig sentiment: the English had violated the constitution and had therefore forfeited their authority. The inherited rights guaranteed under that prescriptive law to the people of Marblehead and to five hundred or so other communities were to be preserved, first through armed resistance and finally through revolution. The trouble was, however, that the lower orders, whose interests were as well served by this position as were the interests of the local gentry, became excited by certain features of Whig rhetoric and were reluctant to be "dissuaded from acting too much on their own judgment." Gerry reported to a friend that "the people feel rather too much their own importance; it requires great skill in gradually checking them to such subordination as is necessary to good government." The necessities of war and economic life moved Elbridge Gerry to sound like a Federalist at certain points in his career and to espouse martial law and a regular army.

He came to the Constitutional Convention declaring, "The evils we experience flow from the excess of democracy." His first concerns were social stability at the local level and the security of property. During the "smallpox war" in Marblehead in 1773–1774, mobs of angry fisher folk had threatened to injure the property and persons of the Gerry family because of their involvement in the erection of a pest house on Cat Island and their promotion of inoculation. All "sense of order and distinction" went out of the people, and the town proprietors (with Gerry's assent) appealed to Governor Hutchinson for the king's protection.

This episode provides a model for the kind of "brushfire federalism" that punctuated Gerry's career. But the basic impetus of his thought went the other way. Legitimate government, he believed, should be expressive of the "genius" of the people and depend upon their virtue. No constitutional arrangement could supply the lack of a public spirit. However, the rigid division of power among national, state, and local authorities would best encourage the survival of the requisite public character of the nation, which Gerry believed had been chosen to set an example to the world. (And Massachusetts, of course, was to set the example for the nation.) Hence Gerry opposed a strong executive, an extensive system of federal courts, and intervention by the government of the United States in the domestic affairs of a state. Gerry did not support the demand of the small-states representatives in the Convention for equality of the states in the national legislature. But that was not important to him inasmuch as he was willing to grant little power to the Congress. Gerry was a small-republic man. None other in that Philadelphia meeting spoke more forcefully for a bill of rights than Gerry. And its utility, once included, he made clear, would be in restraining the federal authority. He cried out against national control of the militia, of state elections, and of federal elections in the states. And though he accepted the Constitution after an unsuccessful attempt to prevent its ratification in Massachusetts, he continued during the remainder of his career to express the same opinion: that limited government was good government, at least at the national level—or as George A. Billias has expressed it, the people should govern themselves "as long as they agreed with him [Gerry] and other local authorities."

After the establishment of the government under the Constitution, which Gerry had refused to sign, he experienced great hostility from the Federalist leaders of Massachusetts society. His letter to the state legislature accounting for his conduct as a delegate to the Constitutional Convention had drawn down upon him highly personal attacks, which questioned not only his judgment but his motives in recommending that the Constitution be approved "only with amendments." But since most people in Massachusetts probably shared Gerry's reservations about the Constitution, he retained a political following and was elected to the First Congress of the United States in February 1789. Serving in the House of Representatives until 1793, he voted sometimes with the Federalists (for instance, on the Bank of the United States and the funding of the debt), sometimes with their opponents (in support of an extremely full bill of rights and for a separate treasury commission beyond Alexander Hamilton's jurisdiction).

After Gerry left the Congress, he was again under attack for contradictory behavior, to which he replied that he was of no party and feared a "nobility of opinion," of ideological orthodoxy, even more than an aristocracy of blood or a faction bent upon its own economic advantage. As a presidential elector in 1797, he supported his friend John Adams but drew further and further away from the Federalists as a party. And when President Adams appointed him, with Charles Cotesworth Pinckney and John Marshall, as part of a diplomatic commission to a hostile France, he became the Federalists' outright enemy because of his role in the XYZ Affair, his disputes with his associates in the American delegation, his secret dealing with Talleyrand, and his apparently pro-French attachments. Gerry did not return to America with Marshall and Pinckney, supposedly because he hoped to prevent war on his own. He expressed a deep fear of French military prowess and was for a time persuaded that only his presence in France could keep the peace. Finally, John Adams called him home in disgrace, and he was ostracized in Boston by men of his own class.

But as a Democratic-Republican, his popularity revived once more. Gerry was the Jeffersonian candidate for governor of Massachusetts every year from 1800 to 1803. He was one of Jefferson's electors in 1804. And in 1810, at the age of sixty-five, he was elected governor of his state. He did little to offend during his first term, but after reelection in April 1811, he harshly attacked the "treasons" of the Federalists, as well as the Federalist clergy, and presided over a redistricting of the state designed to give his party a majority in the Massachusetts Senate. The political maneuver was so outrageous as to attach his name forever to all such proceedings—the gerrymander. In April 1812, Gerry was defeated by Caleb Strong in his bid for a third term as governor, but in the following months he was nominated by the Jeffersonians to be vice-president on the ticket with James Madison. Elected, he took office in March 1813, remaining there the rest of his life. Few Americans of his generation had so much to do with the nation's history, performed on so large a stage, and yet retained an intense identity with their provincial origins as did Gerry. (See Samuel Eliot Morison, "Elbridge Gerry,

Gentleman-Democrat," in *By Land and by Sea* [New York: Alfred A. Knopf, 1953], pp. 181–199; George A. Billias, *Elbridge Gerry: Founding Father and Republican Statesman* [New York: McGraw-Hill, 1976]; Clifford K. Shipton, "Elbridge Gerry," in *Biographical Sketches of Those Who Attended Harvard College, 1690–1771,* vol. 15 [Boston: Massachusetts Historical Society, 1970], pp. 239–259; Eugene F. Kramer, "The Public Career of Elbridge Gerry" [Ph.D. dissertation, Ohio State University, 1955]; James T. Austin, *The Life of Elbridge Gerry, with Contemporary Letters,* 2 vols. [New York: Da Capo Press, 1970]; Albert H. Bowman, *Struggle for Neutrality* [Knoxville: University of Tennessee Press, 1974]; C. Harvey Gardiner, ed., *A Study in Dissent: The Warren-Gerry Correspondence, 1776–1792* [Carbondale: Southern Illinois University Press, 1968]; Margaret C. S. Christman, *The First Federal Congress, 1789–1791* [Washington, D.C.: Smithsonian, 1989], pp. 261–262.)

# CALEB STRONG
January 9, 1745–November 7, 1819
Lawyer and political leader of western Massachusetts

*Old-school Puritan and coauthor of the article on religion in the 1780 Bay State Constitution, the article that preserved in Zion the hegemony of the established Congregational Church. The type of Federalist who viewed government as a means to an end—"discipline" and "virtue"—yet moderate in his attitude toward the uses of power, which is "of an encroaching nature." A firm supporter of the Constitution who from its inception doubted that the Union it institutionalized could long survive: "The territory of the United States is so extensive as to forbid us to indulge in the expectation that we shall remain many years united." A sedate and solid citizen, well liked by the plain people of his state. Not so popular with the gentry of the coastal towns, however, who, in the words of a contemporary, were uneasy with a leader "who calls hasty pudding luxury" and "whose wife wears blue stockings." His good sense was a staple of the Great Convention. Second only to John Adams, was eventually the leading Massachusetts Federalist. Of such personal authority that in the ratification convention that opened in Boston on January 9, 1788, his testimony concerning the plain language, character, and good intentions of the Framers turned the tide in securing the majority needed for adoption.*

Caleb Strong was born in Northampton, Massachusetts, the son of Caleb Strong, tanner, and of Phebe Lyman Strong. He was a direct descendant of John Strong, who had immigrated to that section of the colony after arriving in Massachusetts in 1630. After study with a local clergyman, Caleb entered Harvard College, from which he graduated with highest honors in 1764. Following some experience in humble occupations and trouble with his health, Strong read law with Joseph Hawley and was admitted to the bar in 1772. He was chosen selectman of Northampton in 1774 and served throughout the Revolution on its Committee of Safety. In 1776 he was elected to the General Court and named county attorney, an office he held for twenty-four years. In 1780 he was honored with a seat on the Massachusetts Council but refused appointment to the Continental Congress, as he later refused an appointment to the supreme court of his state, for financial reasons. Caleb Strong in these years was not a rich man; he had not yet achieved distinction in his profession. Yet he grew in favor in the eyes of his neighbors throughout these busy times, in part *because* of his modesty. He served as a state senator from 1780 until 1789 and helped to draft the Massachusetts Constitution of 1780. When chosen as a delegate to the Philadelphia Convention, he had accumulated much experience in American politics. But it was experience at the local level, which explains some features of his perspective upon the business of the Convention.

Strong spoke infrequently that summer of 1787. Much of the time he voted with Elbridge Gerry, who would later become his adversary. He held a "narrow" view of the proper functions of a federal judiciary, arguing that "the power of making ought to be kept distinct from that of expounding the laws." He supported the Great Compromise on equality of state representation in the U.S. Senate and favored leaving to the states part of the responsibility for paying the salaries of Congress. He preferred annual elections for the House of Representatives but was, in the face of southern objection concerning distance and expense, reasonable on the subject, as on all others. He liked the idea of giving the House exclusive power to originate money bills, leaving to the Senate the power of amendment. But he voted against having the president selected by an electoral college. Strong left the Convention before its work was done, sometime late in August, because of sickness in his family. But he created no doubt concerning his support for the document produced there, once it was distributed to the people.

Strong, despite his stature among the delegates to the Massachusetts ratifying convention, said little in the course of its debates. For the most part, he answered questions and provided explanations. He defended compromises, saying that "the southern states have their inconveniences." But his role in the politics of his state was already so secure that he had nothing to prove in supporting the new Constitution, and there was no surprise at his being elected by the Massachusetts legislature as one of his state's original U.S. senators. In Congress Strong vigorously supported Washington's policies, helped draft the Judiciary Act, and presented Hamilton's plan for the Bank of the United States. He was reelected to the Senate in 1793 and served until his resignation in 1796. For a few years thereafter he returned to the private practice of law. But in 1800, when faced by a Democratic-Republican tide and the candidacy of Thomas Jefferson, the leading Massachusetts Federalists chose Caleb Strong as their candidate for governor. He was elected and for eleven of the following sixteen years (1800–1807, 1812–1816) continued in that office, "so good and unexceptionable a man," according to John Adams, that he ran usually ahead of the ticket and was, in the Connecticut River valley, almost unbeatable. He was, generally, a governor who left to his people the management of their own affairs, observing that "inequality . . . arises from the nature of things, and not from any defect in the form of administration of government. All that the best government can do is prevent that inequality which fraud, oppression, or violence would produce."

With the end of Caleb Strong's career came its most dramatic moments. As a Yankee "nullifier," Strong withheld the forces of Massachusetts from full participation in the War of 1812 and moved his state toward secession or a new constitutional convention by means of the Hartford Convention of 1814. According to Strong and his associates among the senior New England Federalists, such measures were clearly within the scope of the U.S. Constitution. A rapid end of the war preserved the Union from a general withdrawal by the old Puritan commonwealths, which felt "deserted" and dispossessed by the Virginia dynasty. Strong's popularity was not injured by these adventures in sectionalism, in which he followed the well-thought-out Federalist doctrine of state sovereignty. He was again elected governor in 1815. However, he chose to retire at the end of this term, returning to Northampton, where he died some three years later, in the midst of his "rebellious" friends. (See Alden Bradford, *Biography of the Honorable Caleb Strong, Several Years Governor of the State of Massachusetts* [Boston: West, Richardson & Lord, 1820]; James M. Banner, Jr., *To the Hartford Convention: The Federalists and the Origins of Party Politics in Massachusetts, 1789–1815* [New York: Alfred A. Knopf, 1970]; *Patriotism and Piety: the Speeches of His Excellency Caleb Strong* [Newburyport, Mass.: M. Blunt, 1808]; Henry Cabot Lodge, *A Memoir of Caleb Strong, United States Senator and Governor of Massachusetts, 1745–1819* [Cambridge, Mass.: J. Wilson & Son, 1879]; Anson E. Morse, *The Federalist Party in Massachusetts to the Year 1800* [Princeton, N.J.: Princeton University Press, 1909]; William Nisbet Chambers, *Political Parties in a New Nation: The American Experience, 1776–1809* [New York: Oxford University Press, 1963]; Richard E. Welch, Jr., *Theodore Sedgwick, Federalist: A Political Portrait* [Middletown, Conn.: Wesleyan University Press, 1964]; Paul Goodman, *The Democratic-Republicans of Massachusetts: Politics in a Young Republic* [Cambridge, Mass.: Harvard University Press, 1964]; Clifford K. Shipton, "Caleb Strong," in *Biographical Sketches of Those Who Attended Harvard College in 1764–1767*, vol. 16 [Boston: Massachusetts Historical Society, 1972], pp. 94–110; David H. Fischer, *The Revolution of American Conservatism: The Federalist Party in the Era of Jeffersonian Democracy* [New York: Harper & Row, 1965]; Margaret C. S. Christman, *The First Federal Congress, 1789–1791,* [Washington, D.C.: Smithsonian, 1989], pp. 334–337.)

# NATHANIEL GORHAM

May 16, 1738–June 11, 1796
Merchant, financier, and land speculator

*Political leader of Massachusetts during and after the American Revolution.
Commercial Federalist. A vigorous, active participant in the debates of the Great
Convention. Of a "lusty . . . agreeable and pleasing manner," according to
William Pierce. In favor of a strong central government—even though he did not
expect the Union to survive: "Can it be supposed that this vast Country including
the Western territory will 150 years hence remain one nation?" One of a large
number of northern Framers whose lives were damaged or destroyed by their
economic and business "adventures" in the years following 1787. Son of
Nathaniel Gorham and Mary Soley Gorham. Descended from John Gorham,
who immigrated to the Massachusetts Bay Colony in 1643. Born at Charlestown.
After only a minimum of education, apprenticed to Nathaniel Coffin, a merchant
of New London, Connecticut, with whom he labored until 1759. On his return to
Charlestown, successful in his own business while still a young man. Entered
politics as the Bay State moved toward war.*

Nathaniel Gorham, after election to the Massachusetts General Court (1771–
1775), was chosen as a delegate to the Provincial Congress (1774–1775), as a
member of the Commonwealth's Board of War (1778–1781), and as a delegate to
the state constitutional convention of 1779–1780. Under the new constitution, he
served in the Massachusetts legislature, first in the upper chamber (1780), then in
the lower house (1781–1787). In the latter assembly he was speaker in 1781, 1782,
and 1785. Even though much of his wealth was lost in the early stages of the
Revolution, Gorham rebuilt his fortune through privateering and speculation, in
property both movable and real. Though not a lawyer, from 1785 to 1796 he sat as
judge of the Middlesex County Court of Common Appeals and in 1788–1789 on
the Governor's Council. From 1782 to 1783 and from 1785 to 1787 he represented
Massachusetts in the Confederation Congress, serving as president of that body
from June 1786 to January 1787. With the dignity of these offices and this public
service behind him, Gorham took his place in the Constitutional Convention. He
chaired the Committee of the Whole and sat on the Committee of Detail. Much of
the time he voted with Rufus King and against Elbridge Gerry and Caleb
Strong—thus canceling his state's voice when the roll was called. But he himself
was heard on more than forty occasions—heard *and* understood.

Nathaniel Gorham's performance in the deliberations of the Framers ex-
emplified the belief that "the business of America is business." Or at least that it
should be, so far as New England was concerned. At one point Gorham declared

that "the Eastern States had no motive to Union but a commercial one," for they could protect themselves and neither feared external danger nor needed the southern states. Disunion, he warned the South, would leave it vulnerable to foreign attack and internal disruptions—as the Revolution had proved. But in return for a navigation act, a tariff, and the "carrying trade," New England might be moved to protect its southern countrymen from their inherent weaknesses. Quid pro quo was his recurring theme in several short speeches.

Gorham also insisted that all the states be given an interest in western lands and suggested that the larger states be broken into smaller units (so as to strengthen the general government). He continued to exhibit the interest in a sound currency and regular tax revenues that he had shown in the Congress: first in a 1783 plan of the New England states to hold their own convention concerning revenue, once the Congress proved to be unable to agree on a monetary policy; and, later, as an emissary from the Congress to New Jersey when that state threatened to withhold its part of the requisition of September 1785. When southerners sought to prohibit the passage of navigation acts in the text of the U.S. Constitution, Gorham asked, "If the Government is to be so fettered as to be unable to relieve the Eastern States [from their commercial problems], what motive can they have to join in it, and thereby tie their own hands from measures which they could otherwise take for themselves?" Yet it was he who voted to extend the slave trade from 1800 to 1808 in return for John Rutledge's support of Massachusetts' views on commerce. Gorham's Federalism showed no ideological passion, no commitment to the grand abstraction of natural rights theory. Questions of interest and practicality stood in their place.

Nathaniel Gorham played no important role in American politics after his service in the Constitutional Convention. Though he did sit in defense of the new Constitution in his state's 1788 ratification convention, for the most part his last nine years were devoted to developing a vast tract of land in New York, which was ceded to Massachusetts as part of a boundary dispute and later sold to Gorham and Oliver Phelps of Windsor, Connecticut. Probably these two men represented a syndicate in the acquisition of 6 million acres. The purchase price was a million dollars, to be paid in three installments and in Massachusetts scrip. The speculators quickly cleared title to 2,600,000 acres in the eastern section of the grant and sold it to settlers. But the Massachusetts paper rose suddenly in value, increasing the true size of the pending debt. As a result, Gorham and Phelps ended bankrupt, ruined, and disgraced. In 1796 Gorham died of apoplexy and remorse, a man once great but fallen, betrayed by the very spirit he had displayed as one of the Framers of the Constitution. (See Orasmus Turner, *History of the Pioneer Settlement of Phelps and Gorham's Purchase and Morris' Reserve* [Rochester, N.Y.: W. Alling, 1852]; Timothy Thompson Sawyer, *Old Charlestown: Historical, Biographical, and Reminiscent* [Boston: J. H. West, 1902]; H. James Henderson, *Party Politics in the Continental Congress* [New York: McGraw-Hill, 1974]; Van Beck Hall, *Politics without Parties: Massa-*

chusetts, 1780–1791 [Pittsburgh, Pa.: University of Pittsburgh Press, 1972]; Joseph L. Davis, *Sectionalism in American Politics, 1774–1787* [Madison: University of Wisconsin Press, 1977]; Robert G. Ferris, ed., *Signers of the Constitution* [Washington, D.C.: National Park Service, 1976], pp. 170–172; Forrest McDonald, *We the People: The Economic Origins of the Constitution* [Chicago: University of Chicago Press, 1958], pp. 43–44.)

# RUFUS KING
March 24, 1755–April 29, 1827
Lawyer, diplomat, and conservative statesman

*Political leader in two northern states. High Federalist, yet in essence a sectional figure. Inclined to value a strong central government both as a stimulant to trade and commerce and as a check on "the madness of democracy." Marked in his childhood with the abuse of his family by destructive mobs. Son of the unfortunate Capt. Richard King, a wealthy merchant and landowner, and Isabella Bragdon King. Born at Scarboro, District of Maine. Educated by the famous schoolmaster Samuel Moody, at Dummer Academy, at Harvard (graduated in 1777), and in the offices of the learned Newburyport (Massachusetts) attorney Theophilus Parsons. Bereft of the support of his family by the collapse of Richard King's business under the stigma of loyalism, and by his early death in 1775. Admitted to the practice of the law in 1780, after a few weeks' military experience during Gen. John Sullivan's unsuccessful expedition to Rhode Island in August 1778. Acknowledged as a master of his profession within only a few years. Elected by Newburyport to represent that community in the sessions of the General Court for 1783, 1784, and 1785. Sent by the Massachusetts legislature as a delegate to the Confederation Congress for 1784–1787. Served on a commission to adjust the boundary between Massachusetts and New York. Completed his term of service to the Bay State as one of its delegates to the Great Convention. Moved to New York after marriage to the heiress Mary Alsop, only daughter of John Alsop, president of the New York Chamber of Commerce.*

Rufus King, at thirty-two, was one of the youngest of the Framers. Yet he was outspoken at the Constitutional Convention, often eloquent but sometimes (according to William Pierce) forceful to the point of "rudeness." Shays' Rebellion strongly affected this young attorney. Before that upheaval he had been suspicious of any system that might turn the future of New England over to a haughty agrarian aristocracy, indifferent to the necessities of trade and maritime commerce, and he had been reluctant to contemplate the creation of a more "national" government than was provided for by the Articles of Confederation. The idea of a Yankee "subconfederation" appealed to him more than the notion of a stronger union of all the former English colonies joined by the Confederation.

As a member of the Congress for Massachusetts, he had already displayed many of the attitudes that he later brought into the Great Convention. One of these was a firm attachment to the mercantile interest, a connection made stronger by his new standing as son-in-law of John Alsop and friend of the leading political and legal lights of Gotham. Another was a horror of political abstractions. By 1786 he had put away any earlier faith he might have had in the common man: "The great body of the people are without virtue, and not governed by any restraints of conscience." To him, equality meant the "unnatural genius" of his age, "the arch enemy of the moral world" whose disposition is to degrade what is worthy, not to raise what is low. To argue conversely was to advocate "principles that do not exist." After independence was achieved, King was quick to assure English friends that "there was no likelihood of our becoming zealous in the propagation of the new doctrines of Liberty and the Rights of Man." At least not if Rufus King had anything to do with the shaping of American policy.

The merit of the Constitution fashioned in Philadelphia, according to Rufus King, was that it did not rest on "romantic speculation" or run to "utopian lengths" in hankering after an experiment in "wild and mischievous doctrines." In the opinion of the delegate from Massachusetts, the Framers had worked wisely and respectfully with the given materials of an already functioning American regime, acknowledging in the process the wisdom that teaches that the true statesman does not argue from definition and "may not apply unqualified metaphysical principles to [his craft]." In King's doctrine, this prudence was admirable because "experience, not abstraction, ought to be our guide in practice and conduct." When the French Revolution came, King hated it as passionately as did any other American of note in his generation. He declaimed against the "detestable principles" of France and foresaw the spread of "barbarism," fathered by "philosophy." Two years before, in Philadelphia, during the summer of 1787, his mind had worked in the same way, on precisely the same assumptions.

In the Great Convention, King was helpful in striking the compromise on the importation of slaves and on the prohibition against a tax on exports. He persuaded his colleagues to include a provision guaranteeing the sanctity of contracts, fought to produce a strong, independent president with a power of absolute veto over legislation by Congress, and defended the separation of powers. But he foresaw the development of the country in the Southwest and expressed his fear that southerners might augment their voting strength by the simple expedient of importing slaves. Although he had introduced and supported legislation in the Confederation Congress to exclude that "peculiar institution" from the territories, he was actually more interested in preventing or discouraging westward settlement than in promoting an issue that "should be considered in a political light only." King was himself a slave owner and the son of a slave owner, and he did not free his last slave until 1812. But as was evident in the remainder of his career, he was prepared to defend the northeastern states against the threat of a southern hegemony. And the issue of slavery, as King admitted to his son in later years, was for him always "a question of *political power* between northern and southern interests."

After the conclusion of the Constitutional Convention, Rufus King made a final gesture in Massachusetts politics by standing for election to the state ratification convention in Boston. He was one of the Federalist leaders in that assembly and played an important role in devising a strategy for his faction in a successful attempt to channel the proceedings toward a decision for approval. As he had in Philadelphia, so in Boston King warned the "children of light" against the "phantom of state sovereignty." Massachusetts could not prosper on its own; union was the way to obtain a monopoly of southern trade and to obtain a market for fish in Spain, acquired at the "trifling" cost of navigation rights on the Mississippi—a cost that only the South and West would be asked to pay. If amendments to the Constitution were in order, let them be subjoined as "changes recommended," not as conditions of ratification. Since the fundamental "law of the land" was now to act upon individuals, Massachusetts would no longer face the danger of too much of a tax burden. And in any case, if the system went wrong, secession always remained as the corrective. At various times throughout his life, King threatened this alternative to national unity: an alternative he expected the West to exercise and once overtly recommended to the Virginian, John Taylor of Caroline. But short of such extremity, New England should be content with the three-fifths formula of counting slaves for both taxes and representation since "it was the language of all America." An accommodation with Spain, a commercial arrangement with England, and cautious dealings with the French—such had been King's program for making use of national unity under the Articles, as, for instance, in the Jay-Gardoqui negotiations and in plans for a subconfederation that could force into existence a nationwide policy on imports, exports, and shipping. There was some danger that the South and West might get New England into a war, but not if the new government refused to authorize big armies for attacks on hostile Indians or their foreign "sponsors." Left to protect itself, the frontier would spread more slowly.

After the Constitution was adopted, Rufus King was elected as one of the original U.S. senators from New York, and he was among the leading spokesmen for the Washington administration in the upper chamber. King argued the case for Hamilton in many crucial circumstances surrounding his financial system. In 1791 he was elected a director of the Bank of the United States. In 1794–1795 he was the principal defender of Jay's Treaty, in support of which he wrote some persuasive essays under the signature "Camillus." In January 1795 the New York legislature reelected him to the Senate. But fatigued with the life of the legislator, King took advantage of the opportunity to become U.S. minister to Great Britain (replacing Thomas Pinckney) when the post was offered to him late in 1795. As minister, he proved to be a successful diplomat and gained the acceptance of most of the English leadership, including King George III. He continued to enjoy that role until he was removed at his own request in 1803. King prevented repeated tensions between his nation and Whitehall from exploding into war, concluded two conventions with the British, and won from them many ex officio concessions—favors granted at least in part because King was such an open Anglophile, especially with reference to England's wars with the French republic and, thereafter, with the empire of Napoleon. However, the same attitudes made King enemies in the United States, particularly his effort to prevent the exile of Irish radicals to America, men full of French ideas "so false and so utterly inconsistent with any practicable or settled form of government."

On his return to New York in 1804 and again in 1808, Rufus King was the Federalist candidate for vice-president of the United States on a ticket headed by a fellow Framer, Charles Cotesworth Pinckney. He purchased an estate on Long Island, played the gentleman farmer, and made good investments. Moreover, he continued to function (especially after Hamilton's death) as one of the respected leaders of a dying political party. But if Federalism was moribund, King's political career was not. Put another way, in Rufus King the political theory of Federalism underwent a metamorphosis, a change that to this day has preserved its influence in the discourse of the republic. For in 1813, when, in a backlash against war with England, King once again won a seat as senator from New York, he was on his way toward developing a new political language, one foreign to the Federalism of his youth and middle years. All this despite the fact that in 1816 he was the last Federalist candidate for the presidency.

Though he avoided the separatism of his old comrades in the Hartford Convention of 1814, and though he collaborated in the war effort once the British began to endanger American coastal settlements, the Rufus King who returned to the Senate was tired of being ruled by southerners and (in the words of a biographer) "hoped for a new sectional alignment of parties." He got his chance to accomplish this in 1819–1820 when the Missouri Territory applied to Congress for admittance to the Union, for Missouri wished to come in as a slave state. King found in this circumstance the engine he required to "stir up a storm in the North." As Robert Ernst has observed, "Although deeply critical of slavery itself, the Senator from New York was primarily and most deeply aroused over the political balance of power. . . . His interest in slavery was primarily political." Or, in Jefferson's opinion, "He [King] was ready to risk the Union for any chance of restoring his party to power." His instrument was the rhetoric of moral advantage, of freedom versus slavery, the argument from definition designed to link North and West—one that foreshadowed Seward and Lincoln in attacking southern influence as something to be isolated as evil. "I hold," said King, "that all laws or compacts imposing any such condition [as involuntary servitude] upon any human being are absolutely void because contrary to the law of nature, which is the law of God." He was ahead of his time in this effort.

At this violation of the "Compromise of 1787" and King's own announced devotion to the sanctity of contract and abhorrence of French abstraction or metaphysical politics, James Madison declared himself to be "truly astonished," adding that if King's position on what the Constitution allowed had enjoyed any support in the Philadelphia Convention, it would have prevented its ratification. Other critics were less generous, calling King a "moral Hypocrite" and accusing him of dishonesty in his account of what had been agreed to in the Great Convention—particularly on the subject of a federal power to exclude slavery from a territory that wanted it. King's crusade was popular in New York; he was reelected to the Senate and served there until 1825.

After his retirement from Congress, Rufus King attempted a second term as minister to Great Britain. But his health broke, forcing in 1826 his return to New York where, at the age of seventy-two, he died the following year. King was a great orator, an able diplomat, and a close student of commerce and maritime law. His notes on the Constitutional Convention are valuable. He also played a role in the writing of the New York State Constitution of 1821. He was a widely read man and authored some useful legislation while in the U.S. Senate. Nonetheless, his was essentially a parochial spirit, a predictable product of his New England upbringing. When in the Congress in 1785, he had proposed for the open lands of the West the New England pattern of township settlement with a corporate life, no large holdings, and a government provision for churches. We should remember that he was doubtful about the Constitutional Convention until convinced it would not endanger established New England modes and orders. Xenophobic, he disliked immigration of most varieties, to say nothing of exposure to strange places and strange ways. Only when he could equate the nation with his portion of it was his patriotism at ease. (See Robert Ernst, *Rufus King, American Federalist* [Chapel Hill: University of North Carolina Press, 1968]; Charles R. King, ed., *The Life and Correspondence of Rufus King*, 6 vols. [New York: G. P. Putnam's Sons, 1894–1900]; Edward H. Brush, *Rufus King and His Times* [New York: Little, Brown, 1926]; James G. King, "Rufus King, Young Statesman of Massachusetts, 1755–1789" [Ph.D. dissertation, Harvard University, 1966]; David H. Fischer, *The Revolution of American Conservatism: The Federalist Party in the Era of Jeffersonian Democracy* [New York: Harper & Row, 1965]; Joseph L. Arbena, "Politics or Principle? Rufus King and the Opposition to Slavery, 1785–1825," *Essex Institute Historical Collections* 101 (1965): 56–77; Dixon Ryan Fox, *The Decline of Aristocracy in the Politics of New York, 1801–1840* [New York: Columbia University Press, 1919].)

# CONNECTICUT

# ROGER SHERMAN

April 19, 1721–July 23, 1793
Shoemaker, surveyor, lawyer, jurist, lay theologian,
and statesman

*Next to Benjamin Franklin, the oldest man in the Great Convention. Mild
Federalist where commerce was concerned, but otherwise distrustful of any great
increase in the federal powers: "No State should be affected in its internal
police," because "it is in the interest of each and of the whole [Union] that they
should be separate within their proper limits." Hence, almost an Antifederalist
in many of his opinions. In Philadelphia to create a "more effective government," but not a "national" government. In some respects a figure left over from
the New England of the previous century, yet withal a most experienced legislator. Described by John Adams (with some understandable exaggeration) as "an
old Puritan, as honest as an angel and as firm in the cause of American
independence as Mount Atlas." Yet according to Connecticut's Jeremiah
Wadsworth, who knew Sherman well, "as cunning as the Devil." Despite his
rustic, plain appearance and country speech, rightly identified by a farmer of his
acquaintance as "twistical"—as skilled a politician as ever came out of colonial
Connecticut. While in the Constitutional Convention, determined to protect the
regime he had done so much to shape. Convinced that "each state like each
individual had its peculiar habits, usages, and manners, which constituted its
happiness." Able to accept the fact that any viable union of the states would have
to rest upon a large variety of disparate versions of the corporate life. Yet eager
to see a government that could promote American commerce, collect taxes, retire
the debt, establish a sound currency, make treaties, raise and supply an army,
and preclude the robbery of one state by another by means of duties. Instrumental in the adoption of the Connecticut compromise, which provided for a bicameral legislature with the states represented equally in one house and
according to population in the other, and in the ratification of the Constitution by*

*Connecticut. Though mayor of New Haven, a man of limited means. A trusted representative of all levels in the society of Connecticut.*

Roger Sherman was born in Newton, Massachusetts, a descendant of Capt. John Sherman of Dedham, Essex County, England, who had settled in Massachusetts ca. 1636. Roger was the son of William Sherman, farmer, cordwainer, and frontiersman, and Mehetabel Wellington Sherman. In 1723 William Sherman moved to Stoughton, Massachusetts, where Roger received some education in the common schools and came under the influence of the local minister, the Reverend Samuel Dunbar, who inspired him to read widely in theology, history, law, and politics. The youthful Sherman also farmed and learned the cobbler's trade. After his father's death in 1741, Roger gathered up his tools and in 1743 moved to New Milford, Connecticut, where his elder brother William was already established. In 1745 he was appointed surveyor for New Haven County and continued in that office when Litchfield County was organized, serving until 1758. In this position Sherman acquired considerable property and began to take an active part in the public life of the township, serving as a town clerk, selectman, deacon of the local Congregationalist church, juryman, school committeeman, and town agent before the assembly. He sat as Litchfield County justice of the peace from 1755 to 1761. In 1756 he became sole owner of New Milford's first store, which he had earlier kept with his brother. Between 1750 and 1761 he published a series of almanacs, which suggests something of the scope of his reading. He also brought out a pamphlet against the circulation of unsound currency. He read law with William Samuel Johnson and in 1754 became a member of the Litchfield bar. When sent by New Milford to the General Assembly in May 1755, he had, at thirty-four, achieved a remarkable alteration in his circumstances from the time of his arrival in Connecticut.

In the years preceding the American Revolution, Roger Sherman continued to represent New Milford in the assembly (1755–1756, 1758–1761), and had some important experience with questions of military finance during the French and Indian War. In 1759 he was appointed commissary for Connecticut troops operating out of Albany, New York. Shortly thereafter, he gave up his law practice and his position as justice of the County Court in Litchfield and moved to New Haven, where he set up a large general store close to the Yale campus. From 1764 to 1766 he was the deputy for New Haven in the General Assembly. In 1766 he was elected to the Governor's Council as assistant, in which office he served nineteen years. In 1765 he became a member of the County Court and justice of the peace in New Haven. In May 1766 he began a twenty-three-year tenure as judge of the Connecticut Superior Court. Sherman also operated a store in Wallingford, Connecticut, and was a well-known figure throughout the state. He was close to the head of the ticket in most elections.

When disturbances over the Stamp Act turned into social disorders and threats to person and property, Sherman broke with his erstwhile friends the Sons of Liberty, because he believed that "their proceedings tend to weaken the authority of the government." Despite his plain origins and popular touch, Sherman despised mob rule throughout his career and once issued a warrant against Benedict Arnold as a check upon lawless radicalism. There was to be no scapegoating of Loyalists in New Haven while he was in charge—and no "unofficial" beatings of enemies of the kind for which Arnold was fined. Yet Sherman was early in his commitment to nonimportation agreements as a peaceful response to hated British legislation, was the head of the New Haven Committee of Correspondence, and even went so far as to organize pressure on New York merchants who had continued to do business with the mother country and had not signed the Articles of Association. During these years Sherman was also a benefactor of Yale College and served as its treasurer from 1765 to 1776. In 1768 the college awarded him an honorary master of arts degree.

For Roger Sherman, as for many other Americans of his generation, the watershed experiences in his decision to practice armed resistance to British power came with the occupation of Massachusetts by the king's troops and the Intolerable Acts, especially the closing of the port of Boston. Before 1773, he had been content to respond to offensive policies initiated by the ministers of George III with protest and commercial retaliation; he also had a few special worries concerning the prospects for appointed bishops and greedy placemen. In the late 1760s, as the almanacs demonstrate, he had been a Whig Loyalist, devoted to the principles of 1688, delighted by victory over France and the "gracious protection of his sovereign lord." The dispute over the Susquehanna lands in Pennsylvania concerned Connecticut more than fears of British invasion and open war. Furthermore, the leading men of the state did not wish to see the people provoked into "division and animosities among themselves," drained of their "public virtue."

Though cautious about "rebellion" and determined that Connecticut should live by its charter and the version of English constitutional theory that vindicated its authority, Sherman had for years entertained an advanced view of the relation of Parliament to the English colonies in North America, maintaining that "the reverse of the Declaratory Act was true, namely, that the Parliament of Great Britain had authority to make laws for America in no case whatsoever." Lexington and Concord, for Sherman, closed the issue of King George III's authority under the Connecticut charter. Yet after attending the original Continental Congress and signing the Articles of Association in 1774, Sherman made no serious objection to the 1775 Olive Branch Petition and was one of its signers. The mainspring of his politics, both at this time and at subsequent stages in his public life, was devotion to the established, well-tested, and long self-governing regime of Connecticut. To protect it, he became a party to the Declaration of Independence, serving with Jefferson, John Adams, Franklin, and Robert Livingston of New York on the committee called upon to formalize that secession with a proper document. Sherman acted to protect an *existing* Connecticut, not to defend some abstract principle.

Sherman was a delegate to Congress from 1774 to 1781 and then again, briefly, from 1783 to 1784. He was perhaps the most energetic, thorough, and regular member. Eventually he became "Father Sherman" to the house, though hated by many "high-toned nationalists," who were made restive by his parsimony, even while they feared and respected his power. Sherman was a signer of the Articles of Confederation and part of the committee that brought these proposals to a vote. He actively supported Connecticut's claims to lands in Pennsylvania and later had a part in the negotiations that surrendered the Wyoming River valley lands for a firmer hold on the Western Reserve in Ohio. He was particularly concerned with the commissariat for the Continental army. Two of Sherman's sons served as paymasters, while a third, Isaac, fought under Washington and rose to lieutenant colonel before the end of the war. For a time Sherman doubted the wisdom of appointing a Virginia aristocrat to command New England troops, and he took special pleasure from the victories of northern generals. "This is the Lord's doing, and marvelous in our eyes!" he declared on hearing of Saratoga, using the idiom of the Good Old Cause. But ultimately he accepted everything in the military arrangements except long enlistments and the prospect of a standing army. He turned his attention to the problems of financing and sustaining American forces in the field.

In the New England conventions called to consider the best policy for controlling prices and supporting the currency of the Confederation, Sherman exerted a considerable influence. He was at the Springfield meeting in 1777, in New Haven in 1778, and at the Philadelphia session in 1780. But he was a realist about the prospects of a currency supported by so small and so irregular a national income. On the question of state emissions of paper money, Sherman was consistently negative. Instead, he called for taxes, retirement of debt, and frugality—cutting back on diplomatic operations, depending on militia rather than on regiments of the Continental Line, paying government purchasing agents by salary instead of with percentage commissions. For a time it appeared that Connecticut merchants, angry with low profits, had deprived Sherman of his seat in the Congress. But soon thereafter, he was reappointed and back in Philadelphia—supporting statehood for Vermont, warning against spending money not yet in hand, insisting on careful accounts. And in the Annapolis session, he was there to promote the common enterprise, scorning such local diversions as "plays, Balls, Concerts, routs, hops, Fandangoes and fox hunting." Cavalier nonsense was not to the taste of this sober statesman. Yet no member of the Congress was more mindful of his responsibility to his electorate.

In the years immediately preceding the Constitutional Convention, Roger Sherman concentrated on politics at the state and local levels. In 1783, at the request of the legislature, he joined with Richard Law to codify and reconcile the statutes of Connecticut, a work finally published as *Acts and Laws of the State of*

*Connecticut*. (Sherman had done essentially the same job in 1768.) In 1784 he was elected the first mayor of New Haven and continued to enjoy that honor until his death. He built a good house, continued with his judicial duties, and presided over the complex and sometimes distressing activities of a large family. In these years his position in New Haven was "almost autocratic." Because he reached the age of sixty-six in 1787, it was reasonable to assume that Sherman was through with the national arena, even though he continued to follow politics with close attention. Yet once Connecticut finally, and with grave reservations, decided to send a delegation to the Great Convention, it was altogether predictable that Sherman—the summary representative of the decentralist sentiments of the state's ordinary citizens—should be chosen after the younger and even more Antifederalist Erastus Wolcott had refused the appointment.

In the Constitutional Convention Sherman spoke at least 138 times and was consistently present except for a brief period (July 20–August 6), just before and during an adjournment to wait for the reports of committees. Many of the rigid Federalists among the Framers feared that the senior member from Connecticut would agree to no more than a "patching" of the system of government under the Articles. They misjudged him. Yet they were correct in expecting that he would give them problems. Sherman had a clear view of the purposes a constitution should serve: "The great end of the federal government is to protect the several states in the enjoyment of [such] rights [as concern local interests and customs] against foreign invasion, and to preserve peace and a beneficial intercourse among themselves; and to regulate and protect our commerce with foreign nations." On June 6 he announced these objectives. Never did he agree that there were others of major importance. Yet it was also his view that "the people immediately should have as little to do as may be about the Government. They want information and are constantly liable to be misled." Add to this his warning that "the constitution should lay as few temptations as is possible in the way of those in power," and there emerges a minimal sort of federal government, neither energetic nor democratic, in which the legislative branch had the greatest share of authority, limited as it might be. "Diversity," he maintained, was itself a "security against the abuse of power." He fostered the Connecticut Plan not only to protect the small states but to protect the states per se. Arguing against the theoretical egalitarianism of James Wilson, he came down sharply against a simplistic view of law in society: "The question is not what rights naturally belong to men, but how [the rights that men enjoy] can be . . . effectually guarded in society." Hence, it would "not comport with their interests if the Federal government were to interfere with the government of particular states."

Sherman had what was for a local-minded man an unusual objection to the inclusion of a bill of rights in the Constitution. According to a biographer, Christopher Collier, "opposition to anything like a Bill of Rights was a function of his states' rights position." For the federal authority to define and guarantee human rights would result in a power of oversight concerning questions related to the internal order of the states. And on the "rights of man," the states were in no way agreed. Or rather, on the "rights of man" *in society*. The dour sage from Connecticut insisted, "State declarations of Rights are not Repealed by this Constitution and, being in force, are sufficient." A federal bill of rights might be either too radical or too conservative, but that was not the important distinction. What signified was, rather, that in either case the language involved would allow the general government to act upon the relations of individuals within the states on the basis of normative distinctions, not procedural rules, and thus would release that government to do whatever it conceived to be "good." Connecticut did not want Pennsylvania and Virginia voting to abolish the "New England Way." Nor would South Carolina agree that Massachusetts should have power to judge concerning slavery in Charleston. In Sherman's opinion, any reference to the "peculiar institution" would be a mistake—excepting perhaps a fugitive-slave clause. The result of official mention would be to extend jurisdiction into areas where it had not existed and would require eventually either approval or disapprobation of an established pattern. On the other hand, if nothing was said either way, slavery could be left where it stood and the necessity to "part with" the Deep South, for which it was a sine qua non, avoided.

Sherman's other objections to a bill of rights were penetrating: if *any* restraints upon the federal authority to regulate the lives of citizens were to be included, then *all conceivable* restraints that were intended also would have to be added, lest silence be converted into license. It was better that the Constitution spell out what the government might do and then reiterate that its "objects were limited." Sherman's reasoning on these questions was as sophisticated as any that appears in the records of the Great Convention. It is understandable that he had the reputation of being "one of the most sensible men in the world."

On the question of the relative importance of the three branches of the proposed federal government, Roger Sherman came down decisively on the side of legislative supremacy. He wished to see the chief executive chosen by the Congress or the state legislatures. Moreover, he thought that the president should serve at the "pleasure" of the Congress. He wanted the national legislature to be involved in the writing of treaties, and he disliked the idea of the presidential veto. Federal judges, he believed, should be limited in power, appointed by the U.S. Senate, and subject to removal by the president upon recommendation of both houses of the Congress. He was ready to question the propriety of allowing the chief executive to remove his own executive appointments or to grant pardons. Sherman feared the political consequences of a standing army and declared, "We can't be too careful of military encroachments." He was directly responsible for the limitations on federal authority over militia in the states. Furthermore, he hoped to keep at that level the process by which conditions for suffrage and office-holding were to be decided. He wanted no canal-making power and no national college, and he doubted that the Congress should have authority to grant commercial charters.

Only within a restricted economic sphere was he any kind of Federalist. Yet he would accept what was "expedient," at least up to a point—so long as the future influence of the states was protected by their equal voice in one house of a bicameral legislature. Sherman wanted the general government to be representative of the states, not the people. He joined the southerners (with whom he may have made a private arrangement in regard to slavery and navigation laws) in blocking the attempt to authorize a tax on exports. He was quick to point out Gouverneur Morris's insertion of a semicolon instead of a comma in the sentence containing a reference to the "general welfare," thus making the clause a sweeping grant of power instead of a limitation on it. Throughout the Convention, Sherman seemed to be involved in almost every important discussion. When a draft had been prepared for submission to the states, he was well satisfied and praised the document as one that "could not have been made on mere speculation."

Sherman was extremely influential in the struggle for ratification in Connecticut, where there was possibly a popular majority against the Constitution, and wrote a series of essays in the local papers urging adoption and assuring the ordinary citizens that "there are few powers vested in the new government but what the present Congress have power to do or request to be done." Because they differ with Sherman on how to read the original U.S. Constitution, some modern scholars have accused him of misleading the people of his state concerning the powers of the new government. Others see Sherman's view of the Constitution as basically sound and those of his critics anachronistic. In the Connecticut ratification convention, he allowed the younger Oliver Ellsworth, his disciple, to carry the burden of debate. Yet Sherman's support was the determining factor in the overwhelming Federalist margin of victory, for many local-minded men were brought over finally by Sherman's example. In 1789 he was elected one of Connecticut's original representatives and was an outspoken member of the First Congress. A hard-money man, he wanted the debt retired in full, supported the main ingredients of Alexander Hamilton's financial "system," and was a figure in the compromise that authorized federal assumption of state debts in return for the location of the permanent capital on the Potomac. He opposed the Bill of Rights, as he had promised, but then accepted it as prudent—given the temper of the people.

At the age of seventy, in 1791, Roger Sherman was elected U.S. senator from Connecticut and concluded his long career of public service in that office. All his politics rested finally on the experience in self-government of "the Godly people of Connecticut," under their colonial charter. Until his death in New Haven in 1793, he labored for his people as a New England equivalent of Patrick Henry, to leave them a "negative" over hurtful innovations. In the Constitutional Convention, he had been Connecticut's member on the Great Committee, which was appointed shortly after he had made the house members aware that unless they attempted accommodation, their business was at a "full stop" and fruitless dissolution was likely. He had also helped to prevent the inclusion of a federal veto power over state laws. Though an Old Light Congregationalist who believed to the end that the "threatenings of divine law against impenitent sinners . . . are [as important] as the promises of the gospel," he had a strong faith in the ability of his neighbors to conduct their own business with probity and justice. His Connecticut was in essence a closed society, a corporate regime of which he approved. He went so far as to raise some doubt about the admission of "persons of different education, manners, and customs," whose immigration might "tend to disturb . . . tranquility."

But despite all his craft, he was a statesman who recognized that debt was a moral question, a provincial who seconded Franklin's belated motion for prayers to be said over the Framers before the opening of their sessions, and a senator who could openly advise his countrymen in a published sermon, "Let us live no more to ourselves, but to him who loved us and gave himself to die for us." Sherman's understanding of what was accomplished in Philadelphia differed drastically from that of James Madison and James Wilson, whose designs for a government he in many respects forestalled. The record of his participation in these events should serve as a correction of simplistic Federalist theories concerning their significance. For it was as much Sherman's Constitution as Madison's or Wilson's. Otherwise, Connecticut would have voted a resounding "no." (See Christopher Collier, *Roger Sherman's Connecticut: Yankee Politics and the American Revolution* [Middletown, Conn.: Wesleyan University Press, 1971]; Roger Sherman Boardman, *Roger Sherman: Signer and Statesman* [New York: Da Capo Press, 1971]; Lewis Henry Boutell, *The Life of Roger Sherman* [Chicago: A. C. McClurg, 1896]; Oscar Zeichner, *Connecticut's Years of Controversy, 1750–1776* [Chapel Hill: University of North Carolina Press, 1949]; Roger Waln, Jr., *Biography of the Signers to the Declaration of Independence,* vol. 3, pp. 199–306, ed. J. Sanderson [Philadelphia: R. W. Pomeroy, 1823]; Julian P. Boyd, "Roger Sherman: Portrait of a Cordwainer Statesman," *New England Quarterly* 5 [April 1932]: 221–236; Richard J. Purcell, *Connecticut in Transition, 1775–1818,* 2d ed. [Middletown, Conn.: Wesleyan University Press, 1963]; H. James Henderson, *Party Politics in the Continental Congress* [New York: McGraw-Hill, 1974]; Bernard C. Steiner, "Connecticut's Ratification of the Federal Constitution," *Proceedings of the American Antiquarian Society* 25 [April 1915]: 70–127; Larry Gerlach, "Toward a More Perfect Union: Connecticut, the Continental Congress and the Constitutional Convention," *Bulletin of the Connecticut Historical Society* 34 [July 1969]: 69–78; Philip Harding Jordan, Jr., "Connecticut during the Revolution and Confederation, 1776–1789" [Ph.D. dissertation, Yale University, 1962]; Forrest McDonald, *E Pluribus Unum: The Formation of the American Republic, 1776–1790* [Indianapolis: Liberty Press, 1979], esp. pp. 291–294; John G. Rommel, *Connecticut's Yankee Patriot: Roger Sherman* [Hartford, Conn.: American Revolution Bicentennial Commission of Connecticut, 1979]; Christopher Collier, "Sovereignty Finessed: Roger Sherman,

Oliver Ellsworth, and the Ratification of the Constitution in Connecticut," in *The Constitution and the States: The Role of the Original Thirteen in the Framing and Adoption of the Federal Constitution*, ed. Patrick T. Conley and John P. Kaminski [Madison, Wis.: Madison House, 1988], pp. 93–112.)

# WILLIAM SAMUEL JOHNSON
October 7, 1727–November 14, 1819
Lawyer, educator, religious leader, and statesman

*A figure of great distinction, both in Connecticut and in all the Confederation, before his election to a seat in the Constitutional Convention. A force for moderation, at Philadelphia and throughout his long career in public life. Decidedly a man of the law, of the great Anglo-American legal prescription, and no democrat. A man who declared in a moment of self-revelation, "I must live in peace or I cannot live at all." A neutral (with Loyalist leanings) during the Revolution, who nevertheless retained the regard of his neighbors even when they favored separation from the mother country. In 1787 perhaps the first citizen of his state. An Old Whig cum Federalist who had honored the English constitution as sovereign before 1776 and who wanted another sovereign law to replace it once independence had been achieved. Son of the Reverend Dr. Samuel Johnson (1696–1777), Connecticut's first native-born Anglican minister, first president of King's College, and a philosopher of note, and of Charity Floyd Johnson, originally of Brookhaven, Long Island. Great-great-grandson of Robert Johnson of Yorkshire, England, who in 1638 had crossed the ocean to assist in founding a "godly commonwealth" at New Haven. Born at Stratford, Connecticut, where his father had a flourishing parish. Educated at home and at Yale, where he graduated in 1744 and took an M.A. in 1747. Also awarded an honorary M.A. from Harvard and an M.A. and LL.D. from Oxford. Trained for the church, but, to Samuel Johnson's great disappointment, turned to the law. Read thoroughly in that discipline under the direction of William Smith, Jr., of New York. Admitted to the Connecticut bar in 1749. Rose swiftly to the head of his profession, with a practice among New York merchants and in his own state. Was chosen for public responsibilities in Stratford as early as 1753 (military). Selectman of his town in 1760. Represented Stratford in the House of Representatives in 1761 and 1765–1766. From 1766 to 1776 (except when in England), member of the Council or upper house of the Connecticut legislature. Colonial agent of his state in London from 1767 to 1771. Reluctantly drawn into the quarrel between the colonies and the British government.*

William Samuel Johnson was one of Connecticut's delegates to the Stamp Act Congress of 1765 and signed the petitions produced by that body. He openly disapproved of every English attempt to raise revenue from North Americans who had no representation in Parliament. After a brief delay, while he doubted the utility of resistance, this American Dr. Johnson became a strong supporter of the colonial embargo on trade with Great Britain—at least until Parliament repealed such distasteful laws as the Stamp Act and the Townshend Duties and revoked the extension of vice-admiralty jurisdiction to a new court in Halifax, where Americans might be tried without a jury of their peers.

While acting as agent for the Connecticut government (and despite his connections in the hierarchy of the Church of England and his 1766 Oxford doctorate in law), he acquired a reputation in the mother country as a spokesman for the "popular party" and a vigorous defender of the right of Englishmen everywhere to the protection of their constitution. But he argued this case on the grounds of legal, historic, and inherited rights—not upon a philosophical doctrine of natural rights. Indeed, he disliked dialectical politics, so much so that he once declared, "Certain political questions, like some intricate points in Divinity, had better never be meddled with. The discussion of them can hardly do any good and will certainly produce much mischief. While they serve to whet the wits of men, they more surely sharpen their tempers toward each other." He called for prudence among his countrymen in their responses to "despotic" English policies and for an avoidance of noisy abstractions, realizing that a revolution against British authority conducted in the name of abstract rights would produce a weak, divided, almost ungovernable nation in the colonies. As the fires of revolution spread among his countrymen, Johnson asked, "When shall we come to a right understanding of these great or at least curious questions of right . . . [and see] that it is dangerous or at least unnecessary to define precisely these deep and difficult objects?" Until 1787 he got no answer.

After returning to New England following his tenure as London agent for Connecticut, William Samuel Johnson did all that he could to further "moderate men or moderate measures. . . . With no others" would he "be concerned." Because of what he had seen in England, he doubted that the ministers of King George III were consciously plotting against the liberties of Americans: "The truth perhaps is that neither side is so bad or have so mischievous designs as the other imagines . . . and [yet] we are in danger of falling together by the ears in the dark." He knew, as early as 1766, that revolution was likely. But he was determined to resist the trend. The thought and the language of the American leaders, those who would most likely inherit authority once the conflict began, disturbed him deeply. In Massachusetts there was an outcry for the rights of man. But for Johnson, the "principles and spirit" of the English constitution were sufficient. He continued as a member of the Governor's Council, the first Episcopalian to be so elevated in Connecticut. He was appointed judge of the superior court and colonel of the militia. And he received the official "thanks of the assembly" for his labors in England. In 1774 he was elected delegate for Connecticut to the Continental Congress. The last of these honors he refused, and the other posts he resigned. Dr. Johnson delayed announcing his disapproval of the Declaration of Independence as long as he could, nor was he about to leave Stratford or bear arms against its citizens. About his American identity, there was never any doubt. But in 1777, when a law required that officers of the Connecticut courts swear an oath of fidelity to the new, independent government of the state, Johnson declined. He returned, for what he thought would be the duration of the conflict with England, to private life.

The circumstance of the Revolution, however, drew Johnson back from the fringes of his society sometime before the war was concluded. In the summer of 1779, after a number of British raids on the exposed coast of Connecticut, his neighbors asked him to negotiate an immunity for Stratford with the threatening British authorities in New York. Reluctantly, the cautious, conservative attorney agreed to intercede, on condition that the townspeople sign a pledge to support and exonerate him should any blame attend the enterprise. On learning of these events, Gov. Jonathan Trumbull and the members of the council found no fault in Johnson's part in this business. But to clear away the confusion, Johnson felt compelled to swear allegiance to the regime. Thereafter his entire situation began to improve, and he resumed the practice of law. Officers of the state government called upon him to plead Connecticut's case in a special court set up to hear the dispute over the Susquehanna lands in Pennsylvania. And in 1784 he was chosen as a delegate to the Confederation Congress for the following year. In that capacity Johnson won for Connecticut a sizable concession in the Northwest Territory. All at once he was again a highly respected figure, mentioned as a probable governor, recognized as the leader of the Connecticut bar, and considered for a college presidency, either at Columbia College or at the College of Philadelphia, later the University of Pennsylvania. Johnson was still a Connecticut delegate to Congress when nominated for a seat in the Constitutional Convention. His was the first name chosen by the Connecticut Assembly.

When he heard of the prospects of an attempt to revise the Articles of Confederation, William Samuel Johnson was opposed. He feared that his countrymen were in a mood to make a bad government worse. Yet, once in Philadelphia, he was pleased by the quality of the various delegations and gave himself to the work at hand. Since 1783 he had been of the opinion that the absence of commercial regulations and the failure to raise revenue had left the Congress without the power necessary to conduct government. And, like most American leaders, he had been alarmed by Shays' Rebellion, which had spilled over the Connecticut border at Sharon. Perhaps, with these eruptions as a backdrop, the "timidity and obstinacy" of the states could be overcome, without endangering their existence or taking away too much of their power. After June 2, when he arrived at the Great Convention, until its work was finally done, Johnson was constant in his attendance at each day's sessions. He joined with his Connecticut colleagues, Roger Sherman and Oliver Ellsworth, in arguing for equal representation for the states in the national legislature—or at least in one of its chambers. Said Johnson, since state governments were not to be destroyed and the new federal authority was "not for the people of America but for the political societies called states which compose the Union . . . they [the states] must, therefore, have a voice in the second branch, if it was meant to preserve their existence, the people composing already the first." Johnson was effective in making his case for the U.S. Senate, with an equal vote for each state. As one of the senior members of the Convention, he spoke eloquently for preserving "some portion of sovereignty" in the states. The Union would be a Union of the states, both federal and national in its design, or no Union at all.

Both Sherman and Ellsworth spoke more frequently than Johnson. Because of their efforts Connecticut got most of what it wanted. Yet combinations with the delegations of other states were necessary to the success of a cautious policy—usually combinations with the men of the South. Johnson was quick to help, to defend the compromise on representation, and even to suggest that the planters be allowed to count their slaves for purposes of representation. "Considerations" of "morality," the Connecticut delegates insisted, belonged only "to the states." His friend Jeremiah Wadsworth reported, "The southern delegates are vastly fond of him." His manners and sweetness of temper were proverbial. Charming and gracious to all, he was a gentleman. But, most important, he set himself against any trend that would lead his country toward a commitment to ideological politics. He remained unwilling to argue from definition. With regret he had come away from the protection of a sovereign law, and to that kind of protection he now hoped to repair: to law and equity based on experience and the English form of jurisprudence. Law and equity, but not disembodied principle, which is easily corrupted into a license for despotism.

From Philadelphia Johnson returned to Connecticut. After a brief trip to New York to accept the presidency of Columbia College, he led the discussion and defended the Constitution in Connecticut's ratification convention. Despite his new assignment in the Empire State, Johnson was chosen as one of Connecticut's original U.S. senators, in which office he served until 1791, when the government removed to Philadelphia. In the Senate he supported Hamilton's financial system and helped to secure the adoption of the Judiciary Act of 1789, expressing always his eagerness to preserve a continuity with English antecedents. His tenure as president of Columbia continued until 1800. In that office he distinguished himself greatly, recruiting a good faculty and establishing a firm foundation for the school's future development. Unlike many college presidents of his day, he kept the spirit of the French Revolution (which he deplored) off the campus of his school. Age and poor health forced his retirement. However, once back at Stratford he revived and lived to the great age of ninety-two, making him the longest-lived of the Framers. In his last years he was instrumental in organizing the Protestant Episcopal church in America—thus fulfilling his father's dream—in addition to being a guide and counselor to the young attorneys and public men of his state and a beloved patriarchal figure. (See Elizabeth P. McCaughey, *From Loyalist to Founding Father: The Political Odyssey of William Samuel Johnson* [New York: Columbia University Press, 1980]; William Allen Benton, *Whig-Loyalism: An Aspect of Political Ideology in the American Revolutionary Era* [Rutherford, N.J.: Fairleigh Dickinson University Press, 1969]; George C. Groce, Jr., *William Samuel Johnson, A Maker of the Constitution* [New York: Columbia University Press, 1937]; E. Edwards Beardsley, *The Life and Times of William Samuel Johnson, LL.D.* [New York: Hurd & Houghton, 1876]; Larry Gerlach, "Toward a More Perfect Union: Connecticut, the Continental Congress, and the Constitutional Convention," *Bulletin of the Connecticut Historical Society* 34 [July 1969]: 65–78; Evarts Boutell Greene, "William Samuel Johnson and the American Revolution," *Columbia University Quarterly* 22 [June 1930]: 152–178; David C. Humphrey, *From King's College to Columbia, 1746–1800* [New York: Columbia University Press, 1976].)

# OLIVER ELLSWORTH
April 29, 1745–November 26, 1807
Lawyer, jurist, and American statesman

*Mild Federalist, but only on the condition that the small states keep their equality of representation in one house of the national legislature. Vigorous defender of states' rights within the federal Union. Warm advocate of the compromise between the sections on the counting of slaves for the purpose of allotting congressional seats. Enemy of the teleocratic or normative approach to the relation of federal power and the internal operations of the member commonwealths: "Let every State import what it pleases. The morality or wisdom of slavery are considerations belonging to the States themselves—What enriches a part enriches the whole, and the States are the best judges of their particular interest. . . . Let us not intermeddle." A great inducement to moderation and confidence in their future within the Union for the southern Framers. A man of the letter of the law from his early youth. After 1789, alarmed at the influence of the French Revolution on some of his countrymen. An Anglophile when American interests were not threatened by English power. As a judge, precisely the kind of person that he was as a Framer, convinced that "it is of more importance, for a judicial determination, to ascertain what the law is, than to speculate what it ought to be." An active member of the Constitutional Convention, where he spoke eighty-four times. A father of the great tradition of the moderate or "cotton" Whigs—the party of Daniel Webster, Rufus Choate, and Robert Winthrop.*

Oliver Ellsworth was born at Windsor, Connecticut, the son of Capt. David Ellsworth and Jemima Leavitt Ellsworth. His great-grandfather, Josiah Ellsworth, had come from Yorkshire, England, to Windsor ca. 1650. Oliver's father intended him for the Congregationalist ministry and had him prepared by the Reverend Joseph Bellamy of Bethlehem, Connecticut. Young Oliver went to New Haven in 1762 but was not happy among the sons of Eli, and at the end of his sophomore year he transferred to the College of New Jersey, from which he was graduated in 1766. Upon returning home, he took up the study of theology but did not long continue in that labor and turned instead to reading in the law, as had many of his friends at Princeton. To support himself in this endeavor, he cut and sold timber and farmed land belonging to his father. In 1771 he was admitted to the bar. He did not prosper rapidly in the law, but slowly he developed a reputation for competence and rectitude. In 1773 his neighbors in Windsor named him their deputy to the General Assembly. Within a few years he was one of the most famous attorneys in Connecticut, with land and houses, money to lend, and interests in many enterprises. His style in speaking and writing turned magisterial, and his appearance became "scrupulously elegant." In 1775 he moved to Hartford and was never far from the center of Connecticut's political life for the remainder of his career.

During the American Revolution Ellsworth committed himself to the patriot cause almost from the beginning. From 1775 he was a member of the Connecticut Committee of the Pay Table, which supervised the state's military expenditures. Two years later he became state's attorney for Hartford County, in which office he continued until 1785. In 1778 he was chosen as one of Connecticut's delegates to the Continental Congress, where he sat until 1783. And in 1779, while serving as deputy from Hartford, he was made a member of the Connecticut Council of Safety, the chief governing body of the state for purposes of defense. From 1780 to 1785, Ellsworth had a place on the Governor's Council. In Congress, Ellsworth was much involved with American maritime concerns. He was appointed to a committee to hear appeals from state courts and admiralty and in that capacity sought to uphold the authority of the general government. He was vigorous in collecting supplies for Washington's army, scrupulous in his management of funds while on the board of treasury, interested in treaties and trade, and eager to bring peace with England, assuming that the restoration of friendly relations with the mother country, once independence had been achieved, would best serve the development of England's former colonies. In the Congress Ellsworth often voted with members of a New England "bloc" and often gave priority to the special concerns of his state. After the conclusion of the war, though he was a confirmed cultural pluralist from his first appearance on the national scene and though he was unwilling to surrender Connecticut's control over its own identity, Ellsworth served gladly with James Madison and Alexander Hamilton on a special committee of the Congress called upon to create a comprehensive system of administration. In 1784 Ellsworth was appointed a member of Connecticut's Supreme Court of Errors and shortly thereafter was named a judge of the Connecticut Superior Court.

Meanwhile, behind the scenes he moved cautiously toward nationalism, writing to Gov. Jonathan Trumbull, "There must, Sir, be a revenue somehow established that can be relied on and applied for national purposes as the exigencies arise, independent of the will or views of a single State, or it will be impossible to support national faith or national existence. The powers of Congress must be . . . adequate to the purposes of their institution. It is possible there may be abuses and misapplications; still it is better to hazard something than to hazard all." In such a cautious spirit and though still a "local-minded" man, Ellsworth went toward the Constitutional Convention, hopeful, as he said in Philadelphia, of "building on the states"—out of their integrity, not at their expense—"our general government."

In the Great Convention the motto of Oliver Ellsworth, in dealing with high Federalists who were likely to spoil the business, was in keeping with his politics at other important times in his life: "Let not too much be attempted." As one biographer, William Garrott Brown, has observed, Ellsworth did not "conceive of the people of the whole country either as the true constituency of the Convention, or as the source of authority for the new government." The sovereignty of the general government, in its restricted sphere, would have to be derived from the states. He would have nothing to do with a theory like James Wilson's—that the Declaration of Independence created one nation, not thirteen. Ellsworth wanted a union that was "partly federal and partly national." It fell to him to make the final motion that every state be represented equally in the second branch of the Congress of the United States (June 29), even as they had been under the Articles of Confederation. He carried much of the burden of debate for the small-states men opposed to the Virginia Plan. The U.S. Senate would be like the House of Lords in the English system—a check on popular majorities. It should not dominate, but it might restrain. "We know," Ellsworth said in Philadelphia, that "the people of the states are strongly attached to their own constitutions. If you hold up a system of general government, destructive of their constitutional rights, they will oppose it. . . . The only chance we have to support a general government is to graft it on the state governments," so that "the U.S. are sovereign on one side of the line dividing jurisdictions—the States on the other"—both having "power to defend their respective Sovereignties."

Ellsworth was opposed to including a federal power of veto over state legislation. Furthermore, he hoped to minimize federal authority over state militias and to preclude by law uninvited federal invasions of states experiencing internal disorders. If the president was not to be chosen by the state legislatures, he recommended that members of the electoral college be selected there. And he favored provision for the salaries of members of the proposed congress through legislation in the states. To the centralizers among the Framers, he issued a warning that looked toward the political difficulty of ratification: "If we are so exceedingly jealous of the state legislatures, will they not have reason to be jealous of us?" Concerning the regulation of suffrage, he spoke to the same effect: "The States are the best Judges of the circumstances and temper of their own people."

Ellsworth's part in the discussion of slavery should be interpreted in the context of these related misgivings about attempting too much. Indirectly he reproached George Mason for being moralistic about the slave trade while continuing as one of America's major slaveholders. He observed with irony that if slavery "was to be considered in a moral light we ought to go farther and free those already in the Country," knowing that the Virginians would agree to nothing of the kind. Ellsworth was a realist who saw the danger of division, probably at the Delaware River, with states ready to "fly into a variety of shapes & directions" if the Framers were doctrinaire. As Connecticut was protective of its own peculiarities, so he opposed disestablishment of the churches in Connecticut. Moreover, in the Continental Congress he had supported a proclamation against "evil amusements," such as "play going, gaming, and horse races." But such sentiments were only advisory. Ellsworth was unusual among his New England "brethren" in recognizing that all Americans did not and would not share in one system of values. If a Constitution was to be produced, every portion of the Union could be asked to agree upon procedures and to surrender whatever authority or practice that was not essential to its well-being—just as Connecticut was willing to give up its preference for an annually elected national legislature, once Abraham Baldwin had explained the inconvenience such an arrangement would impose on Georgia and South Carolina. Slavery, as the Connecticut men understood, was not negotiable if union was to be achieved. Ellsworth, who was the only Connecticut delegate who neither owned slaves nor had slaveholders in his family, had little patience with self-serving declarations. Toward the end of the Convention he admonished his colleagues that time was running short. On or about August 25, most of the discussion being complete, he left Philadelphia— knowing that Sherman and Johnson could represent his views while he saw to his judicial duties in Connecticut.

In the struggle for ratification of the Constitution in Connecticut, Oliver Ellsworth played a central role. In the state convention of January 1788, called upon to judge that document, Ellsworth made a principal address in which he argued that under the terms of the federal compact, "this is a government of strictly defined powers," in which the "particular states retain their sovereignty" where it is not clearly surrendered. Modern scholars, who read the Constitution less well than he, have charged Ellsworth and Sherman with misrepresenting the federal bond. Their distortion of the evidence on this subject is more a reflection of the confusion of our times than a judgment of Ellsworth and Sherman, who understood the Constitution very well.

Ellsworth compared Connecticut, surrounded by states that under the Articles were free to tax its commerce if shipped though their ports, to "Issachar of old, a strong ass couching down between two burdens" (Gen. 49:14). His exposition of the Constitution was accepted by an overwhelming majority at the Connecticut ratifying convention. He also wrote many essays in the press, under the name "Landholder," which urged approval of what had been achieved in Philadelphia. Some of these were in reply to Elbridge Gerry and Luther Martin. They were widely circulated in several states.

From 1789 to 1796, Ellsworth was U.S. senator from Connecticut, in which office he was a firm pillar in the Washington administration. He was the author of the Judiciary Act and instrumental in the adoption of most of Alexander Hamilton's financial program. He wrote the act accepting North Carolina's cession of western lands and another act that provided government for the unorganized territory south of the Ohio River. His embargo on Rhode Island helped compel that troublesome commonwealth to ratify the Constitution and join the Union. He helped persuade southerners to agree to a federal assumption of state debts in return for location of the nation's permanent capital on the Potomac. During his years in the Senate, he was one of its most influential members and is remembered for his role in creating instruments and agencies of the new government.

Ellsworth believed in judicial review as a means of preserving the constitutional balance of powers between the states and the United States. In 1796, President Washington appointed him chief justice of the U.S. Supreme Court, in which office he served until 1800. On the federal bench, Ellsworth was involved in few important cases and showed little disposition to expand the scope of the Court. In *Wiscart* v. *Dauchy,* his ruling (based on his own authority as author of the Judiciary Act of 1789) restricted the review power in cases of equity and is in contradiction to the judicial logic of his successor, John Marshall. Ellsworth also affirmed the authority of the English common law in the courts of the United States. In one instance, he went so far as to enforce it against the British consul in Charleston, South Carolina. In perhaps his most unusual decision, *United States* v. *Isaac Williams,* he maintained that U.S. citizens had no right of expatriation. Justice Ellsworth found the life of a federal judge wearisome and tedious, particularly the long journeys on the circuit.

In 1799, President John Adams named Ellsworth, William Richardson Davie of North Carolina, and William Vans Murray of Maryland to serve as commissioners to the French Republic to negotiate an accord that would adjust the differences that had brought the two countries to the brink of war. The French had been seizing and harassing American vessels under a decree declaring trade with England to be contraband. The American emissaries were dispatched in the expectation that they would deal with Talleyrand and the Directory—the government that had recently insulted the mission of Charles Cotesworth Pinckney, Elbridge Gerry, and John Marshall. Instead, they were confronted with the recently elevated First Consul, Napoleon Bonaparte. The new French government would not agree to reparations indemnifying Americans for losses, but the French did accept a redefinition of contraband that restricted the term to mean military supplies and agreed to follow more responsible and regular policies in their treatment of captured American property. The result of this negotiation was the Convention of Mortefontaine in October 1800. Neither Federalists nor Democratic-Republicans were satisfied with the treaty, though the Congress ratified it in February 1801. Oliver Ellsworth's health had collapsed during the long voyage to Europe, and he was ill during much of the negotiation. Attempting to regain his strength, he tarried a while in France and briefly visited England. The European experience confirmed his opinion of the French Revolution as one that "ignored the selfish nature of man," and he was further convinced of the importance of the English heritage to Americans.

Upon his return to the United States, Ellsworth retired from national politics, though he served again from 1802 until his death in 1807 on the Connecticut Governor's Council. In these last years his health continued to decline, but he remained cheerful and active in agriculture (on his farm near Windsor) and in the affairs of his state. He never encouraged the secessionist tendencies that were so widespread among the New England Federalists following Jefferson's election. Indeed, he refused to do so even though he had in 1794 suggested to John Taylor of Caroline the legality of peaceful secession as an option open to the South. At the time of his death, Oliver Ellsworth was Connecticut's leading citizen, one of the "river gods" of the Connecticut River valley who had directed the state in a temperate course during the difficult period of transition that saw the birth of the republic. (See William Garrott Brown, *The Life of Oliver Ellsworth* [New York: Da Capo Press, 1970]; Richard J. Purcell, *Connecticut in Transition, 1775–1818*, 2d ed. [Middletown, Conn.: Wesleyan University Press, 1963]; Christopher Collier, *Roger Sherman's Connecticut: Yankee Politics and the American Revolution* [Middletown, Conn.: Wesleyan University Press, 1971]; Larry Gerlach, "Toward a More Perfect Union: Connecticut, the Continental Congress, and the Constitutional Convention," *Bulletin of the Connecticut Historical Society* 34 [July 1969]: 69–78; Bernard C. Steiner, "Connecticut's Ratification of the Federal Constitution," *Proceedings of the American Antiquarian Society* 25 [April 1915]: 70–127; Philip Harding Jordan, Jr., "Connecticut during the Revolution and Confederation, 1776–1789" [Ph.D. dissertation, Yale University, 1962]; Michael Kraus, "Oliver Ellsworth," in *The Justices of the United States Supreme Court, 1789–1969: Their Lives and Major Opinions*, vol. 1, ed. Leon Friedman and Fred L. Israel [New York: R. R. Bowker/Chelsea House, 1969], pp. 223–235; H. James Henderson, *Party Politics in the Continental Congress* [New York: McGraw-Hill, 1974]; William C. Dennis, "A Federalist Persuasion: The American Ideal of the Connecticut Federalists" [Ph.D. dissertation, Yale University, 1971]; Ronald John Lettieri, *Connecticut's Young Man of the Revolution: Oliver Ellsworth* [Hartford, Conn.: American Revolution Bicentennial Commission of Connecticut, 1978]; Christopher Collier, "Sovereignty Finessed: Roger Sherman, Oliver Ellsworth, and the Ratification of the Constitution in Connecticut," in *The Constitution and the States: The Role of the Original*

*Thirteen in the Framing and Adoption of the Federal Constitution,* ed. Patrick T. Conley and John P. Kaminski [Madison, Wis.: Madison House, 1988], pp. 93–112; Donald S. Lutz, "Connecticut: Achieving Consent and Assuring Control," in *Ratifying the Constitution,* ed. Michael Allen Gillespie and Michael Lienesch [Lawrence: University Press of Kansas, 1989].)

# NEW YORK

# ALEXANDER HAMILTON

January 11, 1757–July 12, 1804
Soldier, lawyer, statesman, economist, and political
philosopher

*Became a leader of the Federalist party, both in New York and throughout the
nation. Though one of the fathers of the republic, important in the Constitutional
Convention primarily as a foil to milder nationalists, who could appear to be
reasonable in comparison with his attitude toward the concentration of power.
The most extreme nationalist among the high Federalists. With James Wilson and
two or three other delegates, willing to abolish the several states had it been
politically feasible. Yet skilled in state and local politics, and primarily responsible for securing New York's ratification of the document produced in Philadelphia. As one of the authors of* The Federalist *and as author of the doctrine of
implied powers, was a permanent influence on the interpretation of the U.S.
Constitution. A man of extraordinary gifts, almost a prodigy, but possessed of a
supreme self-confidence, with a touch of haughtiness and hyperbole, that earned
him enemies throughout his career. Born on the island of Nevis, one of the
Leeward chain in the West Indies. Natural son of James Hamilton of Ayrshire,
Scotland, fourth son of Alexander Hamilton, the laird of Grange; and of Rachel
Fawcett, the daughter of a French planter and physician. The union of his
parents, perhaps sanctioned by some kind of ceremony, but illegal, and, by
reason of certain irregularities, at best a common-law marriage. Marked
throughout his life by the stigma of his origins. Without a father from an early
age and all but an orphan at eleven. Educated privately on St. Croix, in
apprenticeship to the island firm of Nicholas Cruger; at Francis Barber's school
in Elizabethtown, New Jersey; and at King's College (later Columbia) in New
York, where he was enrolled in 1773. A superb and systematic student and at
seventeen, with the growing dispute between the American colonies and the
ministers of George III, a fledgling orator and political pamphleteer. In the*

*spring of 1776, left school without a degree for military responsibilities in the American army.*

Alexander Hamilton did commendable service as a captain of artillery during the retreat from New York, in the following campaign in New Jersey, and in Washington's winter raids on Trenton and Princeton. But to his good fortune, either some of his writings or his conduct in the field had caught the attention of the commander in chief. Washington's function was so much more than that of general that he required a large staff to sift and organize the information coming into his hands and to execute his orders. He especially needed a secretary with judgment and a skilled pen. As General Washington's aide-de-camp, Hamilton was promoted to the rank of lieutenant colonel, giving him some of the distinction his spirit craved, and then he was thoroughly swallowed up by his military duties for the next four years. He distinguished himself in this role and, in the process, established a reputation and a set of contacts that determined the direction of his future development as a public man. But after a small quarrel with General Washington late in the war, Hamilton asked for and received permission to return to duty in the Continental Line, where, at Yorktown, he won glory in a fierce assault on one of Lord Cornwallis's redoubts—a successful night attack that led to the English capitulation. Following the great victory, Hamilton retired from the army and was elected to the Confederation Congress, where he sat from late 1782 into 1783.

Early study, reinforced by his military experience and the deep-set bias of his mind, disposed Alexander Hamilton to be the consistent "friend to vigorous government"—energetic, "creative," the "national sovereignty, transcendent and entire." From 1778 through 1787, with an ever-growing firmness, Hamilton's view of the American political situation was that once free of George III, the United States should find a sovereign to act in that sovereign's stead and then, with obedience, strengthen that power as best it could. In substitution for Crown and Parliament, some other ground of unity would be required—some American equivalent of the smooth-working complexity of Britain's ancient, inherited regime. Only for a short time, as a politically precocious boy, did Hamilton stand in point of tangency with the radical Whigs and expand upon "the sacred rights of mankind . . . not to be rummaged for among old parchments of musty records [but] written, as with a sunbeam, in the whole volume of human nature by the hand of the divinity itself."

Reading David Hume and leadership experience in the struggles of the Revolution changed these opinions. In 1778 Hamilton spoke chiefly of the right of "self-preservation" if he spoke of natural rights at all. And in any case, even as a youthful enthusiast of independence, the young philosopher never ceased to approve of the English constitution as the "best in the world." The Coercive Acts of 1774, the Prohibitory Acts of the next year, and George III's "Proclamation for

Suppressing Rebellion and Sedition" had forced Americans to give up their hope of an English "league" of states under a common Crown and to consider Parliament as an enemy. Separation from the mother country was, by British policy, made inevitable. But even as independence approached, a guarantee of that liberty for which "he should be as willing a martyr . . . as any man whatever," Hamilton took pause and shared with his friend John Jay his anxiety that "the same state of the passions which fits the multitude . . . for opposition to tyranny and oppression . . . naturally leads them to a contempt and disregard of all authority."

During the year following Yorktown, Hamilton read law, wrote his own manual for legal studies, and in April 1782 was admitted to membership in the New York bar—doing all this while he served as a delegate to the Congress. But the Alexander Hamilton who in 1783 returned from his political service to open an office on Wall Street and begin successfully to practice his profession had lost any regard for democracy that he might have entertained or any patience he might once have had with the sovereignties of the states. In the Congress he had worked hard to make government in the Confederation functional: to collect the impost, to use army pressure in supporting the funding system of Robert Morris, and to pass a diluted revenue plan. And, as he had done even while a soldier, he urged behind the scenes that the government be completely redesigned and set upon a proper financial basis. To that end he secured in 1786 his election as a New York representative to the convention in Annapolis, Maryland, which was to consider the regulation of interstate commerce and other national problems. There, with James Madison and John Dickinson, he persuaded his colleagues to agree upon an address to the states calling for a more general and ambitious assemblage to gather in Philadelphia the following May, to devise such changes in the bonds of their lawful connection "as shall appear to them necessary to render the constitution of the Federal government adequate to the exigencies of the Union." Hamilton (now an elected member of the incoming New York legislature) was responsible for his state's participation in the Annapolis Convention of 1786 and later took the lead in persuading it to send representatives to the Great Convention of 1787. To bestir the magnates of his state, he wrote and spoke of the spread of principles of the "leveling kind" and of the security against despotism that only a new government could provide. With the help of Captain Shays, he temporarily made Federalists out of narrowly local men.

What Hamilton hoped to produce through the law-proposing deliberations in Pennsylvania was not so much a government structured in a particular fashion, with a particular set of institutions, as a power. As Forrest McDonald has written, "What was important was to organize [a government] and to endow it with as much power in relation to the powers of the states as possible." Hamilton accepted the necessity for popular support, for affection and attachment and habit in the operations of an effective republican authority. And he also accepted the need for at least one chamber in the national legislature to be chosen by the people at large. But his final objective, even in these concessions, was to perfect in the United States, on a republican basis (since Americans must have it so), the English political system against which they had just finished making war. His differences with the other Framers resolved themselves into disputes over *which* English political tradition should be fostered on these shores, the heritage of Sir Robert Walpole and the "system" of the commercial Whigs or that of the "Oppositionists," the champions of distributed power, both Tory and Country Whig. The notion of attempting something original and unrelated to the Anglo-American past had little support among the authors of the Constitution. Some of Hamilton's adversaries insisted that the states would not be one unless they were secure in being many and that the nation's origins in established and independent multiplicity be made the basis of its union. Part of Hamilton's response to that insistence bespeaks familiar varieties of military and commercial federalism. Part of it comes from the fact that he was an immigrant who never learned to understand or to work with an American political heritage already in place before the Revolution commenced. But the most important ingredient in the position he assumed in the Great Convention and persisted in as Washington's "first minister" was his dream of an American empire, of national happiness and prosperity, power and glory fostered and encouraged through the agency of government—and particularly by means of financial policy.

Hamilton did not speak frequently while in Philadelphia. During much of the Convention he was in New York, handling pressing personal business and settling a quarrel between friends. Since the two other delegates from his state in most instances neutralized his vote and then, on July 10, canceled it outright by leaving Independence Hall in disgust with the centralist tendencies displayed there, Hamilton found it difficult to attach importance to what he might say or do in answering the obstructionism of John Lansing and Robert Yates. Hamilton first left the Convention on June 29, rejoined it briefly in mid-August, and then early in September resumed his seat and was constant in his attendance until the Constitution was signed. He was present often enough to get his view of the business on the record and to assist some of the less "high-toned" Federalists in defining the alternatives before the house and in resolving consequent disputes. On June 18, after listening quietly as the Convention divided into two more or less distinctive camps, represented by Randolph and Paterson, Hamilton rose to deliver a speech of five hours' duration. The entire address, which shocked many, concerned the necessity for granting sufficient force to the general government.

Since men "are rather reasoning than reasonable animals," Hamilton argued, and will not honor authority merely for reason's sake, they must be acted upon directly by the national power, so that interest, necessity, opinion, habit, respect, and ambition make of them better citizens. Free government was superior to absolute monarchy because it could "interest the passions of the community in its favour" and thus "beget public spirit and public confidence." The security of a government lies thus in attachment and custom, not in devotion to abstract principle or philosophical conviction. But the voice of the people is not the voice of God. And the immediate necessity for the American statesman is to "cure the people of their fondness for democracies." To that end, he recommended that the chief executive of the republic be elected to serve for a life term and that the members of the Senate, acting in the place of a House of Lords, be provided with an equivalent security in office. For thus the great merits of the English constitution might be replicated in America, innovation checked, property made secure, and a modicum of honor and disinterested virtue in office guaranteed—at least if balanced by a House of Representatives chosen on as "broad" a popular basis as was reasonable.

What Hamilton advocated in such addresses was, of course, no tyranny but a regime of the kind Americans, as colonials, had insisted upon *before* the Revolution. He was as attached to liberty in 1787 as he had been in 1775—liberty as he understood it. But he would have no part in fostering either a threat to property by legislative confiscation or a threat of general exploitation and unearned advantage by an aristocratic cabal. Better to leave the permanent interests or divisions of society balanced in an institutionalized tension, with the president to preside over their interplay. "Real liberty," Hamilton declared, "neither is found in despotism or the extremes of democracy, but in moderate governments—if we incline too much to democracy, we shall soon shoot into a monarchy."

Hamilton's objective in advancing his plan was to put his fellow Framers in mind of the importance of "stability and permanency" in government and of the respect of foreign powers that the country would have to earn if it expected to survive. That his model for administration winked at monarchy, he admitted freely. Most probably, the alternative to something close to monarchy *was* (from the appearance of things in the United States of 1787) democratic excess, followed by a "man on horseback," especially once the country had been developed, open lands filled, and widespread inequalities aggravated. His fondest hope was that the Convention would make a fundamental law that Americans would come to love and respect, the kind of law that would diminish the odds in favor of future disorders. He did not expect most of the other delegates to agree with much of what he proposed. To lift the debates toward consideration of a realistic theory of government would be enough. As he foresaw, his colleagues were not about to abolish the states, reduce them to the status of mere administrative districts, or allow the "Governor" (president) to appoint their chief executives. Neither would they give to the national government a veto over legislation in the states nor accord it the power to create state courts. Such arrangements had already occasioned one revolution. And, for this generation, one was enough. William Samuel Johnson, the wise old man of Connecticut, summarized the Convention's reaction to Colonel Hamilton's performance when he declared that "the gentleman from New-York" is "praised by every body . . . [but] supported by none."

In his participation in other debates during the Great Convention, Alexander

Hamilton made few broad generalizations or sweeping proposals and in most cases spoke briefly and to the question at hand. At one point he expressed his distrust of republics and at another indicated that the United States might come to monarchy in the end. He identified the great division among the states as being between North and South, commerce and agriculture—not between small and large. He called the states "artificial," in indifference to their various histories. He objected to the election of the president by any formula not involving the people. And he warned the Convention delegates that they would have to produce something, since there would be no second chance to write a constitution. When the document on which they had agreed left Philadelphia for presentation to the Congress and transmission to the states, it was represented as the approved handiwork of ten delegations "and Mr. Hamilton"—even though he had, on the last day of their gathering, reminded his fellow Framers that "no man's ideas were more remote from the plan than his own were known to be" and continued to speak of it thereafter as a "frail and worthless fabric," a fabric that would need young Mr. Hamilton for a "prop."

Yet, in fairness, no other American did more to secure the adoption of the Constitution by the states than did Alexander Hamilton. In person he organized and conducted the campaign for ratification in New York. And, against great odds, arguing and maneuvering in person, he (with the help of John Jay and Chancellor Robert Livingston) overcame Gov. George Clinton and the political leadership of the Empire State. In the moment of crisis during the ratification convention in Poughkeepsie, the advocates of the Constitution made good use of the approvals voted by other states, of arguments of the benefits that would accrue to New York if it voted yes, and finally of a threat to divide the state—a threat of secession by New York City, which would then join the Union on its own. Hamilton promised that the states would survive the change. The Antifederalists conceded that a new frame of government was needed, that New York could not go its own way, and that prior amendments might make the instrument palatable. Then they gave way.

On the national scene, as one author of *The Federalist*, Hamilton exercised a greater influence. Of the entire collection of eighty-five essays, Hamilton wrote fifty-two; John Jay, five; and James Madison, the rest. All of this was done in the midst of intense political activity in his own area. It was a remarkable tour de force. Hamilton's part in creating the composite *Federalist* of Publius fore-shadowed the view of the nature and purpose of the revised federal union he was to represent during the remainder of his public career. And the same might be said of Madison's contribution. Though in 1788 they appear as Publius in collaboration, what they wrote in that capacity suggested the quarrels soon to divide them. Madison in his essays emphasized the division and limitation of powers within the federal system, Hamilton the good results those powers might produce. Both Madison and Hamilton wrote on subjects suggestive of their own perspectives on what the new government would mean. Hamilton discussed economic concerns and the administrative and judicial functions of the national authority. Madison, in contrast, wrote on political theory and history and on what the government could not do. Both men agreed on the dangers of democracy and the mischief-making propensity of human nature. But Hamilton worked toward employing the passion of that "great beast," the people, to good ends, toward building a practical and progressive politics on a foundation of human weakness, whereas Madison worried about restraining the impact of these shortcomings with a careful set of counterpoints and negations. Hamilton did not concern himself with making the government "control itself." He thought instead of the limitless potential of sovereignty "as to all those objects entrusted to its management." The two men only appeared to approve the same Constitution. Or rather, they favored it for different reasons, with consequences that divided the Union within less than a century.

Alexander Hamilton was appointed, as he had expected to be, the nation's original secretary of the Treasury by President Washington and exercised probably his greatest influence on the subsequent history of the country while in that office. His financial system for funding the national and state debts, for converting those liabilities into a basis for credit and commercial activity, and for organizing the Bank of the United States have been remembered since his time simply as "Hamiltonianism." These policies when, in 1791, combined with his Report on Manufactures and his written opinion for Washington regarding the constitutionality of the Bank of the United States, made Hamilton the target of the opposition party that Madison and Jefferson were finally able to organize. Through that party they were able to redirect the country away from the ambitious designs of the Treasury secretary. The centerpiece of Hamilton's financial magic was, to be sure, little more than a modification of a British institution, the Bank of England, with tariffs added in support. It made some Federalists rich, sometimes at the expense of simple folk who did not understand assumption of discounted paper. Hamilton was, in fact, as Broadus Mitchell has observed, a "holdover from the mercantilist age, utilizing government as an indispensable engine of national improvement." But for his own profit he sought only the immortal renown that belongs to the lawgiver and founder of cities.

Hamilton left the Treasury in 1795, after he had helped to subdue the Whiskey Rebellion and after he had reached the point of open conflict with Jefferson. When the Democratic-Republicans established a party newspaper, with Philip Freneau as editor, Hamilton was ubiquitous in reply and was, in Jefferson's words, a "colossus" and "without numbers . . . an host within himself." Hamilton made the most of Jeffersonian involvement with Citizen Genet and the American enthusiasm for the French Revolution. He participated in discussions of foreign affairs within the Washington administration—once compromising his reputation for probity by communicating his impression of American policy to an English friend, Maj. George Beckwith. And he fought the spread of Jacobinism in America with all his energy. Particularly with his pen did he portray the incompatibility between "democracy" and "Christian civilization." Outside the cabinet he continued to support a pro-British rather than a pro-French connection, emphasizing America's continuing commercial connections with the mother country. Moreover, though he approved of Washington's position of noninvolvement in European conflicts, he did not lose sight of the advantages of war as an instrument for internal transformation of the nation.

Hamilton's conduct in the Treasury and his support of Jay's Treaty had offended the South. By 1798 he was a politically damaged man—even in New York. Differences with John Adams (not his kind of Federalist) worsened his problems. But despite Adams's succession, Hamilton still had friends in the cabinet, a following, and some genuine power. He continued to retain the regard of the former president, who had been (in Hamilton's words) an "Aegis very necessary" to his own role in the affairs of the republic. Along with the aging Washington, Hamilton was called back to military service, and in 1798 he was commissioned a major general. However, American diplomats arranged a settlement with France in the Convention of Mortefontaine and averted the danger of war. Washington died. The quarrel with Adams grew worse. The Jeffersonians decided they could win the election of 1800 without going through with their plans for secession. John Jay would not take his friend's advice about changing the process for selecting electors in New York. And Hamilton's season on center stage in the drama of American politics was at an end.

Or almost at an end. For Alexander Hamilton played a role in the election of his enemy Thomas Jefferson to be the nation's third president—a role that was instrumental in bringing about Hamilton's death. When Jefferson and Aaron Burr received an equal number of electoral votes for the presidency, and the resolution of this impasse fell to the House of Representatives, Hamilton advised his fellow Federalists to support Thomas Jefferson, a mistaken man of principle, over the opportunist Aaron Burr. When Hamilton later placed another check on the boundless ambitions of Aaron Burr, during a New York gubernatorial contest, Burr challenged him to a duel. The Federalist leader accepted Burr's challenge but refused to fire upon his adversary. On the heights of Weehawken Burr was less scrupulous, and gave Hamilton a wound that, on July 12, 1804, at two o'clock in the afternoon, proved mortal. There was a nationwide interval of shock when these events were reported. Revulsion set in against Burr, which, ironically, made of Hamilton's death his final public service.

Much of Hamilton's time in his years out of office had been taken up not by his obligations as party leader but with the responsibilities of a growing family and an active, distinguished, and profitable practice of law. With his wife, Elizabeth, the daughter of Gen. Philip Schuyler, he built a country place, "The Grange"—named after the Hamiltons' ancestral seat in Scotland. He continued to worry about the quality of the nation's leadership, despite the fact that Jefferson was "behaving better" than he had expected. To counter the impact of the organized network of the Democratic-Republicans, he drew up a plan for an organization of his own, the Christian Constitutional Society. About the same time he began to think more and more about religion. He had learned from disappointment and from the death of his son Philip in a duel that his notion of the will was not enough.

It was characteristic of Alexander Hamilton, both as Framer and as servant and leader of the early republic, to be a curious combination of self-confidence and deep desire to demonstrate his own worth. He had perhaps too much faith in "heroes" and "great men" and too little in the nomocratic arrangements that are the essence of civil society. We should take seriously his admonition to Jay that "it will not do to be overscrupulous. It is easy to sacrifice the substantial interests of society by a strict adherence of ordinary rules." In economics as in politics he was anachronistically impressed by the honor that could be achieved by managing people and distressed to think that "America if she attains greatness must creep to it." He liked the great game, and he played it for all the ordinary reasons, but also for "heads." Yet his service in designing, selling, organizing, and financing a viable government cannot be contested. Indubitably, he is the author of one of the accepted views of the American regime. And his insight into the dangers to the nation posed by European ideologies has something to teach us even now. For it was Hamilton who declared of the egalitarians of his day that they were "courting the strongest and most active passion of the human heart, *vanity*." The example of Hamilton, schooled by Blackstone, Hume, and Swift, will not soon be out of date. (See Forrest McDonald, *Alexander Hamilton: A Biography* [New York: W. W. Norton, 1979]; Jacob E. Cooke, *Alexander Hamilton: A Biography* [New York: Charles Scribner's Sons, 1982]; Gerald Stourzh, *Alexander Hamilton and the Idea of Republican Government* [Stanford, Calif.: Stanford University Press, 1970]; Morton J. Frisch, *Alexander Hamilton and the Political Order* [Lanham, Md.: University Press of America, 1991]; Broadus Mitchell, *Alexander Hamilton*, 2 vols. [New York: Macmillan, 1957, 1962]; John C. Miller, *Alexander Hamilton, Portrait in Paradox* [New York: Harper, 1959]; Louis M. Hacker, *Alexander Hamilton in the American Tradition* [New York: McGraw-Hill, 1957]; Nathan Schachner, *Alexander Hamilton* [New York: A. S. Barnes, 1961]; Douglass Adair with Marvin Harvey, "Was Alexander Hamilton a Christian Statesman?" in *Fame and the Founding Fathers*, ed. Trevor Colbourn [New York: W. W. Norton, 1974], pp. 141–159; Linda Grant De Pauw, *The Eleventh Pillar: New York State and the Federal Constitution* [Ithaca, N.Y.: Cornell University Press, 1966]; Harold C. Syrett, ed., *The Papers of Alexander Hamilton*, 26 vols. [New York: Columbia University Press, 1961–1979]; Alexander Hamilton Bicentennial Number, *William and Mary Quarterly* 12 [April 1955]; John P. Kaminski, "New York: The Reluctant Pillar," in *The Reluctant Pillar: New York and the Adoption of the Federal Constitution*, ed. Stephen L. Schecter [Troy, N.Y.: Russell Sage College, 1985], pp. 48–117; Cecil L. Eubanks, "New York: Federalism and the Political Economy of Union," in *Ratifying the Constitution,* ed. Michael Allen Gillespie and Michael Lienesch [Lawrence: University Press of Kansas, 1989].)

# ROBERT YATES
January 27, 1738–September 9, 1801
Lawyer, jurist, and leader of the Revolution

*A decided Antifederalist who in 1788 declared, "There is not a step toward this business that I ever agreed to; nor is there a sentence in it that I will ever agree to." Called by Allan Nevins "the Pym . . . of the revolution in New York." Yet in no sense a champion of popular government, despite his early commitment to American independence. Though of middling origins, comfortable with the hegemony of the Hudson River patroons, having himself married a Van Ness. A slaveholder and a serious Calvinist. Unwilling that the general-welfare clause of the Constitution should authorize ostensibly benevolent interference with "the most trifling concerns of every state." Son of Joseph Yates and Maria Dunbar Yates. Born in Schenectady, but associated throughout his adult life with Albany, the city to which his great-grandfather had immigrated ca. 1700. Given opportunities by his family. Read law with William Livingston after receiving a solid classical education in New York City. Admitted to the bar May 9, 1760, in Albany where, in the town's first ward, he was to become a living institution. An alderman of that city from 1771 to 1775. A member of the Committee of Safety in 1775. Elected to consecutive terms in the Provincial Congress, 1775–1777. Chairman of the New York State Committee on Military Operations, 1776–1777. Member of the Committee of Thirteen, which drafted his state's first constitution.*

In 1777 Robert Yates was appointed justice of the New York State Supreme Court, where he served until 1798. From 1790 until his retirement at the age of sixty, he was the chief justice of that court. In 1789 he was the Federalist candidate for governor, and in 1795 the Antifederalist candidate for the same office. Yates was the floor leader of the Antifederalists during New York's ratification convention, which began at Poughkeepsie on June 17, 1788. But he spoke there only once—to give the lie to what Hamilton claimed he (Hamilton) had said about abolishing the states in the Convention at Philadelphia—and, in view of what he knew of the determination of the Federalists, did not play his part well. Yet he was a popular man in New York, had been unanimously elected by the legislature as delegate to the Great Convention, was the brother of the leading Antifederalist propagandist, Abraham Yates, and was the coauthor of a letter to

Gov. George Clinton in which he and his erstwhile pupil John Lansing explained why they had withdrawn from the Constitutional Convention and had advised their fellow New Yorkers not to approve its results. It was Robert Yates and John Lansing who defined the Antifederalist position in their state, maintaining that the Framers had exceeded their authority, that the document would be "destructive of the political happiness of the citizens of the United States," and that state sovereignty was a better security for civil liberty than consolidated government. In other words, after this letter was published in December 1787, Yates was the natural choice as Antifederalist leader, given his contacts with other Antifederalists all over the country and his knowledge of Federalist arguments. Especially so as George Clinton was restrained by his role as governor.

In view of his party's large majority among the delegates elected to the New York ratifying convention, Yates was overconfident of victory. And among the Antifederalists he was not alone. Though he had a set of notes on what had been said in Philadelphia before his departure on July 10, 1787 (notes first published in 1821), Yates had great difficulty in preparing the "previous amendments," which were supposed to be attached as preconditions of ratification, intended to revise or prevent the creation of a consolidated government. Yates was incapable of doing so even though, in the winter of 1774–1775, he had devised a conservative and confederal plan of government on his own, one that left Americans with a British connection—and demonstrated that Yates was, though Antifederalist, no radical. Yates's silence on alternatives to the Constitution is puzzling.

Robert Yates voted against ratification of the Constitution, knowing that with the threat of New York City's secession from the state, the document would win approval. Yet, once ratification was complete, on the understanding that amendments would be recommended subsequently, he called for acceptance of the new government. Despite his support among people at all levels of the population in New York and despite his two almost successful attempts to win election as governor, the remainder of Yates's career was a slow decline toward obscurity. As an old man, he practiced a little law and served as commissioner in land disputes. He died in greatly reduced circumstances. (See U.S. Senate Document 728, 60th Cong., 2d sess. [1909], p. 205; Alfred F. Young, *The Democratic Republicans of New York: The Origins, 1763–1797* [Chapel Hill: University of North Carolina Press, 1967]; Jonathan Pearson, *Contributions for the Genealogies of the First Settlers of the Ancient County of Albany* [Albany, N.Y.: J. Munsell, 1872]; Stephen E. Sale, "Colonial Albany: Outpost of Empire" [Ph.D. dissertation, University of Southern California, Los Angeles, 1973]; Linda Grant De Pauw, *The Eleventh Pillar: New York State and the Federal Constitution* [Ithaca, N.Y.: Cornell University Press, 1966], pp. 62–63, 86–87, and passim; E. Wilder Spaulding, *New York in the Critical Period, 1783–1789* [New York: Columbia University Press, 1932], pp. 237–238, and passim; Peter C. Hoffer and N. E. H. Hull, "To Determine on the Future Government: Robert Yates' Plan of Union," *William and Mary Quarterly* 34 [April 1977]: 298–306; Carol Spiegelberg,

"Abraham Yates" [M.A. thesis, Columbia University, 1960]; Robert Yates, *Secret Proceedings and Debates of the Convention Assembled in Philadelphia in the Year 1787 . . . from the Notes Taken by the Late Robert Yates, Esquire, Chief Justice of New York, and Copied by John Lansing, Jr., Esquire, Late Chancellor, etc.* [Albany, N.Y.: Webster's & Skinner's, 1821]; John P. Kaminski, "New York: The Reluctant Pillar," in *The Reluctant Pillar: New York and the Adoption of the Federal Constitution,* ed. Stephen L. Schecter [Troy, N.Y.: Russell Sage College, 1985], pp. 48–117.)

# JOHN LANSING
January 30, 1754–December 12, 1829
Lawyer, statesman, and jurist

*Antifederalist, both by principle and by connection. Not frightened by Shays' Rebellion, nor by signs of economic instability. More apprehensive of "the loss of civil liberty" through "coercion" than of the "dissolution of the Union," and thus immune to the central strategy of Federalist rhetoric. In all New York the wealthiest member of his party. And, despite the link with Gov. George Clinton and the Yates brothers, one of the most disinterested. A Hudson River patrician and a slaveholder with a great estate at Lansingborough and forty thousand acres in the Blenheim Patent (Schoharie County, New York), who had doubts about any "energetic" or "consolidated" government. Son of Gerrit Jacob Lansing and Jannetje Waters Lansing. A descendant of Gerrit Lansing, who had emigrated from the Netherlands in the 1640s to settle on the manor of Rensselaerwyck. Born in Albany, and there educated. Read law with Robert Yates. Continued that legal training with the gifted and conservative James Duane of New York City. After admission to the bar in 1775, served as military secretary to Gen. Philip Schuyler. Elected six times to the New York Assembly, from 1780 to 1784 and in 1786 and 1788. In the last two of these terms, chosen as speaker of the assembly. Selected as one of New York's delegates to the Confederation Congress in 1784 and 1785. Mayor of Albany, 1786–1790. New York commissioner in 1786 boundary dispute with Massachusetts and in a later negotiation with Vermont.*

Though still a young man, John Lansing was an experienced political figure when selected with his erstwhile mentor Judge Robert Yates to represent the dominant antinationalist sentiment of his state in the Great Convention. Alexander Hamilton was a third member of the delegation but went as an empty concession to the defeated centralizers of New York City. Lansing and Yates (their families were joined by marriage) went to Philadelphia as men well *instructed,* whether or not the "country party" leaders had given them overt directions. They were authorized to consider a revision of the Articles of Confederation—that much, but no more. Once certain that their associates would attempt something more ambitious, the two New York Antifederalists, on July 10, went home, explaining their reasons for withdrawal in a long, apologetic epistle to Gov. George Clinton.

While in the Convention they were quiet, took notes, and generally supported the position of William Paterson of New Jersey, the spokesman for the small states. Their natural allies, however, were not Paterson, Dickinson, and Read, who accepted the Constitution once an equal voice for each state had been included in the Senate; but, rather, Mercer and Martin of Maryland, Mason of Virginia, and Gerry of Massachusetts, who doubted the wisdom of attempting a completely new frame of government—a government national in its nature and remote from the particularistic "genius" of the local community. Lansing made only one major speech in Philadelphia; on June 16 he delivered an attack on "consolidation." Arguing that the distinct sovereignties of the states should be preserved, he asserted that "all Reasoning on Systems unaided by Experience has generally been productive of false Inferences." He accused the centralizers of being "theoretic" and of desiring a perfection which never existed. (Lansing's notes on the sessions he attended, though not published until 1939, are sometimes useful as a correction of other records, particularly as a supplement to Madison's somewhat selective recall.) His second speech, on June 20, was essentially a gloss upon his earlier presentation, though here he elaborated on his argument against "inequality of representation" with an appeal to the conservative spirit of the American people and the related argument concerning the limited authority of the Convention.

During the June 1788 debates of the New York ratification convention in Poughkeepsie, Lansing shared with Melancton Smith the major responsibility for carrying the Antifederalist side of the debate against such Federalist worthies as Hamilton, Jay, and Chancellor Robert R. Livingston. He had a spirited exchange with Hamilton concerning whether that artful Scot at one point in Philadelphia had actually called for the abolition of the states. Moreover, Lansing made many of the motions for amendment and conditional ratification on which the struggle over the Constitution was finally to turn. His share in these deliberations was distinguished; he argued always from history, experience, and a reverence for an existing political regime. Against a consolidation of the states Lansing invoked the analogy of King Henry IV of France and his "mad scheme" of a united Europe. He saw the specter of despotism once "sword and purse" were under one control. He insisted on the attachment of a bill of rights. He argued against a broad jurisdiction for the U.S. Supreme Court and for an amendment allowing the recall of U.S. senators. But, most important, he sought to include as a condition of New York's ratification the understanding that if the Constitution were not properly amended in a new convention, his state would reserve the right to withdraw from the compact. This motion (and many others) failed because it came too late—and because the Federalists agreed to attach numerous "recommendations" to the act of ratification. Yet Lansing fought to the end.

In 1790 John Lansing was appointed to a seat on the New York Supreme Court, where he served for eleven years and was chief justice from 1798 onward. In 1801 he became chancellor of his state, an office in which he served until 1814. In his final years he was an acknowledged leader of the New York bar. A measure of his reputation for rectitude came in 1804, when the legislative caucus in Albany nominated him as the Democratic-Republican candidate for the governorship. Hamilton advised the Federalists to support Lansing in order to avoid the alternative, Aaron Burr. With such backing in addition to his own merit, Lansing had reason to be confident of election. However, when George Clinton attempted to bargain with Lansing for the appointment of his nephew, DeWitt Clinton, as chancellor as the price of his support, Lansing withdrew from the race. Later Lansing made public his reason for standing aside. He was a consistent figure throughout his public life. Though, according to William Pierce of Georgia, troubled by a small stutter, Lansing was a fine figure of a man, genial and well spoken, with some degree of learning. For a time he was a regent of the University of the State of New York and also took an interest in the development of Columbia College. One December evening in 1829, while in New York City on business, John Lansing left his hotel to post a letter—and forever disappeared under circumstances never explained. (See C. G. Munsell, *The Lansing Family* [New York: private printing, 1916]; De Alva Stanwood Alexander, *A Political History of the State of New York*, 2 vols. [New York: Henry Holt, 1906]; Joseph Reese Strayer, ed., *The Delegate from New York; or, Proceedings of the Federal Convention of 1787, from the Notes of John Lansing, Jr.* [Princeton, N.J.: Princeton University Press, 1939]; Linda Grant De Pauw, *The Eleventh Pillar: New York State and the Federal Constitution* [Ithaca, N.Y.: Cornell University Press, 1966], pp. 56–64, and passim; E. Wilder Spaulding, *New York in the Critical Period, 1783–1789* [New York: Columbia University Press, 1932]; Robert Allen Rutland, *The Ordeal of the Constitution: The Antifederalists and the Ratification Struggle of 1787–1788* [Norman: University of Oklahoma Press, 1966], pp. 259–261; Alfred F. Young, *The Democratic Republicans of New York: The Origins, 1788–1797* [Chapel Hill: University of North Carolina Press, 1967]; John P. Kaminski, "New York: The Reluctant Pillar," in *The Reluctant Pillar: New York and the Adoption of the Federal Constitution*, ed. Stephen L. Schecter [Troy, N.Y.: Russell Sage College, 1985], pp. 48–117.)

# NEW JERSEY

# WILLIAM LIVINGSTON
November 1723–July 25, 1790
Lawyer, statesman, first elected governor of New Jersey

*In the Constitutional Convention, New Jersey's elder statesman and one of the oldest, most prestigious, and respected members when the sessions were convened. Son of Philip and Catharine Van Brugh Livingston. Grandson of the illustrious Robert Livingston, first lord of the manor, and brother of Philip and Peter Van Brugh Livingston. Born at Albany, New York, and raised by his grandmother, Sarah Van Brugh. As a youth lived with missionaries among the Mohawks on the frontier. Educated at Yale and in the law offices of James Alexander, a vigorous Whig. Associated early with such distinguished attorneys as John Morin Scott, William Peartree Smith, and William Smith, Jr. (with whom he prepared a digest of the provincial laws). A successful attorney and a leader in the popular cause. A Calvinist in religion, and constantly in opposition to the more conservative and Anglican DeLancey faction. A member of the New York Assembly from 1759 to 1761, and one of the dominant figures in New York politics until 1769, when his party broke up over the question of resisting British measures. A gifted poet and essayist and author of some of the best early American satire, Livingston then withdrew in disgust from law and politics and moved to Elizabethtown, New Jersey, to enjoy a literary retirement as a gentleman farmer.*

The outbreak of the Revolution drew William Livingston away from the rural peace of Liberty Hall and into the midst of the great events of his time. He was a member of the Essex County Committee of Correspondence and then a delegate to the First and Second Continental Congresses. In June 1776, he left that post to command the New Jersey militia as brigadier general but later that year was called from the field to become the chief magistrate of his state.

Throughout the next fourteen years, until his death in 1790, Livingston was governor of New Jersey. As much as any man, he may be credited with having created the government and institutions of a sovereign state. While the Revolution continued, New Jersey was frequently a battleground of competing armies, and there was a considerable division of loyalties among its population. Yet, with moderation and careful stewardship, Governor Livingston pulled it together and guaranteed its respectable contribution to the struggle for American liberty. In his later years, the people of his state would not let him retire, seeing in his patient and patriarchal presence a summary of what they had fought to achieve. Yet he continued to enjoy whenever possible the pleasures of agriculture and the life of the mind. Though at times a slaveholder, he also gave moderate encouragement to the initial efforts toward the abolition of slavery in his state, cautioning always against coercive schemes to that end.

Governor Livingston said little during the Constitutional Convention, but his name and reputation gave weight to the New Jersey delegation. He performed when present as a moderate Federalist, one of those greatly disturbed by the outcry for paper money and equality in the 1786 riots in New England. He did not arrive in Philadelphia until June 5 and missed many of the debates in July, but he played a major role as chairman of the committee that drew up a compromise on slavery. Returning home, he exercised his potent influence in behalf of ratification and contributed to the speed and unanimity of New Jersey's response. He is a figure of reference when we think of the great role played by aristocratic Whig gentlemen in the formation of the republic. (See Rudolph J. and Margaret C. Pasler, *The New Jersey Federalists* [Rutherford, N.J.: Fairleigh Dickinson University Press, 1975]; Richard P. McCormick, *Experiment in Independence: New Jersey in the Critical Period, 1781–1789* [New Brunswick, N.J.: Rutgers University Press, 1950], pp. 256–258, and passim; Theodore Sedgwick, Jr., *A Memoir of the Life of William Livingston* [New York: J. and J. Harper, 1833]; John Stevens, "William Livingston, Governor of New Jersey," *Magazine of American History* 2 [August 1878]: 484–488; Margaret B. Macmillan, *The War Governors in the American Revolution* [New York: Columbia University Press, 1943]; Dorothy R. Dillon, *The New York Triumvirate: A Study of the Legal and Political Careers of William Livingston, John Morin Scott, William J. Smith, Jr.* [New York: Columbia University Press, 1949]; Harold W. Thatcher, "Comments on American Government and on the Constitution by a New Jersey Member of the Federal Convention," *Proceedings of the New Jersey Historical Society* 56 [October 1938]: 285–303, and "The Political Ideas of New Jersey's First Governor," *Proceedings of the New Jersey Historical Society* 60 [July 1942]: 184–199; Philip Davidson, *Propaganda and the American Revolution, 1763–1783* [Chapel Hill: University of North Carolina Press, 1941]; Milton M. Klein, *The American Whig: William Livingston of New York* [New York: Garland, 1990]; Michael Lewis Levine, "The Transformation of a Radical Whig under Republican Government: William Livingston, Governor of New Jersey, 1776–1790" [Ph.D. dissertation, Rutgers University, 1975]; Carl E. Prince et al., *The Papers of William Livingston*, 5 vols. [Trenton: New Jersey Historical Society, 1979–1990].)

# WILLIAM PATERSON

December 24, 1745–September 9, 1806
Lawyer, statesman, and jurist

*The shortest of the Framers, and spokesman in their company for the special interests of the smaller states. Preeminently a "man of law" and defender of the Anglo-American tradition of inherited legal rights. Born in County Antrim or County Donegal, Ireland, to Richard and Mary Paterson, Ulster Presbyterians who immigrated to North America in 1747. Grew up in Princeton, New Jersey, where his father, a peddler and tinsmith, had settled in 1749. There the elder Paterson opened a store and smithy; the family prospered and young William, following preparation in local private schools, entered the College of New Jersey. On graduation in 1763, he began to read law in the office of Richard Stockton, a signer of the Declaration of Independence, worked in the family business, and took an active part in the cultural and intellectual life surrounding the college. In 1766 he earned an M.A., and two years later passed his examination for the bar. In 1769 Paterson attempted to establish a rural practice of his profession near New Bromley, but in 1772 he returned to Princeton. Shortly thereafter he moved again to South Branch, but did not settle finally in New Brunswick until 1779.*

When the Revolution reached New Jersey, William Paterson was an obscure young attorney with a few influential friends. But the mildly republican stand he took during that conflict propelled him rapidly into a place among the acknowledged leaders of his state. In 1775 he was elected member for Somerset County in the Provincial Congress. In 1776 he was chosen secretary of that assembly and called upon to assist in drafting the state constitution. In the latter enterprise he struggled, under pressure, to preserve what was best in the English legal tradition for the American order of things his neighbors were attempting to create. Also in that cause he served in 1776–1777 as a member of the legislative council and from 1776 until 1783 as the attorney general of New Jersey. Keeping his charge, he was diligent in the prosecution of traitors, Loyalists, and temporizers—and yet careful to restrain his fellow patriots from partisan extremities and lawless acts. During these years he was, in effect, the civic sense of his society on horseback, working at a frenetic pace and becoming in the process the personification of the continuity of law linking colonial past to independent present. From his performance in this role he acquired a great reputation and a confiscated estate, Raritan Plantation, including slaves and a fine house for his family.

Paterson returned to private life and a large, lucrative practice in 1783. But it was inevitable that he would be chosen as a representative from New Jersey, once his state decided in 1787 to participate in the Constitutional Convention. Paterson did not attend the sessions in Philadelphia after the end of July except to return briefly in September for the signing of the Constitution. Yet while he was present, he functioned, formally speaking, as the antagonist in the drama of group composition. The initiative seized with Gov. Edmund Randolph's presentation of what came to be known as the Virginia Plan was blurred when Paterson introduced and won support for an alternative model. The ideas of Randolph, Madison, and the other Virginians had a majority of the delegates behind them. But that majority was not large or firm enough to survive a challenge without making concessions. The process of writing and ratifying a constitution would, if it were to prevail in the states, require near unanimity among the members of the Convention. And it became clear that Paterson's objections to some provisions of the plan preferred by the larger states would have to be accommodated if the meeting were to produce a meaningful result.

The Paterson Plan differed from the proposal of the Virginians in its insistence that the states have an equal vote in a unicameral legislature. It was the position of the New Jersey delegation that it had no authority from its instructions to agree to a government that negated the equal powers of the several states in the nation's legislature: the equality provided by the Articles of Confederation. The rest of Paterson's proposals seemed to create fewer problems: a plural executive, elected by the legislatures; a national judiciary, with specific powers; an authority over trade, taxes, and tariffs; and machinery for adding states and naturalizing citizens. Yet, as has been remarked by Forrest McDonald, the New Jersey Plan was in one respect, apart from the question of representation, more centralist than that of Virginia. For it declared that the component parts of the republic would be "bound" by the "decisions" of the Congress, subject to compulsion by force to ensure their obedience, "any thing in the respective laws of the Individual States to the contrary notwithstanding." This grant of power, making it possible that the Congress might do with the states what it wished, alarmed many of the delegates present in the Convention and was carefully removed from the final version of the Constitution. In its place stands language concerning "the supreme law of the land"—a very different matter.

Yet there was no real contradiction in Paterson's plan. He was never an ardent Antifederalist like Martin, Lansing, or Yates, or even a conditional Antifederalist like Mason or Gerry. Under the Articles of Confederation, the people of New Jersey had been caught in a painful squeeze between the trade and tariff regulations of New York and those of Pennsylvania. Their currency was unsound, and their state did not appear to be viable as an independent economic unit. If other states were to retain their identities, New Jersey would need the protection for its interests that an equal strength in the national legislature would ensure. But Paterson had no objection to the abolition of the states, throwing all Americans into "Hotchpot." And he desperately wanted a change in government to regulate commercial barriers between the states. A federal government dominated by the power of a few of its largest member states is what he could not abide. However, he was a reasonable man and agreed without complaint to a revision calling for a House of Representatives apportioned according to population and a Senate securing the equal representation of the states. Once New Jersey received the concessions on which it insisted, its delegates in the Convention said little; William Paterson, seemingly satisfied, went home. In New Jersey he supported with vigor the instrument he had signed and had, through his statewide acquaintance and numerous contacts, a real influence on the ratification voted in Trenton in December 1787. But the decision there was never in doubt—once the Virginians and Pennsylvanians surrendered the principle of equal representation.

Paterson was elected U.S. senator for New Jersey in the First Congress. While there, he coauthored the Judiciary Act of 1789 and included in it a provision for judicial review. He resigned that post upon his selection in 1790 to be governor and chancellor of his state. The city of Paterson was established during these years, under the charter of Hamilton's Society for Establishing Useful Manufactures granted at the recommendation of Gov. William Paterson. In 1793 President Washington appointed him associate justice of the U.S. Supreme Court. In that office he continued until his death, much of his time in these years being spent in travel to preside over trials on circuit. He participated, as a severe Federalist, in cases concerned with the Whiskey Rebellion, violations of the Sedition Act, and infringements upon the nation's neutrality. Writing the decision in the important case of *Van Horne's Lessee* v. *Dorrance,* he invalidated a Pennsylvania statute as contrary to the Constitution.

It was Paterson's habit to give lectures from the bench on the dangers of conflating justice with abstract "natural rights," on the toxins of metaphysical egalitarianism, and on the real possibility that democratic excesses might produce in the population of America "a set of drones or of idle extravagant wretches [who] live upon the earnings of others" by voting themselves money. The scholarly achievement of his career was the *Laws of the State of New Jersey* (1800)—a work he prepared at the behest of the New Jersey legislature. In it he determined the force still preserved by the prescription of English law in the courts of his state, its limits, and the alterations made in it by acts of the New Jersey legislature since its first establishment in 1702. It was a labor that defined his life. (See Julian P. Boyd, "William Paterson, 1745–1806: Forerunner of John Marshall," in *Lives of Eighteen from Princeton,* ed. Willard Thorp [Princeton, N.J.: Princeton University Press, 1949], pp. 1–23; Gertrude S. Wood, *William Paterson of New Jersey, 1745–1806* [Fair Lawn, N.J.: Fair Lawn Press, 1933]; Daniel A. Degnan, "Justice William Paterson: Founder," *Seton Hall Law Review* 16 [1986]: 313–342; Rudolph J. and Margaret C. Pasler, *The New Jersey Federalists* [Rutherford, N.J.: Fairleigh Dickinson University Press, 1975]; Richard P. McCormick, *Experiment in Independence: New Jersey in the Critical Period, 1781–1789* [New Brunswick, N.J.: Rutgers University Press, 1950];

Leonard B. Rosenberg, "The Political Thought of William Paterson" [Ph.D. dissertation, New School for Social Research, 1967]; Richard P. McCormick, "The Political Essays of William Paterson," *Journal of the Rutgers University Library* 18 [June 1955]: 38–49; Michael Kraus, "William Paterson," in *The Justices of the United States Supreme Court, 1789–1969: Their Lives and Major Opinions,* vol. 1, ed. Leon Friedman and Fred L. Israel [New York: R. R. Bowker/Chelsea House, 1969], pp. 163–174; Leonard B. Rosenberg, "William Paterson: New Jersey's Nation-Maker," *New Jersey History* 85 [Spring 1967]: 7– 40; R. C. Haskett, "William Paterson, Counsellor-at-Law" [Ph.D. dissertation, Princeton University, 1952]; John E. O'Connor, *William Paterson, Lawyer and Statesman, 1745–1806* [New Brunswick, N.J.: Rutgers University Press, 1979]; Mary R. Murrin, "New Jersey and the Two Constitutions" in *The Constitution and the States: The Role of the Original Thirteen in the Framing and Adoption of the Federal Constitution,* ed. Patrick T. Conley and John P. Kaminski [Madison, Wis.: Madison House, 1988], pp. 55–75; Margaret C. S. Christman, *The First Federal Congress, 1789–1791* [Washington, D.C.: Smithsonian, 1989], pp. 310– 312.)

# WILLIAM CHURCHILL HOUSTON
ca. 1746–August 12, 1788
Educator, lawyer, and political leader of New Jersey

*A Framer who attended the Convention for less than two weeks and who, while there, contributed little. Mortally ill with tuberculosis when he got to Philadelphia. Significant as a barometer of political sentiment in the state he hoped to represent. Born in the Sumter district of South Carolina. Son of Captain Archibald and Margaret Houston, later of Anson County, North Carolina. Trained in the Crowfield Academy and by the local Presbyterian clergy. Dispatched at the age of eighteen to the College of New Jersey, where he took the B.A. in 1768, was made master of the grammar school and then tutor. Appointed professor of mathematics and natural philosophy at the College of New Jersey in 1771 and held that position until 1783. Treasurer of the college, 1779–1783. After studying with William Paterson, admitted to the bar in 1781. Resigned from the college in 1783. Briefly a soldier in the New Jersey militia, 1776. In the Provincial Congress in 1776 and the state legislature, 1777–1779; and member of the New Jersey Council of Safety in 1778. Elected to the Continental Congress in 1779 and to the Confederation Congress in 1784 and 1785. Deputy secretary of the Congress, 1785–1786. A vigorous supporter of the steamboat built by John Fitch. While in Congress, authored a memorable essay on taxation.*

William Churchill Houston emerged as a popular attorney in the Trenton area after his resignation from teaching. He was, at various times, clerk of the New Jersey Supreme Court (1781–1788), receiver of continental taxes (1782–1785), clerk of the state assembly, commissioner to settle salary claims by the New Jersey troops, commissioner in disputes between Connecticut and Pennsylvania over the Wyoming Valley claims, and attorney for the East Jersey proprietors in the dividing-line controversy. He served as a delegate to the Annapolis Convention. In 1787 he was a highly respected citizen of his state, but it was expected, even before his withdrawal, that he would not be able to sit through the Philadelphia Convention. Even so, he was named a delegate and given the opportunity to serve, his health permitting. Though absent from most of the Convention, he lived to sign the report of the New Jersey delegates to their state legislature. (See Thomas Allen Glenn, *William Churchill Houston, 1746–1788* [Norristown, Pa.: privately printed, 1903]; Thomas Jefferson Wertenbaker, *Princeton, 1746–1896* [Princeton, N.J.: Princeton University Press, 1946]; Varnum L. Collins, *President Witherspoon, A Biography,* 2 vols. [Princeton, N.J.: Princeton University Press, 1925]; Richard P. McCormick, *Experiment in Independence: New Jersey in the Critical Period, 1781–1789* [New Brunswick, N.J.: Rutgers University Press, 1950]; H. James Henderson, *Party Politics in the Continental Congress* [New York: McGraw Hill, 1974]; James McLachlan, *Princetonians, 1748–1768* [Princeton, N.J.: Princeton University Press, 1975], pp. 643–647.)

# DAVID BREARLY
June 11, 1745–August 16, 1790
Lawyer, soldier, statesman, and jurist

*Able assistant of William Paterson in the preparation of the New Jersey Plan, and a champion of the doctrine of judicial review in American law. A descendant of John B. Brearly of Yorkshire, England, who in 1680 immigrated to the area around Trenton, New Jersey. Son of David and Mary Clark Brearly of Spring Grove. Educated at the College of New Jersey, but took no degree. Early identified with the colonial cause in the conflict with George III. Entered law practice before 1770, probably at Allentown. Colonel of New Jersey infantry regiments from 1776 through 1779. Member of the New Jersey constitutional convention of 1776. Elected chief justice of his state's supreme court in July 1779 and served with distinction for ten years. In 1780 authored decision in* Holmes v. Walton, *in which he overturned a state law allowing for decisions in jury trials where only six jurors were in the box. Ruled the law invalid by reason of its conflict with the organic law, Anglo-Saxon justice understood historically, of which the courts were the proper guardian.*

Of the New Jersey delegates at the Philadelphia Convention, David Brearly had the best attendance record. He served on a committee called upon to distribute seats in the original House of Representatives, and on another committee, formed late in August, whose duty it was to clear up a variety of smaller problems, matters that had been postponed and were yet unresolved when the Constitution was almost complete. For this latter committee, Brearly, acting as chairman, made the official report. His only important speech in almost four months argued in favor of William Paterson's position that the small states would be "destroyed" unless an equal vote was preserved to each of them as a security for their sovereign existence. He also spoke briefly on the advantage of electing the president by a majority of both houses of Congress. Yet he was prepared to see the states abolished completely or made equal in size. Brearly took notes during the Convention, some of which survive. He probably wrote certain sections of Paterson's plan of government.

Though well respected, both in New Jersey and in the Great Convention, Judge Brearly was not a wealthy man. Most of his career was in public service. According to newspaper reports, he was eloquent in his support of the Constitution during New Jersey's ratification convention of December 1787, carrying all objections to the document before him in those debates at Trenton. In 1789 President Washington named Brearly judge of the U.S. District Court of New Jersey, where he served for the final months of his life. In his last years he was Grand Master of the New Jersey Masonic Lodge and vice-president of the Society of the Cincinnati in that state. He was also a delegate to the Episcopal Church's general convention in 1786. (See Richard P. McCormick, *Experiment in Independence: New Jersey in the Critical Period, 1781–1789* [New Brunswick, N.J.: Rutgers University Press, 1950]; Austin Scott, "*Holmes* v. *Walton:* The New Jersey Precedent," *American Historical Review* 4 [Spring 1899]: 3–19; *New Jersey Archives* 36 [New York: AMS Press, 1974]: 29; Robert G. Ferris, ed., *Signers of the Constitution* [Washington, D.C.: National Park Service, 1976], pp. 148–149.)

# JONATHAN DAYTON

October 16, 1760–October 9, 1824
Soldier, lawyer, and land speculator

*A leader of the Federalist party in New Jersey for a quarter of a century. Son of Gen. Elias Dayton of Elizabethtown, New Jersey, who was chieftain of a powerful faction among the New Jersey Whigs. The youngest of the Framers. Elected to sit in the Great Convention in his father's place. Educated at the College of New Jersey, where he earned a B.A. in 1776 and an M.A. in 1783. A soldier in the Continental army, rising to the rank of captain at the age of nineteen. Undisciplined and sometimes careless of his duty. Served under his father and the Marquis de Lafayette. Captured, but exchanged, and returned to service in time for the Battle of Yorktown. A leader in the Society of the Cincinnati throughout the last years of his life. A Presbyterian and a slaveholder. Studied law after the war, received the LL.D. in 1798, and began (often in association with Elias Boudinot) a lifetime of speculation in western lands— lands to which no one in New Jersey had clear right or title.*

Jonathan Dayton, perhaps in consequence of his youth, said little during the Constitutional Convention, but he faithfully followed the leadership of William Paterson and Gov. William Livingston, the acknowledged spokesmen for his state. He did, however, speak on a few occasions and was one of the Framers who announced that he would sign the Constitution though objecting to some of its provisions. Dayton did not arrive in Philadelphia until June 21 but stayed the course once he took his seat. He was hostile to the three-fifths compromise on the representation of slaves, maintained that a simple majority was enough to ratify a treaty, and suggested that the disorders in Rhode Island justified invasion of that state by federal troops. Generally, he was concerned with the rights of the small states. He sat in the Confederation Congress in 1787 and 1788 and was chosen to represent New Jersey in the House of Representatives in the First Congress under the Constitution but declined to serve. He was elected to the House of Representatives for the Second, Third, Fourth, and Fifth Congresses. During the last two of these terms, he was chosen speaker of the house. A vacillating Federalist, he supported most of the programs of his party but had a reputation as a defender of state sovereignty.

The New Jersey legislature sent Dayton to serve in the U.S. Senate from 1799 to 1805. There he opposed the repeal of the Judiciary Act of 1801 but differed with many other Federalists in his support of the Louisiana Purchase (1803). In keeping with New Jersey's position implicit from the original organization of government under the Articles, he was always eager to see new lands opened for settlement in the West. And by that enthusiasm he was politically and morally tainted. Only a fortuitous illness prevented Dayton from accompanying Aaron Burr in his 1806 expedition to carve out an empire from Spanish or American lands in the Southwest. His complicity in that design was, however, well known. Therefore, he was indicted for treason, and, though not finally prosecuted, politically ruined. Nonetheless, he remained popular in New Jersey, continuing to hold office and sitting in the assembly in 1814–1815.

Jonathan Dayton is an example of those Federalists who saw in the new national government a means to general and personal prosperity and to American power and glory. Of New Jersey Federalists, he was among the most controversial—intensely ambitious, abrasive, and often engaged in questionable schemes. But his last years were peaceful and included a final visit with his old commander, Lafayette. His monument is that section of Ohio between the Big and Little Miami rivers in which he developed 250,000 acres and which includes the city of Dayton, named after him. (See Rudolph J. and Margaret C. Pasler, *The New Jersey Federalists* [Rutherford, N.J.: Fairleigh Dickinson University Press, 1975]; George A. Boyd, *Elias Boudinot: Patriot and Statesman, 1740–1821* [Princeton, N.J.: Princeton University Press, 1952]; Anonymous, "Jonathan Dayton, 1760–1824, Patriot and Statesman and Founder of Dayton, Ohio," *New Jersey Genesis* 6 [October 1956]: 113–116; Theodore Thayer, *As We Were: The Story of Old Elizabethtown* [Newark: New Jersey Historical Society, 1964]; Robert G. Ferris, ed., *Signers of the Constitution* [Washington, D.C.: National Park Service, 1976], pp. 156–157; Thomas P. Abernethy, *The Burr Conspiracy* [New York: Oxford University Press, 1954]; Richard P. McCormick, *Experiment in Independence: New Jersey in the Critical Period, 1781–1789* [New Brunswick, N.J.: Rutgers University Press, 1950]; Forrest McDonald, *We the People: The Economic Origins of the Constitution* [Chicago: University of Chicago Press, 1958]; Richard A. Harrison, *Princetonians: 1776–1783* [Princeton, N.J.: Princeton University Press, 1981], pp. 31–42.)

# PENNSYLVANIA

# BENJAMIN FRANKLIN

January 17, 1706–April 17, 1790
Printer, man of letters, diplomat, scientist, and
statesman

*At eighty-one, the oldest of the Framers. In the world at large, the most famous
American of his generation—though, in 1787, not quite the figure that General
Washington was. The benign patriarch of the Great Convention, lending seriousness, order, good humor, and dignity to its proceedings. Bent on good
works, looking for practical solutions to particular problems. A continentalist
since the Albany Congress of 1754, where he had drawn up a plan for a general
American government. Yet of most importance as an aegis for the process of
compromise and composition in which he played only a secondary role. Nonetheless, an influence over the negotiations that produced the most difficult accommodation of the Convention as leader of the committee that proposed an equal
vote for each state in the Senate and a division of seats in the House of
Representatives according to population. With John Dickinson, his old adversary
in Pennsylvania politics, suggested that arrangement not long after the Virginia
delegation had presented its plan of government and New Jersey had made an
answer. Enforced his point with a characteristic homely metaphor: "When a
broad table is to be made, and the edges of planks do not fit, the artist takes
a little from both, and makes a good joint." In that small homily is condensed a
lifetime of experience in business, politics, diplomacy, and pragmatism, which he
brought to bear upon the ideological rigors of the youthful would-be lawgivers
and men of system. Not particularly pleased by the final form of the Constitution,
but firm in his support of it, urging each member of the Convention still present
at its September conclusion to "doubt a little of his own infallibility" and to join
in the necessary experiment of strengthening the general government by signing
the document. With Washington, a powerful inducement to ratification by the
states because of the widespread respect for their opinions among the rank and
file of Americans.*

Benjamin Franklin was born in Boston, Massachusetts, the son of Josiah Franklin, who in 1682 had come to the "Godly Commonwealth" from Northamptonshire, England, and Abiah Folger Franklin, the pious Josiah's second wife. Benjamin was his father's tenth and last son (hence the given name) and the youngest son of the youngest son for five generations. He had some basic tutoring and almost a year at the Boston Grammar School, but his father, a soap and candle maker, lacked the means to provide him with further formal schooling, and therefore the dream of a career in the ministry for the gifted child had to be put aside. Benjamin was for a year or two apprenticed to his father, but he did not like the work and at the age of twelve went to learn the printer's trade with his half-brother, James Franklin. He continued in James's employ until 1723; read widely on his own (especially the English Augustans); wrote under the pseudonym of "Silence Dogood" for his brother's newspaper, the *New England Courant;* and learned his business—publishing the paper himself when James was locked away in jail for offending the authorities.

Finally Benjamin grew restive, determined that James took advantage of him, and ran away at the age of seventeen to Philadelphia, where, according to Franklin's own recollections, he arrived in a disheveled condition, with almost no money yet with little doubt concerning his prospects. He obtained employment as a printer almost as soon as he arrived in Pennsylvania. After misleading encouragement from Gov. William Keith, Franklin planned to set up a shop and voyaged to London to purchase the necessary equipment—with money that Sir William was supposed to advance on credit. When no word or letter of credit came from his erstwhile patron, in 1724 Benjamin found employment in London printing houses, learned more about his trade, and saw a bit of the world. In 1726 he had accumulated the reserves necessary to pay for his return to North America. In the process of preparing for the journey he acquired a new mentor, the Quaker merchant Thomas Denham, who took Benjamin into his Philadelphia firm, taught the boy the mysteries of selling and keeping accounts, and then died in 1728, leaving a portion of his estate to the protégé. For a few months after Denham's death, Franklin went into the service of a senior printer of Philadelphia for whom he had worked before. But soon he gave up training other men's apprentices and with his friend Hugh Meredith set up on his own.

In 1730 Franklin bought out Meredith, took Deborah Reed as his common-law wife, began to publish the *Pennsylvania Gazette* (commenced by another man in 1728), and started his rapid rise to financial independence, political influence, and wide reputation. Out of their shop, the Franklins traded in stationery, books, salves and ointments, news, houses, land, and slaves. Soon Franklin had the contract for all Pennsylvania government printing. He published broadsides, some books, his newspaper, and an assortment of miscellaneous items. Then in 1732 he brought out the first in a series of publications by means of which he reached into households throughout the British colonies in North America. Along the way he became a byword and a mythic figure in expressing the prudent, practical spirit of a new society. Between 1732 and 1758, *Poor Richard's Almanac* came to be second only to the Bible in its popularity in America. Eventually its fame reached Europe, where, along with Franklin's fame as a scientist, it awaited the sage when he arrived in England in 1757.

But first came Franklin's public career as Philadelphia's leading citizen. From 1736 to 1751 he was clerk of the Pennsylvania Assembly, and from 1751 to 1764 he was a leading member of that body. From 1737 to 1753 he was the postmaster of Philadelphia. After asking for the post, he received appointment (with William Hunter of Virginia) as deputy postmaster general for all the colonies, a position he held from 1753 to 1774, during which time he greatly reformed that service. In 1755–1756 he played the major role in organizing the defense of the Pennsylvania frontier against Indian depredations and was elected, at the age of fifty-one, colonel of the Pennsylvania militia. In 1748 he took David Hall as a partner and divided with him the income of the highly successful firm he had established almost twenty years before. Finally, as he had read systematically both to learn and to polish his style while still a boy, as he had founded the Junto for discussion of interesting and instructive topics among his young friends in Philadelphia while still far from established in his profession, in 1743 he proposed by circular letter to correspondents throughout the colonies the creation of an American Philosophical Society—of which he offered, for a time, to serve as secretary.

Franklin's philanthropies were legion. He organized private fire brigades and nonsectarian churches in Philadelphia. With local physicians, he sponsored the building of Pennsylvania Hospital, and he played the central role in founding a preparatory school and college (which became the College of Philadelphia and then the University of Pennsylvania). Franklin reformed the "watch" (police) of Philadelphia, initiated a project for lighting the local streets, and fostered the first circulating library in America. He joined the Masons and became the Grand Master of his lodge. Hardly any project of importance in Pennsylvania got under way without Ben Franklin's being somehow involved in its promotion. The city was proud to have him as its citizen. And when publication of his researches in electricity brought him membership in the Royal Society in 1756, Franklin's neighbors took almost as much pleasure from the honor as did the recipient.

In science or "natural philosophy," Franklin's range of interests ran the gamut from medicine to geology to firsthand observations of whirlwinds, but he was chiefly concerned with knowledge that could be applied to the control of nature. Of course, he invented and promoted his famous stove. He made observations on weather and the Gulf Stream, while on a voyage. He invented the lightning rod and many other practical devices. It was the study of electrical phenomena and his kite that earned him such fame as to inspire the philosopher Immanuel Kant to describe him as "the new Prometheus who had stolen fire from heaven." As a scientist, Franklin enjoyed correspondence with gifted persons throughout the world. His natural philosophy was like his plan in the sphere of ethics, to compose an "Art of Virtue." He looked to results.

In Pennsylvania politics Benjamin Franklin emerged, in company with the cautious Joseph Galloway, as a leader of the Antiproprietary party and opponent of the Penn family and their governors. Because the Penns often prevented legislation, because they were niggardly in their attitude toward taxes necessary for the common defense, and because they left the frontier of the Quaker colony open to attack during the French and Indian Wars, Franklin and his associates favored the revocation of their charter and the creation of a royal government to replace the structures created under the proprietors. Franklin went to London as agent for the Pennsylvania Assembly from 1757 to 1762 to request that the Privy Council set aside the Penns' repeated vetoes of bills for defense. After succeeding in this lesser enterprise, he was in 1764 returned to England to lobby in behalf of the creation of a Crown colony of Pennsylvania. In both these ventures Franklin's objective was one that he had announced as early as 1754, following the Albany Congress, in three letters to Gov. William Shirley of Massachusetts: arbitrary government "must seem hard measure to Englishmen who cannot conceive that, by hazarding their lives and fortunes in subduing and settling new countries, extending the dominion and increasing the commerce of the mother nation, they have forfeited the native rights of Britons."

Proprietary government that left a people helpless went against the English constitution. And so did revenue bills passed by a Parliament that contained no American members. Franklin as agent for Pennsylvania (as he was later to be for Georgia, New Jersey, and Massachusetts) opposed such innovations as imprudent as well as improper, but he was not so outraged by the bills as were his countrymen back in Pennsylvania. As a temperamental diplomat who despised mobs, crimes against property, and seditious printing—and as an advocate of the great advantages of royal government—Franklin did not at first think of associations, boycotts, and tar and feathers as means of resisting the Stamp Act (1765). Indeed, he even recommended that some of his friends be named as stamp distributors and sent over some stamped papers to be sold in his shop, adding in comment, "We might as well have hindered the sun's setting." For a time his American popularity was at a low ebb. There was talk of burning his house. But in the famous "examination" of Franklin by the House of Commons, a preliminary to repeal of the Stamp Act, he comported himself so well and with such lucid eloquence that, once the interview was published, suspicion of his motives disappeared and his reputation was larger than before.

In these long years as agent, Franklin clearly valued the status of the North American colonies *within* the British Empire more than did many of his fellow Americans. An Anglophile, he was a reluctant revolutionary. But never did he doubt that, in some sense, America was one country and England another. True enough, he wished to preserve the English character of the colonies: since "the number of purely white people in the world is proportionately very small," and since "the English [with the Saxons of Germany] make the principal body of white people on the face of the earth, . . . why should the Palatine boors be suffered to swarm into our settlements . . . why increase the sons of Africa by planting them in America, where we have a fair opportunity, by excluding all blacks and tawnys?" Franklin was a conventional xenophobe, made all the stronger in his cultural identity by the pleasure he took from life in England and from a large circle of English friends. Soon he became the American member of the British intellectual establishment—"Dr." Franklin, thanks to a 1759 honorary doctor of laws degree from St. Andrews University. For many years the agent from Pennsylvania had promoted the concept of an internally independent, almost self-governing America within the British Empire—bound together by loyalty to a king and a common history, and by statutory limitation and division of powers. At some point late in the 1760s, Franklin began to doubt that either reason or a common heritage would in the end solve the political problems of British America. To the attention of his countrymen he offered an old Italian proverb: "Make yourselves sheep and the wolves will eat you."

Yet until the time of his return to Pennsylvania in 1775, Franklin struggled to prevent a war between England and its colonies, continued to work for peace even after he had begun to doubt the motives and the judgment of his sovereign lord, King George III. As to the king's ministers, Franklin had never had much confidence in them: the earls of Dartmouth and Hillsborough, George Grenville, Charles Townshend, Lord North. Franklin's friends among the men of power included Edmund Burke, Burke's patron the marquis of Rockingham, and William Pitt, earl of Chatham. But they were rarely in office. In fact, as Franklin's fame grew, and as his position obliged him to bring to Whitehall unpleasant appeals and bad news from beyond the Atlantic, many of the Tory aristocrats grew to resent him. In his turn, Franklin came to believe that the leaders of Parliament "wished to provoke the North Americans into an open rebellion which might justify a military execution and thereby gratify a grounded malice which I conceived to exist here against the Whigs and dissenters of that country." The task of unofficial American ambassador proved to be a thankless one—particularly when Franklin was roundly abused before the Privy Council by Solicitor General Wedderburn when he presented a Massachusetts petition calling for the removal of a royal governor.

The letters of Thomas Hutchinson had, through the offices of other men, come into Franklin's hands, and he had sent them to America to confirm that placemen were giving the English government terrible and disruptive advice, which in folly had been accepted. Franklin observed, "Divine Providence first infatuates the power it designs to ruin." He admitted his role in relaying to Whig leaders in America the purloined letters of Gov. Thomas Hutchinson and Lieutenant Governor Andrew Oliver addressed to officials in London. For his trouble in protecting innocent persons, on January 29, 1774, Franklin was excoriated as an adventurer of "no honour" who had made the term "man of letters" into a "libel"; a miscreant, deserving the "mark and brand," having "forfeited the respect of societies and of men." Immediately Franklin's appointment as postmaster was revoked, and the public relished his humiliation among "the King's friends"—those stalwarts who could with enough money always be persuaded to "vote according to their consciences."

Despite such invective and after the call for a Continental Congress in America, Franklin tried once more to warn of the long, pointless war that was to come. Two of his publications, parodies of the British logic that was driving America toward an appeal to arms, *Rules by Which a Great Empire May Be Reduced to a Small One* and *An Edict by the King of Prussia,* were widely distributed and often remarked. There were hasty consultations with allies such as Pitt and Burke. However, as Franklin by this time foresaw, he was not heard, even by his political lieutenant, Galloway, or by his illegitimate son, William Franklin, the last British governor of New Jersey. When forced into revolution, Franklin went toward the break with firm resolve, though sore of heart. Later, after American freedom had been accomplished and his work for the republic as diplomat in France was concluded, he wrote with some sense of satisfaction to a friend in England on the question of who had been loyal in 1776: "It was [for Americans] a resistance in favour of a British constitution, which every Englishman might share in enjoying, who should come to live among them; it was resisting arbitrary impositions, that were contrary to common right and to their fundamental constitutions, and to constant ancient usage. It was indeed a resistance in favour of the liberties of England, which might have been endangered by success in the attempt against ours." The Franklin who reached Philadelphia just in time to serve in the Second Continental Congress and to be the oldest signer of the Declaration of Independence was no magically transformed figure but rather a man of the prudent English Enlightenment, the friend of David Hume and champion of history as a "moral study"—the same person who had gone to England in 1764 to make a Crown colony of Pennsylvania.

Benjamin Franklin was not long reestablished as an American-in-residence before he was called upon to resume his role as American-abroad, a role for which he provided the original definition. But first he had almost eighteen months at the administrative center of the American Revolution. Franklin was elected to the Congress within days of his arrival home. For a few weeks he was quiet, digesting the scene. Fighting had already occurred at Lexington and Concord. An army was in the making. To satisfy the moderates in Congress, he agreed to one last petition to the Crown. But he expected to accomplish nothing, despite the "olive branch" temperance of its appeal. And in July he proposed his own "Articles of Confederation and Perpetual Union." They were rejected as premature, but they served as a basis for the Articles prepared later by John Dickinson.

From the beginning of official American diplomacy with the formation of a congressional committee to seek outside support for the Revolution, Franklin had a hand in the business. Indeed, "unofficial" suggestions from a French envoy that aid would follow upon a Declaration of Independence made Franklin a vigorous advocate of that measure. He served with Thomas Jefferson (as his editor) on the committee called upon to prepare the document. With John Adams and Edward Rutledge, Franklin was commissioned to meet with his old friend Lord Howe, on Staten Island, to inform him that future peace negotiations would have to accept the independence of the colonies as a predicate for the settlement of difficulties. Franklin presided over the Pennsylvania Constitutional Convention of 1776, which reflected some of his favorite constitutional theories. He established the U.S. postal service. He wrote instructions for the first American emissaries. And he went on a winter journey to Canada to stir the flames of revolution in Canada. However, when the French urged serious consideration of a treaty of friendship, Franklin, because of his international stature and his previous visits to and wide acquaintance in France, was asked, even though he was soon to reach the age of seventy, to sail across the seas and represent his country. His service as American "commissioner" or minister to France from 1776 to 1785 was the triumph of his career, revenge upon the English, and directly instrumental in the achievement of American independence.

While in France, Franklin acted out the details of a favorite myth of the French intellectuals—the legend of a bygone Golden Age, where before they had been confused and corrupted by the impedimenta of a complex social identity, men lived in a simple polis, according to the leadings of nature and the dictates of reason. In France Franklin could adopt the identity of a citizen of the Republic of Letters, even though he could not be a Frenchman. Therefore he could present himself as a citizen of the world—and America as the proper habitat of such beings—and manifest an interest in America's survival, which France, as the most enlightened of nations, could share with him. The canny townsman of Philadelphia, in his fur hat, was thus a new Solon or Lycurgus—a symbol for French hopes for a better future of their own. No wonder he secured for Washington the loans and gifts, fleets and armies that helped win the war.

In France Franklin was the hero as litterateur or savant. The French were fascinated by the old man in plain dress who came, instead of the trivial aristocrats to whom they were accustomed, to represent an infant republic. He visited Voltaire and joined a lodge of Freemasons, flattered French ladies, set up a press at Passy, attended meetings of the Academy of Sciences (of which he was a member), and persuaded the foreign minister of Louis XVI, the Comte de Vergennes, that the interest of his master was to ensure American independence, lest the Anglo-Saxons make a premature peace and release England's power to concentrate on its natural enemy. Finally he became a cult figure, not a diplomat, whose image could be found in French households and be recognized at all levels of French society. As an unofficial overseas "secretary of state," Franklin encouraged privateering, bought supplies, dispatched assistants to other countries, issued passports, treated with "unofficial" English representatives, and, in the end, in 1783, negotiated a general peace in the Treaty of Paris.

Some younger American diplomats complained of Franklin's methods in conducting the business of the republic in France. The Congress ignored them and refused Franklin's offer to resign. Indeed, Congress kept him in France long beyond the time when he wished to retire. Because of France's attitude toward the aging sage, there was little choice. In Philadelphia, the French envoy had announced that no other ambassador would do. Finally, upon the arrival of Thomas Jefferson, Franklin was free to go home. He had talked the French into deep and dangerous involvement in a war that brought them only revenge and moral self-satisfaction. And he had then persuaded the English to accept American ownership of the West, as far as the Mississippi. Franklin played his cards as they came and enjoyed the game. Approaching eighty, he still believed that the advantage of being a "reasonable creature" was that "it enables one to find or make a reason for everything one has a mind to do." No other American, however zealous, could have done the job he did at Versailles.

When Franklin reached Philadelphia in September of 1785, he was seventy-nine. Almost immediately he was elected president of the Supreme Executive Council of Pennsylvania, in which office he served for three terms. He would have little time for work on the *Autobiography,* a book he had begun a decade earlier while still in England, or for correspondence with friends, or for his favorite types of natural observation. The public business of Pennsylvania— along with his new Society for Political Enquiries—used up most of his remaining energy. At first Franklin was not selected to be a delegate from his state to the Great Convention. Though he had long urged a revision of the Articles of Confederation, it was thought that he would be physically unable to attend the meeting called to that purpose. But when his health improved, he became in late March, by unanimous vote of the legislature, an addition to the company of the Framers. In France, according to John Adams, "Franklin's reputation was more universal than that of Leibnitz or Newton, Frederick or Voltaire." In Philadelphia he was simply the wise old grandfather of the republic, the philosopher as tradesman. In that capacity he served in the Convention, attending almost every session.

Benjamin Franklin's contributions to the drafting of the U.S. Constitution were in his support of a provision that allowed for easy naturalization of foreign immigrants, in his opposition to property limitations on the suffrage, and in his regular appeals for moderation, in one case calling for a minister to pray over his fiercely determined younger colleagues. "How has it happened," he asked, "that we have not hitherto once thought of humbly applying to the Father of lights to illuminate our understandings? . . . [I] believe that without his concurring aid we shall succeed in this political building no better than the Builders of Babel." Franklin opposed giving the executive absolute veto power over the proposed Congress, and he did not approve of allowing a president to seek a second term. He feared the development of an order of American "placemen" and therefore contended that a chief executive (which he would have preferred to replace with a council) and his aides should receive no salary. Money bills, he believed, should originate in the lower house of the Congress, where the "public spirit of our common people" would be represented, and should not be rewritten in the U.S.

Senate. He seconded Mason's motion for a council to advise the president, moved to include a federal power for building canals, and opposed a financial test for holders of federal office. Finally, he called for a careful definition of treason relating to its prosecution, as well as for explicit procedures for impeachment and trial of a chief magistrate. Peace and order required clarification in these areas, so that tyranny and political harassment might be avoided.

At times Franklin jested, chiding the enthusiasts with small analogies and humorous tales. Some of his speeches were prepared in writing, and read for him by James Wilson. In good spirits, meaning as he had at twenty-five to "keep his friends in countenance," he accepted the role to which circumstances assigned him in the four months of deliberation. He had a genuine confidence in the future of the then ramshackle combination of "little republics"—especially once it became a bona fide Union and not just a loose confederation. And though not entirely satisfied with the Constitution produced by his associates, he was moved by its completion to prepare a peroration for the entire Convention and to make his famous remark concerning the "rising sun" and the emblem on the back of Washington's chair.

Benjamin Franklin died thirty months after the adjournment of the Constitutional Convention. Twenty thousand people attended his funeral, and his death was remarked throughout the western world. Clearly, he summarized one side of the American character. As Carl Becker has written, Franklin was satisfied with "the best possible rather than the best conceivable worlds." And he made it—and himself—up as he went along. As we learn from his masterpiece, the *Autobiography* (1781, 1818), he was by practice an "amiable chameleon," an eminently practical man who could write for his Quaker friends an antislavery petition to a Congress that, as he well knew, could not accept it, and at the same time keep a slave (belonging to his son-in-law) in his own house. His old age was not troubled by these contradictions. Certainly the Franklin who balanced "freedom of the press" with a "liberty of the cudgel," a freedom to assault obnoxious and trouble-making journalists with legal impunity, was not the conventional champion of human rights. The "rights of man," for him, meant self-government and perhaps a gradual movement toward constitutional monarchy in a country such as France. But it did not prohibit the state, in defending itself and the liberty of its citizens in a free country, from calling upon a man for all the property that he possessed.

Despite his devotion to the nation's future prospects as a free country, Franklin thought at times that he might leave America to live among his friends in England or France. But only as an American living abroad. To one of his countrymen he observed, "We are the sons of the earth and seas and, like Antaeus, if in wrestling with Hercules we now and then receive a fall, the touch of our parents will communicate to us fresh strength and ability to renew the contest. Be quiet and thankful." Benjamin Franklin's entire career is a comment on what he meant by such advice. (See Carl Van Doren, *Benjamin Franklin*

[Westport, Conn.: Greenwood Press, 1973]; David F. Hawke, *Franklin* [New York: Harper & Row, 1976]; Leonard Labaree et al., eds., *The Papers of Benjamin Franklin,* 28 vols. to date [New Haven, Conn.: Yale University Press, 1959–]; Gerald Stourzh, *Benjamin Franklin and American Foreign Policy* [Chicago: University of Chicago Press, 1954]; William S. Hanna, *Benjamin Franklin and Pennsylvania Politics* [Stanford, Calif.: Stanford University Press, 1964]; Benjamin H. Newcomb, *Franklin and Galloway: A Political Partnership* [New Haven, Conn.: Yale University Press, 1972]; Carl Becker, *Benjamin Franklin* [Ithaca, N.Y.: Cornell University Press, 1946]; J. A. Leo Lemay, ed., *The Oldest Revolutionary: Essays on Benjamin Franklin* [Philadelphia: University of Pennsylvania Press, 1976]; Robert F. Sayre, *The Examined Self: Benjamin Franklin, Henry Adams, Henry James* [Princeton, N.J.: Princeton University Press, 1964]; M. E. Bradford, "Franklin and Jefferson: The Making and Binding of Self," in *A Better Guide Than Reason: Studies in the American Revolution* [La Salle, Ill.: Sherwood Sugden, 1979]; Bruce I. Granger, *Benjamin Franklin: An American Man of Letters* [Ithaca, N.Y.: Cornell University Press, 1964]; D. H. Lawrence, *Studies in Classic American Literature* [New York: Doubleday, 1953]; Edward S. Corwin, "Franklin and the Constitution," *Proceedings of the American Philosophical Society* 100 [Fall 1956]: 283–288; Paul W. Conner, *Poor Richard's Politicks: Benjamin Franklin and His New American Order* [Westport, Conn.: Greenwood Press, 1980]; William George Carr, *The Oldest Delegate: Franklin in the Constitutional Convention* [Newark: University of Delaware Press, 1990]; Ormond Seavey, *Becoming Benjamin Franklin: The* Autobiography *and the Life* [University Park: Pennsylvania State University Press, 1988]; Esmond Wright, *Franklin of Philadelphia* [Cambridge, Mass.: Harvard University Press, 1986]; "Benjamin Franklin: A Reassessment," *Pennsylvania Magazine of History* [October 1987], whole issue; Verner W. Crane, *Benjamin Franklin and a Rising People* [Boston: Little, Brown, 1954]; J. A. Leo Lemay, "Benjamin Franklin," in *Major Writers of Early American Literature,* ed. Everett H. Emerson [Madison: University of Wisconsin Press, 1972], pp. 205–243; Mary E. Rucker, "Benjamin Franklin," in *American Literature, 1764–1789: The Revolutionary Years,* ed. Everett H. Emerson [Madison: University of Wisconsin Press, 1977], pp. 105–125.)

# Gouverneur Morris
January 31, 1752–November 6, 1816
Statesman, diplomat, lawyer, planter, and financier

*Though a representative of Pennsylvania in the Constitutional Convention, by way of an appointment that he did not seek, more properly identified with landed magnates of New York's Whig aristocracy. The least sanguine of the Framers, but one of the most brilliant. Grandson of Lewis Morris I, and youngest son of Lewis Morris II, lords of the manor and justices of the King's Bench. Born at Morrisania, the family seat in Westchester County, to his father's second wife, Sarah Gouverneur Morris. Of distinguished Dutch, Huguenot, Welsh, and English ancestry. Educated in a French school at New Rochelle, in the Academy of Philadelphia, at King's College, and in the law offices of William Smith. Destined by birth, training, and ability for a life of public service and political importance.*

Gouverneur Morris's portion from his father was £2,500, the "best education that's to be had," and a network of connections by blood and marriage with the great families of two states. Of this, as with everything else that came his way, he made the most. He was admitted to the bar at the age of nineteen, and, by the time the American Revolution had directed his talents into another channel, he had given signs that he might have had a distinguished career as an attorney. Like his father and grandfather, both of them great defenders of colonial rights under the English constitution, he was, even while away from his original profession, devoted to the concept of liberty as achieved through law.

He gave to this commitment his unqualified support at important points throughout his career. Therefore, he was uneasy about the possibility that radical egalitarian consequences might emerge within the English colonies in North America as a side effect of the struggle to win some kind of independence, and he was slow to align himself with the warmer spirits among the Sons of Liberty. For a long time he continued to hope for a peaceful reconciliation: an accommodation guaranteeing to British America an internal autonomy and right of self-determination. When that hope dimmed following the publication of the Intolerable Acts and the appearance of a British fleet off Sandy Hook, he threw himself wholeheartedly into the effort to create in America a completely separate, strong, and united republic: one that could restrain the spirit of that great reptile, "the Mob." As did half of his family, including his eldest brother, Lewis Morris, third lord of the manor and signer of the Declaration of Independence, he became a rebel in order to control a revolution—so that New York might not become a democracy in the process of becoming free.

Morris's participation in the American Revolution began with his election as a delegate from a meeting of Westchester freeholders to the Provincial Congress convening in New York City in May of 1775. There young Morris distinguished himself by his ideas on currency, his moderation, and his freedom from cant. With other young aristocrats, he offered himself as a soldier in February of 1776 but was returned to his seat in the Provincial Congress when the Continental Congress refused to organize the battalion planned by the gentry of New York. In the Provincial Congress he was among the first to call for a final break with Great Britain, though he preferred it should be done quietly lest the people be excited into "rashness and presumptions." He was among the authors of New York's constitution of 1777—a document that required compromise with Robert R. Livingston on behalf of slavery and with John Jay in the cause of religious intolerance. After Sir William Howe had occupied the city of New York, Morris served on a committee charged with coordination of the defense of the Hudson River counties and the northern border of the state. He observed the campaign that ended in victory at Saratoga, reported on the fall of Ticonderoga, and was a severe inquisitor into the activities of Loyalists, some of whom had been his friends. As a part of the inner Council of Safety, he helped to run the state from its little capital at Kingston.

New York sent Gouverneur Morris to a seat in the Continental Congress in 1778. There he displayed a great concern for military operations, became a friend of Lafayette, and gave constant support to the leadership of General Washington, whom he admired and had met the year before. For the Congress he spent part of the winter of 1778 at Valley Forge. Later he authored legislation for military reforms, supervised much of American diplomacy, wrote pamphlets to negate the blandishments of British offers of amnesty, and planned invasions of Canada. He wrote the instructions that Franklin carried to France and the plan for a final peace with England. He drew plans for a treasury board that anticipated Hamilton's grand design of a decade later. And when in May of 1779 he lost his place as a member for New York (by "neglecting" that state's desire to prevent the independence of Vermont), he moved to Philadelphia, set up a law practice, and in 1781 joined Robert Morris as assistant superintendent of finance—a post he held until 1784.

Robert Morris was himself responsible for the election of his friend, lieutenant, and business partner to a place in the Pennsylvania delegation to the Philadelphia Convention. Gouverneur Morris did not particularly wish to take part in these deliberations, since family business following the death of his mother greatly occupied him in New York. But, apart from the absence of a few weeks, he did attend the Convention with regularity and spoke more frequently (173 times) than any other member of that body. He brought to it wit, good humor, great oratorical gifts, and a completely formed political philosophy. His unsentimental evaluation of human nature often shocked his opponents in these debates. The depravity of men was his axiom. And for advanced views of a metaphysical human equality, he had only cheerful contempt: "He who wishes to enjoy natural Rights must establish himself where natural Rights are admitted. He must live alone." This doctrine is more Hobbes than Locke. And to moderate it, Morris would add only that the natural law of life is that men "live in society" and "do what that condition requires." The foundation of his doctrine was a commitment to the sanctity of property as the basis of civilization. Financial and commercial confusion under the Articles was, however, only a part of his politics in 1787. The rest he argued from definition and the record of human history.

According to Gouverneur Morris, the form of government that the Framers were ready to attempt should "depend upon the established institutions and the political maturity of the people." And in this teaching he seemed moderate indeed. He expected to preserve the states and voted to deny Congress the veto over their legislation. Yet he could be as ruthless for the new sovereign that he had in mind as he had been against the old. Where deliberation failed, other means of effecting change would have to be considered. Even before the Convention officially opened, it appears that he suggested to the members already in Philadelphia that the equal representation allowed to the small states in the Continental Congress might be, on this occasion, denied them by fiat if they would not agree to such an arrangement. He made the same threat concerning Delaware's role under the new government when Gunning Bedford spoke of foreign alliances for that tiny commonwealth. Small, unreasonable states might be abolished with the sword. Yet his argument was not contradictory, for he maintained that the choices before the house were so severe, between a strong government and a despotism following civil war, that republican scrupulosity about consensus was a luxury he and his associates could ill afford.

Gouverneur Morris was, among the Framers, almost the definition of a high Federalist. What he wanted from Philadelphia was a government strongly national in character. He called for a president elected for life or, failing that, eligible for reelection. He preferred a federal property qualification for freeholder suffrage and an appointed Senate, chosen by the president, serving without pay and for life. Unlike most of the Framers, he expected the Supreme Court to have broad review powers. His model for a new United States was clearly undemocratic. "Give the votes to people who have no property," he said, "and they will sell them to the rich," or else vote themselves the possessions of those more prosperous.

Morris's proposals were anathema to most of the southern delegates. Though he himself had recently inherited slaves and, in the view of many, had a flavor of sectional prejudice, he made the only serious attacks on the institution of slavery itself (as opposed to the slave trade) offered during the Convention. He advocated a power to tax exports, an end to the slave trade, and a suspension of the three-fifths compromise on the political representation of slaves, probably because it allowed the slaveholders to augment their power. He was also negative about the admission of new states from the West: "The Back members are always most averse to the best measures." He articulated a fear that the South and the West would get "the maritime states" into wars. Yet he pretended to speak for "America" and the "rights of mankind." However, he accepted the important compromises, once they were achieved, and was so respected for his gifts of style and language by friends and adversaries alike that the task of preparing the final draft of the Constitution was placed in his hands.

After the adoption of the Constitution by the states, Morris went to Europe to pursue his business interests, traded in commodities and debts, promoted speculations in land, and in 1790, acting for President Washington, opened unofficial negotiations with the British concerning trade, frontier forts, reparations for stolen slaves, and the exchange of diplomatic representatives. He accepted an appointment early in 1792 as U.S. minister to France. During the dark days of the Terror, he was the only foreign minister who kept to his post in Paris. He had tried, while still a private citizen, to save the government and the life of Louis XVI. Morris was, in fact, entrusted with the king's private funds not long before his execution. And, as American minister, he made his house a refuge to a great many who had, in his presence, flirted with advanced ideas, which Morris had warned against. Morris was, as his valuable diary indicates, appalled by the fanatical ideology of the Jacobin republic. The French recognized this attitude, and, in consequence, requested his recall. His time in France made the gentleman from New York if anything more conservative than he had been before, and more appreciative of the stability of the new government. But he remained overseas another four years, active in trade, in travel, and in his various "adventures." Once home, he rebuilt the mansion on his estate. He was elected U.S. senator for New York in 1800 to fill out another man's term. In that capacity he supported the Louisiana Purchase, even though it might mean the addition of new southern states, and urged that the United States take a hand in suppressing the slave uprising in St. Dominique. The French Revolution, he thundered, had released a poisonous doctrine upon the world. Any measure calculated to restrain the ideologically disguised imperial ambitions of France deserved the approbation of those responsible for the future of the American republic.

A Jeffersonian majority in the New York legislature prevented the reelection of Morris in 1802. Undeterred, he retired to Morrisania and private life. In the years remaining he continued to prosper in trade. He married and had a son. He was generous with his friends and with worthwhile public causes. The tall figure with the wooden leg (he had lost the leg in an accident at the age of twenty-eight) was a familiar sight on Wall Street and at great public occasions, such as those when he delivered the eulogies for Hamilton and George Clinton. In 1810 he was appointed by the legislature as chairman of a board of commissioners called upon to build the Erie Canal. His other significant involvement with things political came in 1812, when, outraged by America's tacit alliance with Napoleonic France in a war with England and against the best interests of "Christian civilization," he called for the secession of New York and New England from the Union. Morris's pamphlet, "Address to the People of the State of New York," led to the Hartford Convention of 1814. It argued the legality of secession on the evidence of his experience in the Constitutional Convention of 1787 and from a high Federalist point of view. Morris lived to see his plan of secession fail, but he enjoyed as a consolation the restoration of the Bourbon dynasty in France.

Gouverneur Morris was an eminently civilized American and a great patriot. An Old Whig, loyal to the values represented for him by his distinguished ancestors and the mentors of his youth, he embraced a politics of experience and was scornful of the regnant abstractions of Enlightenment radicalism. He is a correction of the conventional view of the Framers as speculative men of "big ideas." Yet he was an advocate of the abolition of slavery, by moderate and gradual means, in his own state, even though he had no faith in the "rights of man" ordinarily associated with such a position. His part in the Great Convention and in early American politics indicates something of its complexity. And his influence on the document is greater than we are often led to believe. (See Max M. Mintz, *Gouverneur Morris and the American Revolution* [Norman: University of Oklahoma Press, 1970]; Howard Swiggett, *The Extraordinary Mr. Morris* [Garden City, N.Y.: Doubleday, 1952]; Theodore Roosevelt, *Gouverneur Morris* [Boston and New York: Houghton Mifflin, 1888]; Beatrix C. Davenport, ed., *A Diary of the French Revolution by Gouverneur Morris,* 3 vols. [Boston: Houghton Mifflin, 1939]; Daniel Walther, *Gouverneur Morris: Witness of Two Revolutions* [New York: Funk and Wagnalls, 1934]; Jared Sparks, *The Life of Gouverneur Morris, with Selections from His Correspondence and Miscellaneous Papers,* 3 vols. [Boston: Gray & Bowen, 1832].)

# GEORGE CLYMER

March 16, 1739–January 24, 1813
Merchant, banker, signer of the Declaration of
Independence, and leader of the movement toward the
Revolution in Pennsylvania

*A commercial Federalist, but also affected by Pennsylvania's experience with mob rule and "the excesses of democracy." A quiet, thoughtful, modest man. Of little influence on the debates of the Framers, but respected by his colleagues for his services to the infant republic and for his strength of character. Throughout his life an admirer of the satires of Jonathan Swift. More of a strict republican than most of those present in the Great Convention. Best known for his work in financing the American war effort and for his role as a leader of the Continental Congress after the independence of the colonies had been declared. A man of wealth, but possessed of a genuine popular touch. Religious, and probably Quaker by origin, but a member of the Episcopal Church during his maturity. A generous contributor to the cultural life of his city, where he became a well-loved figure and ornament of public occasions. A courageous peacemaker.*

George Clymer was born in Philadelphia, the son of Christopher Clymer and Deborah Fitzwater Clymer and grandson of Richard Clymer, who had immigrated to that city from Bristol, England. George was orphaned in his infancy and grew up under the guardianship of his uncle, William Coleman, a substantial figure in the commercial life of the Quaker Commonwealth. After some schooling at home and a course of reading in Coleman's considerable library, Clymer became a clerk in the counting house of Robert Ritchie and, later, an associate of Reese Meredith and his son, also merchants of note. Eventually Clymer became a partner in this firm, which he combined with his uncle's business after Coleman's death. His rise was marked by membership in the Philadelphia Common Council, 1767–1770. He also married into the Meredith family and in 1773 was, as America's quarrel with the mother country intensified, a man of mark in the business life of Pennsylvania.

Clymer was strongly opposed to the mercantilist economics of the British Navigation Acts. In his view, they restricted the development of firms like his own in a fashion that was unfair to colonials—making of them something less than freeborn Englishmen. In 1773 he headed an ad hoc committee that compelled officials of the Crown charged with enforcing the Tea Act to resign as consignees and withdraw from the service of George III. He was one of the first in Philadelphia to call for complete independence. And he helped underwrite the ensuing conflict by exchanging all his own specie for Continental currency. Clymer was a member of the Pennsylvania Council of Safety and one of the first two treasurers of the new system of government established by the Continental Congress. In 1776 he was elected a delegate from his state to that assembly and took his seat in time to sign the Declaration of Independence, after its adoption. In Congress Clymer soon became a man of all work, active in promoting the general loan (money borrowed from American citizens to finance the Congress), building links among the various states, inspecting the army in the field at Ticonderoga, and directing the defense of his city when the Congress, under threat of British invasion, removed to Baltimore. Clymer actually worked to the point of physical collapse. British troops vandalized his home in Chester County, and the war almost destroyed his fortune. Yet he persisted, returning to Congress for two additional terms (1777, 1780–1782), where he continued to assume a variety of responsibilities.

Clymer also served in the Pennsylvania legislature from 1780 to 1782 and from 1784 to 1788, where he opposed the ill effects of the radically democratic Pennsylvania constitution of 1776 and advocated a return to something like the traditional structure of state government under the proprietors, with a clear division and limitation of powers and no threat of mob rule. Once, in the expectation of educating his children, Clymer retired to Princeton, New Jersey, assuming that independence had been achieved. (Earlier, he had attempted to withdraw from public life while still living in Pennsylvania.) But duty drew him back to Philadelphia, where, in the midst of the city's worst experience of radical demagogy, he helped defend the home of his colleague James Wilson ("Fort Wilson") against the attack of an armed mob. Despite his horror at such outrages,

Clymer continued to have confidence in the deliberate sense of the American people, as reflected by republican institutions.

In the Great Convention George Clymer (who had liked the old government under the Articles) opposed a tax on exports, warned against rapid expansion in the West, and objected to restrictions on Pennsylvania's taxing power over commerce passing through its territory. He opposed the provision of an authority to give binding instructions to members of Congress. In general he was silent, ever present and supportive of whatever his friend George Washington seemed to approve. In the Pennsylvania legislature it was Clymer who made the motion for a state ratification convention, and he labored successfully in organizing Federalist forces to win the battle there. Upon the adoption of the U.S. Constitution, Clymer was elected to a seat in the House of Representatives of the First Congress (1789–1791) and then appointed a collector of the excise taxes on spirits brewed in Pennsylvania (1791–1794).

Retiring to private life, he encouraged various worthwhile civic causes, including the Pennsylvania Academy of the Fine Arts and the Philadelphia Society for Promoting Agriculture. He continued a career in banking fostered by his original association with the Bank of North America and later served as the first president of the Bank of Philadelphia. Unlike his former associate Robert Morris, he prospered as part of the system he had helped to create. Clymer disliked the French Revolution once it became an "armed doctrine" but did not approve of efforts to crush republicanism in France. As he grew older, his identification with the Federalist party declined. A careful man, he illustrates the pattern of American leaders who were "radicals" for the Revolution, but did not expect independence to disturb the internal order of their society. In his old age, he was one of Philadelphia's honored citizens, respected by all ranks of society. (See Robert L. Brunhouse, *The Counter-Revolution in Pennsylvania, 1776–1790* [Harrisburg: Pennsylvania Historical Commission, 1942]; H. James Henderson, *Party Politics in the Continental Congress* [New York: McGraw Hill, 1974]; Robert Waln, Jr., "George Clymer," in *Biography of the Signers to the Declaration of Independence,* vol. 4 [Philadelphia: R. W. Pomeroy, 1823], pp. 173–246; Harry Simpson, ed., *The Lives of Eminent Philadelphians* [Philadelphia: William Brotherhead, 1859], p. 211; John Bach McMaster and Frederick D. Stone, *Pennsylvania and the Federal Constitution, 1787–1788* [New York: Da Capo Press, 1970], pp. 704–706; Robert G. Ferris, ed., *Signers of the Constitution* [Washington, D.C.: National Park Service, 1976], pp. 154–156; Charles H. Lincoln, *The Revolutionary Movement in Pennsylvania, 1760–1776* [Philadelphia: University of Pennsylvania Press, 1901]; Richard A. Ryerson, "Leadership in Crisis. The Radical Committees of Philadelphia and the Coming of Revolution in Pennsylvania, 1765–1776: A Study in the Revolutionary Process" [Ph.D. dissertation, Johns Hopkins University, 1973]; Harry Martin Tinkcom, *The Republicans and Federalists of Pennsylvania, 1790–1801: A Study of National Stimulus and Local Response* [Harrisburg: Pennsylvania Historical and Museum

Commission, 1950]; Walter H. Mohr, "George Clymer," *Pennsylvania History* 5 [October 1938]: 282–285; Jerry Grundfest, *George Clymer: Philadelphia Revolutionary, 1739–1813* [New York: Arno Press, 1982].)

# THOMAS MIFFLIN
January 10, 1744–January 20, 1800
Merchant, leader in the Revolution, soldier, and
Pennsylvania politician

*A popular political figure in his state at the time of the Constitutional Convention, but of no influence on its deliberations. A mild commercial Federalist and a man of considerable wealth, but of no consistent political philosophy. Important in Pennsylvania for his conspicuous role in bringing the state to a full commitment to the struggle for American independence. Born in Philadelphia, of distinguished Quaker origin. Son of John and Elizabeth Bagnell Mifflin. Educated in a Quaker school, at the College of Philadelphia, and in the countinghouse of William Coleman, a Philadelphia merchant often associated with John Mifflin's enterprises. At twenty, Thomas Mifflin visited Europe, and upon his return to Philadelphia, entered a trading partnership with his brother George. In business, entirely successful, but drawn to politics by his concern for colonial rights. Outspoken in his opposition to the Stamp Act and instrumental in the adoption of nonimportation agreements. With Charles Thomson, Benjamin Rush, and George Clymer, a leader in the popular movement to establish committees of correspondence. Four times elected to the Provincial Assembly (1772–1776) and sent by that body to represent Pennsylvania in the First and Second Continental Congresses, where he was one of the youngest and most radical members.*

Soon after the opening of hostilities at Lexington and Concord, Thomas Mifflin was elected a major in one of the first regiments raised in Pennsylvania, and on June 23, 1775, he was appointed Gen. George Washington's aide-de-camp. He took part in the siege of Boston, but in August of 1775, he was persuaded to accept the post of quartermaster general of the Continental army, a position he held (except for a brief interval during the 1776 campaign in New York) until March 1778. In the beginning he was an efficient quartermaster, though he longed for martial glory, and on a few occasions distinguished himself under fire. In December of 1775, he was commissioned colonel and in May of the following year promoted to the rank of brigadier general. However, much of his reputation was due to his status as a soldier-politician who had the backing of a sizable faction within the Continental Congress.

For a time Washington made good use of Mifflin's influence in Philadelphia and often employed him as liaison with congressional and state authorities. Mifflin was present at the battles of Trenton and Princeton, was appointed major general in February of 1777, and was assigned the duty of preparing the defenses of Philadelphia. On several occasions his speeches persuaded soldiers to stay with the army even in the dark days after the retreat from New York through New Jersey. Moreover, he brought fresh troops from Pennsylvania to participate in Washington's reconquest of most of New Jersey. But he grew to overvalue his own military importance, became jealous of Washington's other officers, tired of his duties as quartermaster, and gradually withdrew from direct involvement in the war effort, citing "reasons of health." Once Philadelphia had fallen to Sir William Howe, Mifflin pressed upon Congress his request dated October 8, 1777, that he be allowed to resign his military offices.

However, Mifflin was not officially relieved of his responsibilities as a soldier until February of 1779, or of his responsibility for Washington's commissary until March of 1778. During this period when he was neither in nor out of the army, he became a willing tool of American political leaders who were dissatisfied with General Washington's leadership and determined to replace or restrain the Virginian in his role as commander in chief. Mifflin's assistants failed completely in their duty to provide for the encampment at Valley Forge during the dreadful winter of 1777–1778. The affairs of Mifflin's department degenerated into a great confusion, and he was called upon to face a court martial once his records had been presented and not approved. The charges included idleness, duplicity, and criminal partiality—putting the interests of a faction and state ahead of the needs of the country. Meanwhile, Gen. Thomas Conway and Gen. Horatio Gates were put forward by some radical spirits in the Congress and the army as better suited to the military purposes of a "revolutionary people" than the cautious George Washington. Mifflin and Gates were appointed to a congressional Board of War to oversee the activities of forces in the field, and Thomas Conway was appointed inspector general. Evidence of collusion linking these officers and their patrons in the Congress with a design to force Washington's resignation came to light. And they, instead of Washington, were injured. General Gates, with difficulty, was able to extricate himself from the collapse of the "Conway Cabal." General Conway was forced out of the army, and Thomas Mifflin's often repeated request that he be allowed to resign was finally honored. Though his involvement in the maneuvering against Washington and his mismanagement as quartermaster general discredited Mifflin and denied him any role of importance in national politics under the Constitution, he retained favor among the people of Pennsylvania.

After his withdrawal from the army, Mifflin rose quickly in Pennsylvania politics, in which he had never ceased to be involved even while a soldier. He was reelected to the state assembly in 1778 and to the Confederation Congress from 1782 to 1784. Ironically, he was the president of that body when General Washington returned to it his commission as commander in chief. On the state level, Mifflin opposed the radical democrats who called for cheap money and price controls, fought to revise or cancel the radical Pennsylvania constitution of 1776, and at the same time successfully continued to represent himself as the champion of the ordinary citizen and enemy of the "wicked Tories." After three more years in the legislature, he was elected to the Supreme Executive Council of Pennsylvania in 1788 and succeeded Benjamin Franklin as its president. In 1789–1790 he was also chairman of the state constitutional convention that replaced Pennsylvania's radical constitution of 1776 with a more conservative one. Mifflin was elected Pennsylvania's first governor under this new instrument in 1790 and served in that office for nine years, the three terms allowed by the constitution. After leaving that office, he served a final year in the state legislature.

The paradox of Thomas Mifflin's public life is summarized by the distance between the form of his political appeal and the substance behind it. According to his erstwhile friend Benjamin Rush, Mifflin's popularity was "acquired by the basest acts of familiarity with the meanest of the people. He avoided the society of gentlemen, and cherished that of mechannicks." Yet on most days, Mifflin rode from his estate in the suburbs to his office dressed in the full uniform of a general, astride a fine horse, and followed by a retinue of servants in livery. He ended his career as a Jeffersonian. But apart from a few pleasantries with the French ambassador and a reluctance to quash the Whiskey Rebellion, nothing in his policy or conduct greatly offended the social and economic leaders of Philadelphia, especially the Quaker merchant princes, whose political support Mifflin retained long after he had forfeited his membership in their religious community. Though he died in financial straits and was buried at public expense, though he had run through a great fortune and was notoriously fond of the bottle, though his political career was more a matter of eloquence and a pleasing exterior than of fixed and well-considered beliefs, Thomas Mifflin was a hero to the people of his state. (See Kenneth R. Rossman, *Thomas Mifflin and the Politics of the American Revolution* [Chapel Hill: University of North Carolina Press, 1952]; Forrest McDonald, *We the People: The Economic Origins of the Constitution* [Chicago: University of Chicago Press, 1958], pp. 61–63; J. Edwin Hendricks, *Charles Thomson and the Making of a New Nation, 1729–1824* [Rutherford, N.J.: Fairleigh Dickinson University Press, 1979]; David F. Hawke, *In the Midst of a Revolution* [Philadelphia: University of Pennsylvania Press, 1961]; Harry Martin Tinkcom, *The Republicans and Federalists of Pennsylvania, 1790–1801: A Study of National Stimulus and Local Response* [Harrisburg: Pennsylvania Historical and Museum Commission, 1950]; Robert L. Brunhouse, *The Counter-Revolution in Pennsylvania, 1776–1790* [Harrisburg: Pennsylvania Historical Commission, 1942]; William Nisbet Chambers, *Political Parties in the New*

*Nation: The American Experience, 1776–1809* [New York: Oxford University Press, 1973]; Ronald M. Baumann, "The Democratic Republicans of Philadelphia: The Origins, 1776–1797" [Ph.D. dissertation, Pennsylvania State University, 1970]; Richard A. Ryerson, "Leadership in Crisis. The Radical Committees of Philadelphia and the Coming of Revolution in Pennsylvania, 1765–1766: A Study in the Revolutionary Process" [Ph.D. dissertation, Johns Hopkins University, 1973].)

# THOMAS FITZSIMONS

1741–August 26, 1811
Leader of the Revolution in Pennsylvania, vigorous nationalist, militia officer, and one of Philadelphia's "merchant princes"

*Commercial Federalist par excellence, also led to advocate a stronger national government by threats of disorder in Pennsylvania. Described by his contemporaries as "an aristocrat" and, unlike his friend George Clymer, not restrained in his politics by questions concerning the aboriginal "rights of man." Roman Catholic, one of two in the Great Convention. Born in Ireland, but immigrated in his youth to Philadelphia, where he went into trade. Married (in 1761) Catherine Meade, the daughter of the powerful and wealthy Robert Meade. With his brother-in-law formed a partnership under the name of George Meade and Company, which prospered in the West India trade.*

Upon the outbreak of the American Revolution, Fitzsimons—first cautiously and then enthusiastically—endorsed the patriot cause. During the war he commanded a company of militia, which he had raised himself (1776–1777), and was a member of the Philadelphia Committee of Correspondence, the Council of Safety, and the Navy Board. His firm provided fire ships for the protection of the city, gathered supplies for military use, and in the last years of the conflict, donated five thousand pounds to the Continental army. In 1782 Fitzsimons was elected to a seat in the Confederation Congress, where he urged payment of the government's debt to its soldiers and the retirement of other debts owed by the Confederation. Though an opponent of the ultrademocratic Pennsylvania Constitution of 1776, he was elected a member of the Pennsylvania Council of Censors, and from 1785 to 1789 was a powerful member of the state legislature. A founder of the Bank of North America, he was one of its directors from 1781 to 1803.

In the Great Convention Fitzsimons was regular in his attendance, but he said little to distinguish himself. He favored a constitutional restriction on the rights of suffrage, a provision allowing states to continue to charge duties on commerce originating outside their borders, the reservation of high national office to men of means, and the right of Congress to tax imports and exports. However, he believed that both the Senate and the House of Representatives should have a hand in drafting treaties with foreign powers, and that Congress should have the authority to improve navigation or port facilities. Generally, he voted with the high Federalists, following the lead of Robert Morris. In their company, he helped to persuade the Pennsylvania legislature to call a ratification convention soon after the Constitution had been completed.

When the new government was established, Fitzsimons served in the House of Representatives for three terms (1789–1795). In Congress he was an energetic advocate of the program of Alexander Hamilton. He called for a high tariff, retirement of the national debt, and internal improvements. Then, after defeat by a Democratic-Republican, he returned to Philadelphia. There he became president of the Philadelphia Chamber of Commerce and director and president of the Insurance Company of North America. But he held no further public offices except for a place on an arbitration commission established under the terms of Jay's Treaty. Even so, in his final years he continued to enjoy some political influence, opposing Jefferson's Embargo of 1807–1809, and recommending that the first Bank of the United States be rechartered. Fitzsimons suffered great losses as a consequence of the collapse of the empire of Robert Morris; like so many of the Framers from a commercial background, he went into financial bankruptcy. Thereafter his fortunes and his reputation improved, but were never completely restored. Fitzsimons was a generous contributor to his church and for many years a trustee of the University of Pennsylvania. A dignified man and a friend to the Irish citizens of his city, he was a philanthropist throughout his life. (See Robert L. Brunhouse, *The Counter-Revolution in Pennsylvania, 1776–1790* [Harrisburg: Pennsylvania Historical Commission, 1942]; Henry Simpson, ed., *The Lives of Eminent Philadelphians* [Philadelphia: William Brotherhood, 1859], pp. 372–373; Robert G. Ferris, ed., *Signers of the Constitution* [Washington, D.C.: National Park Service, 1976], pp. 163–164; John Bach McMaster and Frederick D. Stone, *Pennsylvania and the Federal Constitution, 1787–1788* [New York: Da Capo Press, 1970], pp. 706–707; Charles H. Lincoln, *The Revolutionary Movement in Pennsylvania, 1760–1776* [Philadelphia: University of Pennsylvania Press, 1901]; Richard A. Ryerson, "Leadership in Crisis. The Radical Committees of Philadelphia and the Coming of Revolution in Pennsylvania, 1765–1776: A Study in the Revolutionary Process" [Ph.D. dissertation, Johns Hopkins University, 1973]; J. A. Farrell, "Thomas Fitzsimons," *Records of the American Catholic Historical Society of Philadelphia* 39 [September 1928]: 175–224; Henry Flanders, "Thomas Fitzsimmons," *Pennsylvania Magazine of History and Biography* 2 [October 1878]: 306–314.)

# JARED INGERSOLL, JR.

October 27, 1749–October 31, 1822
Lawyer and political leader of postrevolutionary Pennsylvania

*In the Great Convention, the Antifederalist from Philadelphia, chosen by the commercial Federalists who controlled the legislature of his state as a token concession to the minority. Actually convinced before 1787 that a stronger central government was necessary to the future of the United States. Never really a democrat, though concerned about state sovereignty and the financial needs of a general government. Spoke only once in the Constitutional Convention, to specify that he "did not consider the signing, either as a mere attestation of the fact, or as pledging the signers to support the Constitution at all events," but as the best thing to do at the time. Born in New Haven, Connecticut. Son of Jared Ingersoll, Sr., one of the leading Tories in America, and Hannah Whiting Ingersoll. Father a representative of the colony of Connecticut in England, and later stampmaster general of all New England under the Stamp Act. Rendered unpopular by his acceptance of this appointment. Moved by Whitehall to Philadelphia, where the Crown had made him a vice-admiralty court judge for Pennsylvania.*

*The younger Jared Ingersoll was educated in the best schools of Connecticut; at Yale (from which he graduated with a B.A. in 1766); by reading in the law (primarily with Joseph Reed in Philadelphia, after his family's relocation there in 1771); and at the Middle Temple (1774–1776). Admitted to the Pennsylvania bar in 1773. Advised by family to be absent from the country as the Revolution approached. No longer a Loyalist when, after a two-year tour of Europe and some association with Benjamin Franklin in France, he returned to Philadelphia late in 1778. Shortly thereafter, a patriot, even though his father had been driven into retirement and exile for refusing to approve American independence. Attorney for President Joseph Reed of the Executive Council of Pennsylvania and for the powerful merchant Col. Charles Pettit, an Antifederalist into whose family Ingersoll had married. Later attorney for the even wealthier Stephen Girard. Linked to the Constitutionalists, who supported the democratic Pennsylvania Constitution of 1776 and local autonomy for the states, by personal associations. Understandably, a cautious person. A devout Presbyterian and an old-fashioned "man of the law," with a fine practice in a community of distinguished attorneys. Member of the Continental Congress for Pennsylvania, 1780–1781. Probably silent in the Constitutional Convention because of the anomaly of his situation within the Pennsylvania delegation.*

After the establishment of a government under the federal Constitution, Jared Ingersoll, Jr., served on the Philadelphia Common Council in 1789 and as attorney general of Pennsylvania from 1790 to 1799 and from 1811 to 1817. From 1800 to 1801 he was U.S. district attorney for Pennsylvania. Displeased by the conduct of Jefferson's first administration, he was identified as a mild Federalist for the remainder of his life. He was the choice of Pennsylvania Federalists for the vice-presidency in 1812, but, essentially, he was not a political man. In 1791, Ingersoll was admitted to practice before the U.S. Supreme Court, and in that arena he participated in some of the Court's most famous early cases, including *Chisholm* v. *Georgia* (1793) and *Hylton* v. *United States* (1796). In these actions, Ingersoll contended generally for a strict construction of the Constitution and against the doctrine of implied powers. He was attorney for Sen. William Blount of Tennessee when Blount was threatened with impeachment for plotting to persuade Britain to conquer Louisiana and Spanish Florida. In 1820–1821, at the end of his career, Ingersoll served briefly as presiding judge of the District Court for the City and County of Philadelphia. At the time of his death at the age of seventy-three, his son, Charles Jared Ingersoll, was already established as a leader of the American bar, though in his legal philosophy he was the antithesis of his traditionalist father and grandfather. (See Charles Jared Ingersoll, "Jared Ingersoll," in *The Lives of Eminent Philadelphians*, ed. Henry Simpson [Philadelphia: William Brotherhead, 1859], pp. 594–596; Robert G. Ferris, ed., *Signers of the Constitution* [Washington, D.C.: National Park Service, 1976], pp. 175–176; Franklin Bowditch Dexter, *Biographical Sketches of Graduates of Yale College, with Annals of the College History*, vol. 3 [New York: H. Holt, 1903], pp. 184–187; Horace Binney, *Leaders of the Old Bar of Philadelphia* [Philadelphia: Sherman and Sons, 1859]; Lawrence Henry Gipson, *Jared Ingersoll: A Study of American Loyalism in Relation to British Colonial Government* [New Haven, Conn.: Yale University Press, 1920]; John Bach McMaster and Frederick D. Stone, *Pennsylvania and the Federal Constitution, 1787–1788* [New York: Da Capo Press, 1970], pp. 707–709; H. James Henderson, *Party Politics in the Continental Congress* [New York: McGraw-Hill, 1974]; Harry Martin Tinkcom, *The Republicans and Federalists of Pennsylvania, 1790–1801: A Study of National Stimulus and Local Response* [Harrisburg: Pennsylvania Historical and Museum Commission, 1950]; W. M. Meigs, *The Life of Charles Jared Ingersoll* [New York: Da Capo Press, 1970], pp. 18–25.)

# JAMES WILSON

September 14, 1742–August 21, 1798
Lawyer, jurist, political philosopher, "projector," land speculator, and statesman

*Signer of the Declaration of Independence and of the Constitution. Architect of the Pennsylvania Constitution of 1790. A theoretical democrat and a high*

*Federalist who in much of his career lived in conflict with the spokesmen for the popular cause, both in Pennsylvania and elsewhere in the country. A metaphysical progressive who thought of the state as an instrument for the pursuit of perfection, believing at the same time that government had "the right of acquiring everything without which its perfection cannot be promoted or obtained." A philosopher of democracy who first attacked slavery and then bought slaves. A dialectician who could "bewilder truth in all the mazes of sophistry, and render the plainest proposition problematical." Able, through "the power of moral abstraction," to recommend that we love men far away, "so unknown, or so distant as to elude the operation of our benevolence." Yet unable to act the part of kinsman to members of his own family left behind in his native Scotland or to pay his debts to the relatives and friends who launched him on his American career, even when they needed the money and he did not. A man of noisy sentiment and moral intuition, but apparently a humbug—particularly in his expansive expressions of faith in the common man and in the future of America. Never so interested in the will of the people as in the sponsorship of the "better sort" with the hope of making money. Capable, without hesitation, of putting his own opinions in place of the preferences of his constituents because he knew how they would have felt "if possessed of equal information." Among the Framers, second only to Gouverneur Morris in the frequency of his speeches (168) in the Philadelphia Convention. Perhaps a precursor of American political thought, but in 1787 not representative of the frame of mind that produced the U.S. Constitution.*

James Wilson (nicknamed "James de Caledonia") was born in Fifeshire, near the university town of St. Andrews in Scotland. He was the eldest son of William Wilson, yeoman farmer and elder of the kirk, and Alison Landale Wilson, a strong-willed woman. After early schooling in the Cupar Grammar School, young James proceeded to St. Andrews, where in 1757 he was granted a scholarship. He commenced a course of studies that was expected to lead into a career in the ministry of the Church of Scotland. However, when James's father died in 1762, the young man withdrew from St. Mary's, the theological college of the university to which he had transferred upon completion of his B.A. in the previous year, and took a job as a tutor in a gentleman's house. This occupation did not satisfy the ambitious young Wilson, who believed himself destined for a higher station. Friends and relatives were happy in North America. In 1765 he asked for an equivalent opportunity and was given it by the little village of his boyhood—by the Annans, Balfours, Landales, and Wilsons. With a stake and a brief taste of the merchant's life in Edinburgh, James set sail for the New World.

Upon his arrival in Pennsylvania, armed with letters of reference, Wilson received almost immediate appointment as tutor in Latin at the College of Philadelphia. He was given an honorary M.A. by the small school and became recognized as a man of learning and ability. Shortly thereafter (again with aid from a kinsman), he arranged to read law in the offices of the distinguished John Dickinson. In 1767 Wilson was admitted to the Pennsylvania bar. The following year he set up practice in Reading, Pennsylvania. Two years later, he moved westward to Carlisle, married into a family of local importance, and began to prosper among his litigious Scotch-Irish neighbors.

Soon he had half the legal business in the county and cases throughout the state, as well as in New Jersey and New York. He gave literary lectures at the College of Philadelphia. He traded in land, bought slaves and a big house. In 1774 he was chosen as chairman of the Carlisle Committee of Correspondence and was elected to the Provincial Assembly. He finished a manuscript that he had first drafted in 1768, entitled *Considerations on the Nature and Extent of the Legislative Authority of the British Parliament* (1774). In this work he maintained that since "all men are, by nature, equal and free," Parliament could have no authority over Englishmen in America, who were connected to the mother country only through obligations to a common king—provided that king did not "withdraw his protection" from them. The skill displayed in this performance helped propel James Wilson into the forefront of leadership in a Pennsylvania moving steadily toward independence; and from that rank he did not retire.

In 1775 Wilson was sent by Pennsylvania to be one of its delegates in the Second Continental Congress. There he joined forces with the conservative leaders of the "old regime" in Pennsylvania politics, the spokesmen for the "Proprietary party" and balanced government under the charter of the Penns. With his old mentor, John Dickinson, and Robert Morris, Wilson approached with hesitation the fateful prospect of outright revolution and permanent separation from Great Britain. Wilson's theme in his *Considerations* had been the desirability of something like the British Commonwealth that emerged later in history. In February of 1776, he prepared a reaffirmation of that doctrine, though (according to Wilson's own interpretation of the event) he carefully coupled it with conditions designed "to lead the public mind into the idea of Independence." This strategy was too abstruse for the Congress, which refused to publish the document. As the pressures of war gathered, Wilson put aside his reservations and voted—almost reluctantly—for the Declaration of Independence.

By this time he had already lost much of his following among Pennsylvania radicals. Yet he persisted in representing his state with the best of his energy and judgment. Wilson called the democratic Pennsylvania Constitution of 1776 "the most detestable that ever was formed." Even so, his enemies continued him in the Continental Congress until September of 1777. He served on committees urging the states to relinquish frontier lands (he wanted the general government to confirm his titles in the West); calling for a national power to collect taxes and raise a revenue; and negotiating a treaty of friendship with the Indian tribes of the Northwest. In keeping with his position in the Great Convention, he also called for representation in the Congress according to the concentration of free white population and for an end to voting by states.

After leaving Congress, Wilson delayed briefly in Maryland and then moved his home from Reading to Philadelphia, where he became counsel for many wealthy Loyalists, *avocat general* for the French maritime and commercial courts in the United States, the political leader of the merchant aristocracy, an investor in privateering, and an advocate for land-jobbing companies and banks. In arguing a case for the Bank of North America—a bank of which he was a director—he maintained that "the United States have general rights, general powers, and general obligations, not derived from any particular states, nor from all the particular states, taken separately; but resulting from the union of the whole." In this language there is clear evidence that, well before the Constitutional Convention, Wilson was already the friend of implied authority and what would later be called the doctrine of inherent power, the enemy of state sovereignty, and the supporter of a notion of natural rights as applying more to the conflict of "the weak against the strong" than to the quarrel of "the citizen against the state."

Abandoning the faith of his youth, Wilson became an Anglican—though, in truth, he was more a Deist. He moved in the highest circles—and perfected the stiff, haughty manner that made him a much-hated figure in his state: so hated that, in the fall of 1779, the people of Philadelphia formed themselves into a militia on its way to being a mob and besieged Wilson's house, as if it "had been the local headquarters of the British Grenadiers." Wilson's conservative political associates, hearing rumors of the attack, armed "Fort Wilson," fired on the multitude when it arrived, suffered and gave many casualties (both dead and wounded), and, once troops arrived to restore peace, dispatched the Caledonian to refuge in the country. This support in a moment of crisis did not signify that Wilson actually enjoyed the personal loyalty of many friends. Contemporary records indicate that he was a cold man, with no gift for fellowship. But in 1782, he did retain the respect of the conservatives (called Republicans) in Pennsylvania politics. For in that year, as they recovered control of the legislature, they returned Wilson to his old seat in the Congress—a seat which he also occupied in 1785–1787. They were unable to prevent the repeal of the Bank of North America's charter, but with the selection of James Wilson, they did lay the groundwork for the Constitutional Convention.

During the Convention Wilson was almost unique among the Framers in reasoning from a systematic philosophical position, resting on a general metaphysic, to recommend that particular provisions be included in the Constitution. Wilson came to the deliberations with a set of assumptions concerning American politics and the meaning of the Articles of Confederation not shared by many of his colleagues. First of all, Wilson never accepted the historic and well-established multiplicity of cultural identities reflected in the thirteen state governments as a given of any viable plan for a stronger union. Indeed, Wilson denied, in the face of all evidence and opinion, that the states were sovereign in their connection through the Articles of Confederation. His argument (supported by few American thinkers before the antebellum debates concerning slavery and secession) was that the states were dissolved, along with the tie to England, by the Declaration of Independence; and that the Continental Congress represented "the people of the United States," taken collectively, who are the "We" of the Declaration. He called the states "imaginary beings" and asked his fellow Framers "to proceed by abstracting as much as possible from state governments." Elsewhere he added that, as to the purposes of union, the states "should be considered as having no existence."

Perhaps the explanation of Wilson's animus against the states is, as some scholars have argued, that, like some of the other recent immigrants among the Framers, he could not recognize the importance of the old colonial divisions as a locus of political emotion and personal loyalty, even in the process of creating a federal union. Although he was later to be the proponent of a theory of dual sovereignty that was used to pacify the Antifederalists (and, by a curious inversion, to augment the authority of the general government and the federal bench), one *and* many was a doctrine he could not comprehend. Or it may have been that the reality of American politics present in the Constitutional Convention offended his uniformitarianism, his love for the ecumenic dream of King Henry IV of France, or his Scottish "common sense" philosophy. But another plausible explanation of his conduct was the unwillingness (or inability) of the Continental Congress to grant him those rich appointments and valuable western lands that he so earnestly desired. In the records of the Great Convention, there is also support for the theory of Pennsylvania Antifederalists that Wilson had in mind an appointment as chief justice of the United States.

Wilson opposed the Great Compromise on representation of the states in the Senate with more vehemence and determination than was shown by any other champions of the proportional Virginia Plan. His charge against the formula finally adopted was that it violated "the inherent, indisputable and unalienable rights of men." And, with absolutely no effect on his fellow Framers, he made the same complaint against Madison's plan to attach a property qualification to the franchise; against schemes such as the electoral college for an indirect selection of presidents; against requiring a two-thirds vote for the ratification of treaties; and against related provisions. Yet, despite his official obeisance to the unadulterated "will of the people," he taught another doctrine on the assignment of powers to the Supreme Court. These he wished to see both extensive and detailed—including a power to review (with the chief executive, whom he also exalted) the actions of Congress even before they faced any challenge at law. Wilson was an overt champion of judicial activism, of "legislation" by the courts, and of the "imperial presidency," in a company to whom such notions seemed foreign. Wilson was "inelastic, doctrinaire and full of bombast"—going so far as to suggest that the highest purpose of union was the "reformation" of the

American mind. Though he served on the Committee of Detail, whose members composed the first draft of the Constitution, the theory that he was a major influence on the final form of the document is unsupported, a myth of those scholars who prefer his teaching to that of the Framers of genuine importance. Wilson is perhaps most useful in directing attention to what the authors of the Constitution did not intend for it to mean.

Though often disappointed in the Convention, James Wilson was the dominant figure in the Pennsylvania ratifying convention of 1787. There he placated Antifederalists with promises that "all rights not specifically given to the general government" were "reserved to the states"—and that therefore no bill of rights was needed to complete the Constitution, since such definitions were properly the business of the "sovereign" states, who could make and enforce their own versions of "universal truth." For days he held the floor, answering all objections to the federal compact—often with arguments he had not used in the Great Convention. Here his oratory was at its best—so brilliant that his friend Benjamin Rush spoke of the performance as "a blaze of light." And, in his major address to this gathering of delegates from throughout his state, he held out a vision of America's future, a dream of power and glory moving westward, filling those who owned a share in it with "awe and apprehension"—of a land so vast, with such infinite potential, that it was rich beyond the wildest dreams of avarice. In these remarks, and in his earlier October 6, 1787, speech in the State House yard, soon after the adjournment of the Constitutional Convention, Wilson carried the case for the proposed federal Constitution in Pennsylvania.

Upon the installation of President George Washington and the formation of the government under the Constitution, Wilson did not receive the highest judicial honor. Though he directly solicited the post of chief justice of the Supreme Court, and though the most important Federalist in Pennsylvania, Robert Morris, had lobbied to win him the job, Washington recognized the problems that might issue from Wilson's passion for speculation, from the rumors of his debts, and from riots like the one in Carlisle, Pennsylvania, in January of 1788—the climax of which was a burning of Wilson in effigy. Washington wisely turned away from the proud, learned Scot, called by his enemies "Lieutenant-General of the Myrmidons of power," and appointed John Jay of New York. Wilson was, however, offered the position of associate justice, which he accepted. Soon after his elevation to the Court, he was asked to give a course of lectures in the law at the College of Philadelphia, of which he was a trustee. The results of this labor, published mostly after his death, were the first studies of their kind to be produced in North America—an attempt to create an American jurisprudence based on consent instead of authority. Wilson had a central and positive role in writing the Pennsylvania constitution of 1790. He began, at the behest of the state legislature, a complete digest of the laws of Pennsylvania. Finally, it appeared that his efforts in so many fields of endeavor, his great energies, were beginning to bear fruit. It was rumored that Wilson had become one of the richest men in the country. America was "the home of limitless progress," said he. And "it is the glorious destiny of man to be always progressive." But what some authorities have referred to as the "compulsive and irrational" dimension of his commitment to progress of a personal kind was beginning to catch up with him.

Between 1792 and his death in 1798, James Wilson plunged more and more deeply into land speculation. He was a large investor in the Illinois-Wabash Company. He bought an interest in one of the infamous Yazoo companies, as well as lands in Pennsylvania and New York. At the same time, he was adventuring in commercial and manufacturing schemes. Depression and war in Europe—a war that curtailed immigration—dried up investment funds and lowered the value of frontier properties. Still, Wilson came up with larger and larger designs, asking Dutch investors to buy 500,000 acres through him and to ship over their own immigrants to purchase the land.

In intervals between these frantic efforts to shore up his financial empire, Wilson did a little business as federal judge, rode the circuit, and wrote an important opinion in *Chisholm* v. *Georgia,* in which he argued, from his familiar definition of the Union as representing the whole people of the United States and not a bond between the people of the states, that a citizen of one state could sue the government of another state—in this case, a state where Wilson had lands. His object was to "develop" the intention of the Framers. The Eleventh Amendment to the Constitution canceled this ruling—and reproached the Federalists on the Court for reaching after unwarranted authority. Wilson's opinion was called a "rhapsody," and contemporaries spoke of his willingness to "twist any text" to strengthen the power of the general government. Perhaps he, and not Marshall, was the father of judicial review based on implied powers. But he went about the task with the same lack of scruple that he displayed in his land dealings and therefore provided no aegis for his successors in imaginative construction of the fundamental law. Finally, his colleagues on the Court reminded him that it was "of more importance to ascertain what the law is, than to speculate what it ought to be."

In the end, creditors began to call in his notes. The Congress refused to shore up his claims. Hundreds of thousands of dollars were due. Wilson, though a justice of the Supreme Court, fled, "hunted," in his own words, "like a wild beast." Twice he was arrested. Ironically, he found final shelter in the South, with his friend Justice James Iredell at Edenton, North Carolina. There, of a "nervous fever," crying out in remorse, he died in shame—one of the most curious, brilliant, gifted, and distressing figures in the political history of the country. (See C. Page Smith, *James Wilson, Founding Father, 1742–1798* [Chapel Hill: University of North Carolina Press, 1956]; Arnaud B. Leavelle, "James Wilson and the Relation of Scottish Metaphysics to American Political Thought," *Political Science Quarterly* 57 [Fall 1942]: 394–410; Ralph A. Rossum, "James Wilson and the 'Pyramid of Government': The Federal Republic," *Political*

*Science Reviewer* 6 [Fall 1976]: 113–142; Geoffrey Seed, *James Wilson: Scottish Intellectual and American Statesman* [Millwood, N.Y.: KTO Press, 1978]; W. E. Obering, *The Philosophy of Law of James Wilson: A Study in Comparative Jurisprudence* [Washington, D.C.: Catholic University Press, 1938]; Robert G. McCloskey, "James Wilson," in *The Justices of the United States Supreme Court, 1789–1969: Their Lives and Major Opinions,* vol. 1, ed. Leon Friedman and Fred L. Israel [New York: R. R. Bowker/Chelsea House, 1969], pp. 79–96; Ralph A. Rossum, "James Wilson," in *Encyclopedia of the American Constitution,* vol. 4, ed. Leonard W. Levy et al. [New York: Macmillan, 1986], pp. 2067–2070; Robert Waln, Jr., "James Wilson," in *Biography of the Signers to the Declaration of Independence,* vol. 6, ed. John Sanderson [Philadelphia: R. W. Pomeroy, 1825], pp. 113–175; Robert L. Brunhouse, *The Counter-Revolution in Pennsylvania, 1776–1790* [Harrisburg: Pennsylvania Historical Commission, 1942]; Randolph G. Adams, ed., *Selected Political Essays of James Wilson* [New York: Alfred A. Knopf, 1930], pp. 1–43; Robert G. McCloskey, ed., *The Works of James Wilson,* 2 vols. [Cambridge, Mass.: Harvard University Press, 1967]; John Bach McMaster and Frederick D. Stone, *Pennsylvania and the Federal Constitution, 1787–1788* [New York: Da Capo Press, 1970]; George W. Carey, "James Wilson's Political Thought and the Constitutional Convention," *Political Science Quarterly* 17 [1987]: 49–107; Garry Wills, "James Wilson's New Meaning for Sovereignty," in *Conceptual Change and the Constitution,* ed. Terence Ball and J. G. A. Pocock [Lawrence: University Press of Kansas, 1988], pp. 99–106; James A. Schact, "Architect of the Constitution: James Wilson," *Wisconsin Bar Bulletin* 60 [May 1987]: 32–36.)

# ROBERT MORRIS
January 31, 1734–May 8, 1806
"Merchant prince" of Philadelphia, financier of the
American Revolution, and banker

*Called "the Great Man," with a mixture of irony and respect. At the time of the Constitutional Convention perhaps the wealthiest man in North America. Another commercial Federalist. With Roger Sherman, a signer of all three of the nation's basic documents: the Declaration of Independence, the Articles of Confederation, and the U.S. Constitution. Yet a conservative in almost every sense of the term. The most influential member of the Pennsylvania delegation to the Great Convention. A large, confident, and jovial figure; one who could write to a friend, "I have never failed to get the better of my Enemies on the day of Trial." Not a learned man, but ingenious, described by a political contemporary as one who in argument "bears down all before him." By 1787, greatly hated by* *those who believed he had profited improperly from his services to the patriot cause. Born in or near Liverpool, England. Brought to Maryland at the age of thirteen by his father, Robert Morris, a tobacco merchant. Orphaned shortly thereafter (1750) and left with little schooling and an inheritance of about $7,000.*

Morris was apprenticed in his early teens in the countinghouse of Charles Willing, which became the firm of Willing, Morris and Company when Robert came into his majority. Later, under a succession of names this trading and banking house prospered and survived to act an important part in supplying weapons and ammunition to an infant Continental army. And Robert Morris, as a very young man, became one of the leading citizens of the thriving commercial city of Philadelphia.

In 1765 Morris signed the nonimportation agreement to protest the Stamp Act. In October of that year he was part of a local committee that forced the collector of the stamp tax to close his office. Yet he was no rebel—just one of a host of American merchants who had learned to despise English mercantilist economic policy as it affected American business. And he never regarded the idea of independence from the mother country as anything more than a desperate last resort. However, for "the Principles of the British Constitution . . . [he was] content to run all hazards." On St. George's Day, April 23, 1775, when news of the Battle of Lexington reached Philadelphia's leading citizens in the midst of their annual celebration of their English inheritance, Morris realized that a mortal struggle was in the offing and decided to stand with his adopted city.

In close sequence, he became a member of the Philadelphia Committee of Correspondence (1775–1776), of the local Council of Safety (1775–1776), and of the Pennsylvania Provincial Assembly (1775–1776). From 1775 to 1778 he sat in the Continental Congress, where he quickly became important in organizing his countrymen for the purposes of defense. The Congress bought through his firm, arranged for transport and credit, and borrowed from it. Morris helped to plan coastal fortifications, to sponsor privateers, to build an American navy, and to instruct American diplomats sent abroad. He made money out of his patriotism, but he gave good value for his services. With John Dickinson, he opposed the Declaration of Independence; yet, unlike Dickinson, he signed it in August of 1776, some time after it had been approved. He put his hand to the instrument of revolution even though he continued to hope for an eventual restoration of a tie with England. From 1776 to 1779, 1780 to 1781, and 1785 to 1786, he occupied a seat in the Pennsylvania legislature under the state's constitution—a system of government of which he completely disapproved. And during a period of three crucial years, 1781–1784, he held the office of superintendent of finance under the Articles—the highest civilian position created by the Confederation.

Morris's long struggle to bring solvency to the Congress and support to

American armies in the field went through several stages before he was given sole authority over those enterprises. First of all, he purchased tobacco in the name of the government for trade with France, Holland, and the West Indies. In 1778 he served as chairman of the Committee on Finance. And, once the authority of that body expired and Morris withdrew to the Pennsylvania legislature, he often, in the name of George Washington, applied directly to the states for supplies and money. He continued to borrow money for the government on his own credit, when nothing else was available and emergency action was required, for he had faith that the future of America was one of "Power, Consequence and Grandeur." Moreover, he was one of the few Framers who understood how the transformation of the country would come about. From his position at the center of the nation's commercial life, he could foresee where present trends might lead.

On assuming virtually dictatorial authority over the confused and disordered finances of the new nation, Morris made use of his remarkable skills. He pledged to the Congress, "The United States may command everything I have except my integrity, and the loss of that would effectually disable me from serving them more." As superintendent, Morris eliminated many previously authorized army posts, offices, and agencies; had expenses reported directly to him; instituted a system of purchase contracts; secured new French and Dutch loans; and raised some money from the requisitions he persuaded the Congress to levy. With his own reputation and about $5 million, he instituted regularity where chaos had been. He established plans for a sinking fund to reduce outstanding notes, as retirement became convenient. Yet he disavowed responsibility for direct payment on demand for past debts, leaving such for subsequent settlement by Congress. When Washington needed to pay the army under his command in order to march it south to Virginia, Morris, in person, rushed coin to motivate the uneasy northern regiments into assenting to a campaign far away from home.

Despite his hopes, Morris was unable to convert the business of his office as superintendent into a basis for a stronger union of the states or to assume all outstanding war debts under the Confederation. But he moved the government some distance in that direction, toward agreement with the idea that federal taxes should be used to pay the war debt. The prospect of such arrangements worried the decentralists in Congress and the state governments, who knew that Morris would use his authority to increase the importance of the general government. Therefore, the policy that Morris advocated was never seriously implemented— and was, indeed, contrary to the letter of the Articles. But, in any case, Morris had done an amazing job.

Another expedient for changing the administration of the nation's business from a "rope of sand" into a lasting bond was the 1781 chartering, under Morris's supervision, of the Bank of North America, which opened its doors in January 1782 with $400,000 capital. The financier mingled the affairs of the Confederation with those of the Bank, and both with enterprises of his own. He prospered from this network of connections. But that possibility, and the means to it, had been accepted by the Congress when they had first asked Morris to control the nation's purse strings. Even so, envy and abuse, charges and accusations, compelled him to give over the task of "preaching to the dead" and wait for a more auspicious moment to reform the country into what he believed would be something economically viable, with a coercive power to raise a revenue. What he feared was that the states would pay their debts to the Confederation by honoring the claims of creditors within their own boundaries and would then subtract that sum from what he expected them to send to the general treasury. In one sense, Morris's plan for a powerful national government was a victim of American military success. That unity and economic cooperation would be as important in peacetime as in war was difficult to argue *after* a war fought for liberty, against a remote sovereign insisting on its power to tax.

Out of office, Morris acquired a contract with the Farmers-General of France for a monopoly of the tobacco trade with that country. He revived his old dream of developing Orange Grove plantation on the Mississippi (in Louisiana) with hundreds of slaves and every improvement. He had bought a large country house outside Philadelphia, rebuilt his home in that city, and made plans for an even grander "palace." He participated again in state politics, working to revise the Pennsylvania Constitution of 1776 and to protect his bank. He sent ships to Iberia and the Orient, to the West Indies and the southern states. And when the Annapolis Convention was called, Robert Morris made certain that he was a delegate to that meeting. When his state answered the call from Annapolis for a larger convention to be held in Philadelphia in May of 1787, Morris led the ticket in the legislature's selection of Pennsylvania's delegates.

Once in the Convention, Morris was surprisingly silent for a man of such self-confidence and obvious influence. But he knew his limitations. Moreover, Gouverneur Morris and James Wilson were both present to speak for him, except when Wilson sounded too "democratic." And General Washington was in the chair. To these particulars, Morris had addressed himself. Before the formal opening of the Convention, he had unsuccessfully argued that the votes of the states should be weighted according to their population and their property. Morris seconded a motion that senators be appointed to serve "on good behavior"—for life. Otherwise he kept silent and worked behind the scenes as host for much of the social activity of the gathering. Moreover, once the Constitution was signed, Morris put the great resources of his influence to work in supporting ratification, especially among public creditors—security holders who, as a group, had an interest in the establishment of the proposed federal government.

In 1789 Robert Morris was elected one of Pennsylvania's original U.S. senators, and he served in that office until 1795. Senator Morris voted the Federalist line. He played a major role in the maneuvering that brought the nation's capital to the District of Columbia. But, once the new government was fully in operation, Morris began to speculate heavily in frontier lands. Inflation in the price of securities, along with an international financial contraction, collapsed his empire. In 1797 came bankruptcy, and in 1798, arrest and confinement for failure to pay debts. Yet despite his ruin, his pride, and his huge debts, Robert Morris was a generous man and a patriot. Though untouched by democratic dogma or the abstractions of his sometime-enemy/sometime-employee Thomas Paine, Morris was full of public spirit, brave, and farsighted. He was a supporter of the Episcopal Church, of which his brother-in-law, William White, was the Pennsylvania bishop, and of many public causes. When released from the Prune Street debtors' prison in 1801, Robert Morris was a broken man. His protégé, Gouverneur Morris, had secured an annuity to Mrs. Robert Morris, on the returns from which the family lived modestly. In a little house not far from the scenes of his fame, death came to Robert Morris in his seventy-third year. (See Eleanor Young, *Forgotten Patriot, Robert Morris* [New York: Macmillan, 1950]; Clarence L. Ver Steeg, *Robert Morris, Revolutionary Financier* [New York: Octagon Books, 1976]; Ellis Paxson Oberholtzer, *Robert Morris, Patriot and Financier* [New York: Burt Franklin, 1969]; John Bach McMaster and Frederick D. Stone, *Pennsylvania and the Federal Constitution, 1787–1788* [New York: Da Capo Press, 1970], pp. 703–704 and passim; E. James Ferguson, *The Power of the Purse: A History of American Public Finance, 1776–1790* [Chapel Hill: University of North Carolina Press, 1961]; E. James Ferguson et al., eds., *The Papers of Robert Morris, 1781–1784,* 7 vols. to date [Pittsburgh: University of Pittsburgh Press, 1973–]; H. James Henderson, *Party Politics in the Continental Congress* [New York: McGraw-Hill, 1974]; Frederick S. Rolater, "The Continental Congress: A Study in the Origin of Our Public Administration, 1774–1781" [Ph.D. dissertation, University of Southern California, 1970]; Robert Waln, Jr., "Robert Morris," in *Biography of the Signers to the Declaration of Independence,* vol. 5, ed. John Sanderson [Philadelphia: R. W. Pomeroy, 1824], pp. 189–375; Henry Simpson, ed., *The Lives of Eminent Philadelphians* [Philadelphia: William Brotherhead, 1859], pp. 702–722; Forrest McDonald, *We the People: The Economic Origins of the Constitution* [Chicago: University of Chicago Press, 1958], pp. 54–57, and his *E Pluribus Unum: The Formation of the American Republic, 1776–1790* [Indianapolis: Liberty Press, 1979], pp. 50–57; William Graham Sumner, *The Financier and the Finances of the American Revolution* [New York: Dodd, Mead, 1891].)

# DELAWARE

# JOHN DICKINSON

November 8, 1732–February 14, 1808
Lawyer, planter, statesman, and political philosopher

*One of the most prominent members of the Convention, and a leading citizen of both Pennsylvania and Delaware for twenty years prior to that meeting. Possibly the most learned of the Framers; undoubtedly the most undervalued and misunderstood member of their notable company. The only one of the Fathers of the republic to play a role in every significant moment in its history from the Stamp Act Congress of 1765 through the 1787 deliberations in Philadelphia. Best remembered as "the Penman of the Revolution."*

Born in Talbot County, Maryland, John Dickinson was the son of Judge Samuel Dickinson and Mary Cadwalader Dickinson, both Quakers. With his older brother, Philemon, he grew up in Delaware in Kent County, in an elegant house that still stands southeast of Dover. As an heir to a substantial property (six square miles), he was first educated privately and then in the offices of John Moland, a leader of the Philadelphia bar. Young John finished this preliminary training in 1753 and was then dispatched to London and the Middle Temple for four years of the best of English legal preparation. On his return he established himself in his profession, eventually becoming one of the most respected of American attorneys. In 1760 Dickinson was elected to the assembly of Delaware, where he served as speaker. In 1762 he won a seat as a Philadelphia member of the Pennsylvania legislature. There he became a champion of the proprietary government, opposed to all plans to cancel the charter of the Penns and substitute in its place direct supervision by officers of the Crown. He cherished the old constitution of Pennsylvania, even though, as he admitted, it was subject to abuse, for it embodied a pious respect for the political rights of colonials, particularly in regard to self-government. A new constitution granted by the king might not. Even at this stage in his career, Dickinson was more concerned with preserving established liberties than with reaching after new ones. He put his trust in law, not men, and never feared to be made unpopular by opposing some momentarily popular idea.

After a struggle with the faction led by Benjamin Franklin, Dickinson was not reelected to the Pennsylvania legislature in 1764. However, he remained a political force by exercising his abilities as a pamphleteer. In 1765 he produced *The Late Regulations Respecting the British Colonies . . . Considered*. He was the author of resolutions agreed to in the Stamp Act Congress. And in 1767–1768 he issued, first in the newspapers and then as a book, his *Letters from a Farmer in Pennsylvania*, a work that made him, in the space of a few months, the recognized spokesman for the North American colonies in their disputes with the aggressive policy of the ministers of George III. Sustained by this surge of American acceptance and international acclaim, he was, in 1770, returned to his seat in the Pennsylvania legislature, where he played a dominant role in the sequence of events that resulted finally in the independence of the United States. In that year he married Mary Norris, daughter of the wealthy Isaac Norris, long a leader of the Philadelphia commercial establishment, and thus reinforced his already considerable position in the local aristocracy. Dickinson's home near Philadelphia, Fairhill, became, for a time, the center of public life in the state. In December of 1776 British troops burned it in retaliation—thus identifying John Dickinson as one of those most directly responsible for what the British saw as a "rebellion."

In 1771 Dickinson, speaking for the Pennsylvania legislature, drafted a "Petition to the King" seeking redress of grievances. He became, in 1774, the chairman of the Philadelphia Committee of Correspondence and later in that year was appointed a member for Pennsylvania in the Continental Congress. For his colleagues in Congress he wrote the *Declaration and Resolves of the First Continental Congress* (1774) and the *Declaration of the Causes of Taking Up Arms* (1775). He was also the author of the anthem of the Revolution, the "Song of the Farmer," and of much else besides. In all these roles Dickinson labored to define the quarrel with the imperial government in England in terms of the common political heritage in the English constitution and the prescriptive rights of Englishmen. If there had to be a revolution, and he knew it was likely that there would be, he was determined that it should be accomplished on the proper grounds. He feared an internal transformation of American society in a radically democratic direction, as prophesied by some excited voices in New England, as much as he feared the armies of George III: he feared the one as a product of the other. The protection of known and proven modes and orders was the purpose of every public gesture of his life—though in moments of extremity he could agree to prudent change, when no other method for conserving could be found.

In such a spirit, after long resistance and a try at almost every alternative, Dickinson accepted the Declaration of Independence, though he did not vote for it, made the best speech of his life against it, and left his post in Congress to assume the duties of brigadier general of the Pennsylvania militia rather than grace with his presence the moment of its adoption. Dickinson's objections to a final break with England in July of 1776 included disapproval of the timing of the measure (before a union of the states had been achieved, a new "house" prepared to replace the old) and disapproval of Jefferson's vehement language. But the core of his anxiety was not circumstantial. It had to do instead with his unwillingness to agree to a definition of his America as an entity now completely "outside" the stream of British history: as a reflection of fashionable ideas in contrast to the legal and customary continuity he had been trained to defend. Even after American independence had been achieved, he continued to resist such an abstract definition of its significance.

Dickinson composed the first draft of the country's original instrument of government, the Articles of Confederation; and, following the clamor caused by his principled stubbornness in July of 1776 and a brief retreat to home ground in Delaware, he was returned by his old neighbors to serve in the Continental Congress for 1779. In their name in that session of Congress he signed the Articles he had helped to write. Dickinson served as a private soldier in the Battle of Brandywine and aided his entire region in defense planning and preparation in the face of invasion.

In 1781 he became president of Delaware. From 1782 to 1785, in a vindication that followed the electoral defeat of the extreme democrats in the Quaker State, he was the president of Pennsylvania. For a two-month period, Dickinson was the elected chief executive of two states. After retiring to Delaware and the Dickinson estate in 1785, he was called upon again to attend (and chair) the Annapolis Convention of 1786 and in 1787 to lead the Delaware delegation to the Constitutional Convention. In support of the end product of that gathering, Dickinson wrote a series of essays entitled *The Letters of Fabius,* a work that bears an interesting comparison to *The Federalist Papers.* In his remaining two decades of life, he continued to give effective political support to the cautious, decentralized conception of the federal Union outlined in that final work of advocacy—most of the time as a Jeffersonian Democrat. He championed the view of a balanced regime of divided powers, which he had bespoken in the Great Convention.

John Dickinson's role in the Philadelphia debates was less than his stature would have led his contemporaries to expect and more than subsequent scholarship has been willing to allow. One explanation of this intermittent performance is that he missed some of the discussion because of illness. Another is his uneasiness with the idea of concentrated power, a stronger national government and what it might mean to the nation's future. But Dickinson did have an important share in the shaping of the Constitution, despite sickness and temperamental fear of change. And that portion of his public life played out within the Convention was in keeping with, and drew its authority from, all that he had said and done before in his country's service.

Throughout the Constitutional Convention, from the time of his initial remarks, John Dickinson championed both the necessity for a new instrument of government able to raise money, provide for defense, conduct foreign affairs, and establish a currency and also the need to preserve and protect the "agency" of the sovereign states within the new system. He was the first delegate to suggest that the states have equal representation in the Senate. He voiced a concern with the possibility that the Supreme Court might intrude into matters not properly under its jurisdiction—such as the domestic institutions of the states. And he warned repeatedly against proposed innovations that had nothing to recommend them but speculation and theory: innovations that violated what was already ineluctably "given" in the pattern of American life. An instance of Dickinson's protective concern for institutions rooted in place and history, *grown* but not *made,* is his constant reference to the advantage of giving influence, in the Congress and in other features of the fundamental law, to the thirteen state legislatures. For these assemblies, operating from the colonial beginnings and through the Revolution, were in his opinion the particular repositories of Americans' already existing liberty as a people and the proper source for local charters of liberty. Let there be a bill of rights in Virginia, for Virginians, to be interpreted by them. In Delaware, let there be another, different bill of rights, read by different men, and in the Constitution, careful delimitation, not subject to subsequent construction by the federal courts, of the distinctive spheres and responsibilities of state and national governments. In these arguments Dickinson reasoned from experience and the record, from authority and analogy—particularly to republican Rome and England, but never from definition. Among the Framers he is the chief spokesman for the Old Whig tradition so important to subsequent American political thought. And he is responsible for one of the most influential interpretations of the American Revolution.

Dickinson was in agreement with the more decided Federalists in the Convention that there was a danger of fostering democratic excesses by the creation of a new government; with many of his associates he foresaw the ominous prospect of a greedy proletariat in America's future, a propertyless mass ready to vote itself the properties of others. But he also agreed with the decided Antifederalists that concentrated national authority might readily be converted into an instrument for creating an artificial aristocracy of "placemen," friends of the administration in power made wealthy by economic privilege and sponsorship. To avoid these doleful alternatives and to secure the nation's political temperance, a careful distribution of powers was absolutely required. Hence Dickinson's many references to the example of the English constitution. Though Americans, from their own history, could not reproduce English institutions, they should, with the materials at hand, attempt to produce their effect, and thus should erect such a government as would allow the virtue of Americans to express itself through forms suited to their "genius," reflective of their "deliberate sense" of themselves.

For Dickinson, despite the peculiarity of his Quaker origins, was an American Burke, the faithful steward of an old regime. Like his Irish counterpart, he had the passion of a convert for an acquired religion: a devotion to an American variant of English constitutionalism, rooted in Saxon antiquity and enthroned as sovereign in 1688. Neither wealth nor enlightenment was, in his view, a primary reason for strengthening the Union. Instead, the reasons were the preservation of an inherited way of life and the liberty needed to practice it—the kind of liberty for the sake of which the Revolution had been fought. Finally, Dickinson's view of the Constitution was of a document that any reasonable Antifederalist could accept. The jealous vanities of the several states could not be allowed to stifle the general government, as they had the old Congress, but otherwise the states were the objects of his special care in Philadelphia. For he identified them as the sources of our attachment to the political bond, the American version of the ancient patterns of English life and law that produced stability in the mother country. Nor did Dickinson, at the end of his political career, struggle in vain. None of his important arguments was effectively challenged in the Convention. And it was his kind of Constitution, as represented by his speeches in the Convention and in *The Letters of Fabius*. He is, with Charles Cotesworth Pinckney of South Carolina, definitive of the moderate Federalist position of 1787–1788 and a key to the meaning of what was achieved.

In his last two decades John Dickinson lived as a private citizen in Delaware, kept a fine house in Wilmington, farmed his acres in Kent County, collected an edition of his essays, advocated a moderate approach to the abolition of slavery in his state, and counseled his neighbors against rash and imprudent conduct of every kind. He broke with the Federalists because, in his view, they had violated the fundamental law hammered out in Philadelphia. (See Charles J. Stillé, *The Life and Times of John Dickinson, 1732–1808* [New York: Burt Franklin, 1969]; John H. Powell, "John Dickinson, Penman of the American Revolution" [Ph.D. dissertation, University of Iowa, 1938]; James M. Tunnell, Jr., "John Dickinson and the Federal Constitution," *Delaware History* 6 [Fall 1955]: 288–293; M. E. Bradford, "A Better Guide Than Reason: The Politics of John Dickinson," in *A Better Guide Than Reason: Studies in the American Revolution* [La Salle, Ill.: Sherwood Sugden, 1979], pp. 79–96; John Dickinson, "The Political Thought of John Dickinson," *Dickinson Law Review* 39 [October 1934]: 1–14; H. Trevor Colbourn, *The Lamp of Experience: Whig History and the Intellectual Origins of the American Revolution* [Chapel Hill: University of North Carolina Press, 1965], pp. 107–119; Robert L. Brunhouse, *The Counter-Revolution in Pennsylvania, 1776–1790* [Harrisburg: Pennsylvania Historical Commission, 1942]; Milton E. Flower, *John Dickinson: Conservative Revolutionary* [Charlottesville: University Press of Virginia, 1983]; James H. Hutson, "John Dickinson at the Federal Constitutional Convention," *William and Mary Quarterly* 40 [April 1983]: 256–282; Stanley K. Johannsen, "Constitution and Empire in the Life and Thought of John Dickinson" [Ph.D. dissertation, University of Missouri, 1973]; Forrest and Ellen Shapiro McDonald, "John Dickinson and the Constitution," in *Requiem:*

*Variations on Eighteenth-Century Themes* [Lawrence: University Press of Kansas, 1988], pp. 85–103; John Willson, *John Dickinson: The Letters of Fabius* [Hillsdale, Mich.: Hillsdale College Press, 1992].)

# GUNNING BEDFORD

1747–March 30, 1812

Lawyer, jurist, and political leader of Delaware

*The stormy petrel of the Constitutional Convention, and an influence upon its deliberations through his fierce devotion to the interests of his adopted state. Born in Philadelphia, educated at the College of New Jersey (later Princeton), where he was Madison's roommate, and in the law offices of Joseph Reed of Philadelphia. He was admitted to the Pennsylvania bar, and then he moved, first to Dover and later to Wilmington, where he began to practice his profession. Ostensibly Bedford did some military service during the Revolution; but he is not to be confused with his soldier cousin of the same name, a politically prominent Delaware contemporary. To distinguish himself from his kinsman, who was Colonel Bedford and then Governor Bedford of their state, Bedford the Framer styled himself Gunning Bedford, Jr. Throughout their careers, the two men often worked toward the same ends, as, for instance, in Delaware's ratifying convention of December 1787, where the Constitution was first approved by a state.*

Gunning Bedford was, by turns, an elected member of the Delaware legislature, the state council, the Continental Congress, and the Federal Convention of 1787. He was chosen as a member of the Delaware delegation to the Annapolis Convention but did not attend. From 1784 to 1789 he was the attorney general of his state. In 1789 President Washington appointed him the first federal district judge for Delaware, in which office he performed until his death.

Most of Bedford's adult life was spent in public service. Yet he was a man of modest means. In person he was large and convivial, corpulent and direct. His powers as an orator were considerable; William Pierce describes him as a "bold and nervous speaker" with "a very commanding and striking manner." In theory, and later as a judge, he was a moderate Federalist. Yet he was nonetheless prepared to threaten the Philadelphia Convention with the possibility that the small states might make foreign alliances of their own if a constitution protecting their influence and integrity were not agreed to by the delegations of Massachusetts, Virginia, and Pennsylvania—the great powers represented on that floor. "Do your worst," he challenged. His firmness at a crucial point helped to force the compromise on equal representation in one chamber of the national legislature—a concession Delaware had set as a condition for its agreement to a firmer bond of union. He thereby strengthened the hand of Mason, Dickinson, Gerry, and other moderates in restraining the more ardent centralizers present in that assembly.

Bedford was originally suspicious of the motives of certain leading figures in the Convention. But he came, by stages, to favor replacement of the Articles of Confederation with an instrument able to protect his neighbors from foreign enemies *and* the high tariffs of Maryland and Pennsylvania. Moreover, he hoped to see Delaware acquire an interest in public lands to the west. He was opposed, however, to giving Congress a power to veto state legislation and reluctant to assign great authority to the president or the Supreme Court. He was regular in his attendance at the Convention, spoke frequently, and was a member of several committees. He gave his support to the important compromise that resulted in a final agreement. After ratification, his role in Delaware politics was as a trusted adviser to the Delaware establishment. He was a mild abolitionist but considered slavery to be a concern of the sovereign commonwealths. Twice he was a presidential elector, and for years he championed the cause of education in his city. He illustrates the peculiarity of Delaware Federalists: enthusiasm for a stronger government rooted in essentially provincial concerns, made necessary by the size of their state. (See John A. Munroe, *Federalist Delaware, 1775–1815* [New Brunswick, N.J.: Rutgers University Press, 1954], pp. 105–109, and passim; Robert G. Ferris, ed., *Signers of the Constitution* [Washington, D.C.: National Park Service, 1976], pp. 143–144; Henry C. Conrad, *Gunning Bedford, Junior*, no. 26 in a series [Wilmington: Historical Society of Delaware, 1900]; George H. Ryden, *Delaware—The First State in the Union* [Wilmington: Delaware Tercentenary Commission, 1938]; Richard A. Harrison, *Princetonians: 1769–1775. A Biographical Dictionary* [Princeton, N.J.: Princeton University Press, 1980], pp. 131–135; Harold J. Littleton, "Gunning Bedford, Jr., and his Home, Lombardy Hall," in *Fully, Freely, and Entirely* 1 [Winter 1985]: 4–5.)

# GEORGE READ

September 18, 1733–September 21, 1798
Signer of the Declaration of Independence (though
he opposed it), lawyer, jurist, and political leader

*A high Federalist, though careful of the interests of the smaller states. With John Dickinson, the leader of the Delaware delegates. Author of the instructions that forced them to hold out for an equal voice in Congress for each of the states. Son of John Read of Dublin, Ireland, and Mary Howell Read. Born in Cecil County, Maryland, into a family of considerable means. Episcopalian. Educated at Alison's Academy at New London, Pennsylvania, and in the offices of John*

*Moland, a distinguished Philadelphia attorney. Admitted to the Philadelphia bar in 1753, but soon relocated to New Castle, Delaware, where his family then resided. A punctilious lawyer of profound learning and large practice while still a young man. Appointed attorney general for the three lower counties by the Crown in 1763, a post he held until late in 1774. Opposed to the Stamp Act and an advocate of nonimportation. Elected to the legislature of his colony in 1765. Like his friend John Dickinson, a very reluctant revolutionary, and no democrat. Sent by Delaware to the First Continental Congress in 1774. A member of the Second Continental Congress, which in July of 1776 declared for American independence. The only member of that body to vote against the resolution of independence and still sign the Declaration. The presiding officer and dominant member of the Delaware state constitutional convention of 1776. Guaranteed in that labor that revolution against external British authority would not bring about radical change within his society. Member of the Delaware legislative council from 1776 to 1779. Became acting president of Delaware in September 1777, after the capture of President John McKinley. Unremitting in his efforts in that office in the task of civil and military preparation. Relieved as president of Delaware in March of 1778 and, by reason of ill-health, of his post on the council in the following year. Assented with reluctance to the Articles of Confederation because they did not guarantee Delaware's access to western lands or set proper limits on interstate tariffs and taxation. Appointed judge of the Court of Appeals in Admiralty by the Confederation Congress in 1782. Returned to the Delaware legislative council from 1782 to 1788.*

George Read was one of Delaware's delegates to the 1786 Annapolis Convention and in the next year was dispatched to Philadelphia. In the Constitutional Convention he spoke strongly of the advantage of doing away with the states as separate political entities and, failing that unlikely political expedient, of the necessity for giving Congress the power to repeal state laws. However, these arguments were clearly part of a rhetorical strategy designed to protect the people of his state from political impotence and to secure for them as much influence as could be acquired. He was among those Federalists made uneasy by talk of holding goods in common and the cancellation of debts. He attended almost every session of the Convention and spoke on numerous occasions, almost always briefly but to the point. He wished senators to hold office "during good behavior," or at least for nine-year terms, and for the president to have the largest possible appointive powers. Though uncertain of the authority of the Philadelphia Convention, he feared the combination of the great states might reduce Delaware to a "cipher," and in the face of their designs, once threatened to lead a walkout. Yet he was eventually satisfied that the proposed government was not "putting new cloth on an old garment," and on his return to Delaware he was instrumental in securing early ratification.

George Read was U.S. senator from Delaware under the Constitution from 1789 until 1793. While in Congress, he voted consistently for the Federalist program. On September 18, 1793, he resigned from the Senate to become the chief justice of his state, a position he held until his death. Never a man of great wealth, Read enjoyed his estate on the Delaware, his gardens, his servants, and his repose. Socially, he was one of the most conservative of the Framers and a strong influence over the politics of his state. Quiet and composed, a lawyer's lawyer, and a man of the prescription, he was a force for order in his world, a moralist of the "public virtue" in the early life of the republic. (See William T. Read, *The Life and Correspondence of George Read, Signer of the Declaration of Independence* [Philadelphia: J. B. Lippincott, 1870]; John A. Munroe, *Federalist Delaware, 1775–1815* [New Brunswick, N.J.: Rutgers University Press, 1954]; George H. Ryden, *Delaware—The First State in the Union* [Wilmington: Delaware Tercentenary Commission, 1938]; Robert G. Ferris, ed., *Signers of the Constitution* [Washington, D.C.: National Park Service, 1976], pp. 206–208; Margaret C. S. Christman, *The First Federal Congress, 1789–1791* [Washington, D.C.: Smithsonian, 1989], pp. 313–314; Robert Waln, Jr., "George Read," in *Biography of the Signers to the Declaration of Independence*, vol. 4, ed. J. Sanderson [Philadelphia: R. W. Pomeroy, 1823], pp. 21–83.)

# RICHARD BASSETT

April 2, 1745–September 15, 1815
Planter, lawyer, jurist, and local political leader

*Though a man of wealth and influence in his own region, one of the silent, inconspicuous figures in the Constitutional Convention. Son of a tavern keeper, Michael Bassett, who deserted his wife, Judith. Richard Bassett was born in Cecil County, Maryland, and raised by his kinsman, Peter Lawson, from whom he inherited the six-thousand-acre estate of Bohemia Manor, near the Delaware line. In his youth Bassett read law, first at home and then in Philadelphia. In 1770 he received a license to practice in Dover, Delaware, where he kept a townhouse. He had another home in Wilmington. And it was to his adopted state that his public life belonged.*

During the Revolution Bassett was a captain in the Delaware Council of Safety. He was a member of the Delaware constitutional convention and sat in both houses of the state legislature. In 1786 his associates in that body sent him as one of their representatives to the Annapolis Convention and in the following year dispatched him as part of the Delaware delegation to Philadelphia. There he followed closely the leadership of John Dickinson. He was also a member of the Delaware ratifying convention, which on December 7, 1787, gave its unanimous support to the federal Constitution.

In the remainder of his political career, Richard Bassett had a considerable part in the political affairs of Delaware and in the government of the republic. From 1789 to 1793 he was a U.S. senator. From 1793 to 1799 he was chief justice of the Court of Common Pleas in his state, and from 1799 to 1801 he was governor of Delaware. In that year John Adams named Bassett, a loyal Federalist, as one of the notorious "midnight judges." He was confirmed in this appointment, but the Democratic-Republicans abolished his seat on the U.S. Circuit Court, and he spent the remainder of his life in retirement.

Richard Bassett was one of the most devout of the Framers. He converted to Methodism during the Revolution and became a close personal friend of Bishop Francis Asbury, who held meetings on his plantation. Bassett freed his slaves and then employed them as hired labor. But he was no egalitarian or champion of radical change. Rather, he was a pillar of the older order in Delaware, an aristocratic order that preserved its authority through the Revolution and into the early years of the new nation. When in the Senate, he usually voted with the southern Federalists but opposed Alexander Hamilton's financial system. He was a mild Federalist, best remembered for his contributions to the development of his chosen church. (See Robert E. Pattison, "The Life and Character of Richard Bassett," *Papers of the Historical Society of Delaware* 29 [1900]: 3–19; Robert G. Ferris, ed., *Signers of the Constitution* [Washington, D.C.: National Park Service, 1976], pp. 142–143; Henry C. Conrad, *History of the State of Delaware* [Wilmington, 1908]; John A. Munroe, *Federalist Delaware: 1775–1815* [New Brunswick, N.J.: Rutgers University Press, 1954]; and George H. Ryden, *Delaware—The First State in the Union* [Wilmington: Delaware Tercentenary Commission, 1938]; William Henry Williams, *The Garden of American Methodism: The Delmarva Peninsula, 1769–1820* [Wilmington, Del.: Scholarly Resources, 1984], pp. 99–102 and passim; Margaret C. S. Christman, *The First Federal Congress, 1789–1791* [Washington, D.C.: Smithsonian, 1989], pp. 226–228.)

# JACOB BROOM

1752–April 25, 1810
Surveyor, farmer, merchant, entrepreneur, banker,
and civic leader of Wilmington, Delaware

*A quiet man of moderate views, and one of the least influential of the Framers. Son of James Broom, blacksmith, and Mary Willis Broom, a Quaker of Chester, Pennsylvania. Jacob Broom took little part in the American Revolution. But he was, from his early years, a man of mark in Delaware, active in the development of his state, repeatedly burgess and chief burgess of his native town of Wilmington, and a member of the state legislature from 1784 to 1787 and 1788 to 1789. In 1786 he was appointed delegate from that assembly to the Annapolis Convention and in the following year was named again to represent Delaware, this time in the larger meeting at Philadelphia. There he voted consistently as a commercial Federalist. During the debates he made only one significant speech—against premature adjournment without agreement upon a draft to send to the states. He was one of those who contributed to Delaware's early approval of the document. And he continued in the Federalist faith throughout the remainder of his days.*

Contrary to the usual report, Jacob Broom was no "plain man" out of place in a gathering of notables. He built the first cotton mill in Delaware, served as the first postmaster of Wilmington, was a developer of lands, scientific farmer, and justice of the peace. Almost every significant commercial venture initiated in his proximity received his support, as did educational and religious enterprises. When the Du Pont family arrived in the United States, they settled on lands purchased from Jacob Broom. He was first director and then chairman of the board of directors for the Bank of Delaware (1806–1810). In the years following the Constitutional Convention, Broom prospered greatly. He became clearly one of the leaders of the Federalist oligarchy in his state. His son, James M. Broom, served a term as a Federalist member of the House of Representatives. A grandson was Native American party ("Know Nothing") candidate for president in 1852. (See William W. Campbell, "Life and Character of Jacob Broom," *Papers of the Delaware Historical Society* 51 [1909]: 1–37; John A. Munroe, *Federalist Delaware, 1775– 1815* [New Brunswick, N.J.: Rutgers University Press, 1954]; Robert G. Ferris, ed., *Signers of the Constitution* [Washington, D.C.: National Park Service, 1976], pp. 150–151 and 233–234; George H. Ryden, *Delaware—The First State in the Union* [Wilmington: Delaware Tercentenary Commission, 1938]; Betty C. Homan, "The Elusive Jacob Broom—Signer," *Daughters of the American Revolution Magazine* 121 [1987]: 860.)

# MARYLAND

# LUTHER MARTIN

ca. February 20, 1748–July 10, 1826
Lawyer, soldier, jurist, and Maryland legend

*Antifederalist. The tireless champion of the sovereignty of the states. Most vigorously engaged in the Constitutional Convention when he heard it argued that Maryland was not sovereign before the adoption of the Articles of Confederation but a mere "political subdivision" of a nation created by the Declaration. Most himself when declaring, "I consider it an incontrovertible truth, that whatever by the constitution government may do, if it relates to the abuse of power by acts tyrannical and oppressive, it some time or another will do." Of the opinion that only hypocrisy or "total ignorance of human nature" could justify a great concentration of powers in the general government. A serious classical republican, yet convinced that loose talk about "equality of liberty and rights" would result in "mobocracy . . . scorching, feverish, convulsive." Even less a democrat than most of the Federalists in the Great Convention. Committed to the proposition that the political rights of Americans had their proper repositories in the several member commonwealths of the Union, and not in some state of nature. A cheerful pessimist. An Old Whig and a legalist. Probably, with William Paterson, his friend from college days, a coauthor of the New Jersey Plan. Certain that the aim of the Federalists was "to leave the states at the mercy of the general government, since they could not succeed in their immediate and entire abolition." In fifty-three speeches, fought them all the way. Left the Convention early in order to avoid being present at the signing. Continued throughout the remainder of his life, even when identified by party as a Federalist, in the position he had represented in Philadelphia. In his generation one of the most eminent lawyers in America, and a great original.*

Luther Martin was born near New Brunswick, New Jersey. He was the son of Benjamin and Hannah Martin, pious evangelical Protestants of English stock whose ancestors had come to New Jersey from Massachusetts in the middle of the seventeenth century. Though Luther's father was a farmer, he managed to send the boy to the College of New Jersey, from which he was graduated with honors in 1766, after two years' preparation in the grammar school and four years in the college. Upon receipt of his diploma, Luther Martin went immediately to Maryland, where he obtained a teaching position in Queen Anne's County on the Eastern Shore. At that time he swore the required Oaths of Abjuration and Test and promised to conform to the Church of England. For the remainder of his career, he was a member and supporter of the Maryland social and political establishment—perhaps the most conservative of the old colonial regimes, which changed little after independence and was suspicious of even that small degree of external authority over its affairs represented by the Articles of Confederation.

After three years of teaching at the academy in Queenstown, Martin began to read law, first with Solomon Wright, the father of one of his students, and then with Samuel Wilson of Back Creek, Maryland. In 1770, with debts mounting, Martin took another school at Onancock in Accomack County, Virginia. But in September of 1771, the pedagogical period of his life ended when he presented himself at Williamsburg to be examined for admission to the Virginia bar by George Wythe, the future chancellor, and John Randolph, the king's attorney general. After succeeding in this examination and qualifying for practice in Accomack County, Martin looked away from the tidewater to the newer settlements along the frontier, where lawyers were not so plentiful. And in 1772 he took a tour west, all the way to Fort Pitt, meeting on his journey some of the principal men in those parts, including Capt. Michael Cresap, his future father-in-law. When he returned, he found that a situation had opened for him in the local courts, and he was shortly thereafter licensed in Maryland. Within two years his income was "at or near £1000 per year."

In 1774, upon the outbreak of revolutionary sentiment in most of the American colonies, even conservative Maryland was caught up in the times. In the company of the squires, Martin was elected to the Committee of Observation in Somerset County. In December of that year he was a delegate to the Provincial Congress at Annapolis. He was also active in restraining the Tories in his portion of the state. As a patriotic gesture, he became engaged in the manufacture of salt and had some practice in the Maryland and Virginia courts established by the independent state governments. In these years Martin established a close friendship with Samuel Chase, Maryland political leader and future justice of the U.S. Supreme Court. He was drawn further and further into the politics of transition. And when Sir William Howe published a broadside designed to foster Tory sentiment in Pennsylvania, Delaware, and the Eastern Shore of Maryland, Martin wrote a "humble address" in reply. It caught the eye of his influential neighbors, and in February of 1778 he was appointed attorney general of the state of

Maryland, a post he held for the next twenty-seven years, the longest incumbency in such an office in the history of the republic to this date.

As attorney general Luther Martin became something like an institution in the life of his state. The post left him free to continue in a practice of his own and gave him a kind of security in both a financial and political sense. Moreover, it taught him the importance of a "state *independent* and *sovereign*," of the effect of the Revolution on Maryland, as nothing else could have done. During the Revolution he was a fervent prosecutor of active Tories, of whom there were a number in Maryland, and he sent several of them to the gallows. For a few months he served with the Baltimore Light Dragoons, an elite cavalry unit, when it was dispatched to Virginia to face Col. Banastre Tarleton in the campaigns that led to Yorktown. In the course of his legal responsibilities he traveled to every corner of his state and became familiar with the people, their occupations, attitudes, religions, and various ways of life.

To supplement this considerable social and political experience, Martin made use of the scholarly resources available to him as attorney general and undertook a careful and profound study of the law. He purchased confiscated property in Baltimore, married Maria Cresap, and concentrated on becoming not only the leading attorney in Maryland, but also the best. His figure in old-fashioned dress became a familiar sight on the streets of that thriving port city. Bemused in thought or buried in a book—he was so preoccupied and near-sighted that, according to legend, on one occasion when he accidentally bumped into a cow that had wandered onto Baltimore Street, he tipped his hat, apologized, and continued on his way. Martin's arguments in the courts even at this early date became famous for their orotundity, antiquarian scholarship, otiose circumambient development, and irresistible conclusion.

In 1784 Luther Martin was elected to the Confederation Congress, but because of official obligations he could not attend. However, when in 1786 the Maryland legislature decided to send delegates to the Constitutional Convention and when many of the state's other leading men refused to serve because of their fear that in their absence a "paper money bill" might be proposed in the legislature, Luther Martin felt himself obliged to accept appointment. He arrived in Philadelphia to take his seat on June 9, 1787, and continued to act his part as Framer until September 4, when he and his fellow Antifederalist, John Francis Mercer, left the meeting in disgust to return to Maryland to organize opposition to ratification.

Some scholars argue that Martin rejected the Constitution simply because of its hostility to state monetary and debtor-relief experiments—because he was a supporter of Samuel Chase. But this view does Martin an injustice and is belied by the comprehensive political doctrine with which he confronted the proposals of the Federalists. In Martin's opinion, the general government existed to support and protect the political integrity of the states to which the people had surrendered their sovereign political rights by long usage and continuous participation.

A federal government should prevent foreign invasion and the abuse of one state by another. When it fails to do so, "the time may come when it shall be the duty of a State, in order to preserve itself from the oppression of the general government, to have recourse to the sword." Martin did not defer to the ingenuity of James Madison, the dialectics of James Wilson, or the personal authority of George Washington. On June 27 and 28, he gave his reasons for voting against them all: If the "General Govt. was meant merely to preserve the State Governts," then what the Federalists proposed would not suffice. Optimistic talk about the wonders a revised union might bring impressed him not in the least. Throughout his life he was of the persuasion that "the man who pretends to expect by universally republicanizing the world, to effect the perfectibility of human nature, the perfectibility of human reason, and the perfectibility of human happiness, or to introduce a millennium on the earth," should be treated as "an enthusiastic visionary . . . or a crafty villainous imposter."

Contrary to the popular misunderstanding of his role in the Convention, Luther Martin did not go to Philadelphia to be a spoiler or mere obstructionist. He was ready to see a revision of the Articles. As noted above, he had a hand in devising a plan of government of which he approved. And some of his specific proposals, such as an electoral college for choosing the president, were finally adopted by the Convention. He served amicably on the committee that produced the compromise on representation in the Senate. Moreover, on July 14, he moved to adopt the committee's report, "to make trial of the plan, rather than do nothing." Even though he owned slaves, Martin opposed on normative grounds any authorization allowing the continuation of the slave trade. He disapproved of including federal judges in a council of revision or of neglecting to specify the scope of their authority. He wanted no federal power of veto over legislation in the states. But he also disliked leaving with the states the power to prevent creation of new commonwealths out of their frontier holdings and chided James Wilson for his selective indifference to the reality of political bodies.

In his view, senators should be compensated by the communities they were to represent, and the states left to subdue their own internal rebellions and to govern their own militias. He voted against allowing reelection of presidents and feared the creation of a "royal party" through the power of appointment. He disliked the "elastic clause" (Article I, section 8), which permitted whatever legislation seemed necessary to the exercise of powers granted, and opposed the authorization of a direct tax, unless the states first failed to meet their quotas. He supported freedom of religion but saw no harm in a mild religious test to keep "pagans and atheists" out of offices of trust. With George Mason, he said a word in behalf of leaving an option for relief of debtors and emission of paper money— to protect the poor when specie became scarce.

Martin objected to the secrecy of the proceedings of the Constitutional Convention. He doubted that the people of the states would approve of the results but suggested that the Constitution be sent to the state legislatures and then, after amendments had been recommended, reconsidered in a second, and perhaps a third, convention. Hasty approvals, he observed, would strengthen suspicion that the entire business was a plot by monarchists and advocates of special power for large states. Yet he also moved that acts and treaties adopted by the U.S. government "shall be the supreme law." He wanted a new constitution, but only if produced under the proper conditions, containing the necessary provisions. Those Framers who could tolerate only their own plans of government he accused of "pride," as with "master-builders." Founding was not to his taste, but rather preserving. On all of these points he told the other Maryland delegates how he stood when they met in private session, and in a private conversation with George Washington, he was equally candid. Hence he went back to Annapolis eager to expose the centralists "whose object and wish it was to abolish and annihilate all State governments, and to bring forward one general government, over this extensive continent." Better two or more confederacies than a unity of the wrong kind.

In 1788, after presenting a lengthy address to the Maryland legislature, Martin published it as *The Genuine Information, Delivered to the Legislature of the State of Maryland, Relative to the Proceedings of the General Convention, Lately Held at Philadelphia*. He also placed sections of this pamphlet and other essays opposing the Constitution in newspapers in Maryland and other states. He was a delegate to the Maryland ratification convention held in Annapolis in April of 1788, but he was literally unable to speak because of laryngitis. He did, however, change his attitude toward the Constitution following the adoption of the Bill of Rights, particularly in view of the Ninth and Tenth amendments. Once Thomas Jefferson, whom he had never admired, became the head of the opposition party, Martin came to identify himself with at least part of the position of his old adversaries, the Federalists. He wrote frequently for the political press. He prepared a careful reply to Jefferson's abuse of his father-in-law, Colonel Cresap, in *Notes on the State of Virginia*.

In the following years his law practice continued to expand and provided him with more business than he could manage. His income was more than $10,000 a year. Frequently he had cases before the federal courts. Changes in the Maryland judicial system moved Martin to retire as attorney general of that state in 1805. From 1813 to 1816 he was chief justice of the Baltimore Court of Oyer and Terminer, where he lectured juries on democratic "wickedness" and "licentiousness." From 1818 to 1822 he was once again, briefly, attorney general. However, during most of this late period of service to his state, he was unable to perform the duties of his office because of a paralytic stroke he suffered in 1820. Often his energies were dispersed in too many directions. And, throughout his career, he had a reputation for drinking a great deal more than was seemly. Justice Joseph Story described the famous and successful advocate as "poor and needy; generous and humane; . . . negligent and profuse." But in the courts, in legal brief and argument, the pieces of his life came together, and Luther Martin was most at home.

The cases that earned him a lasting reputation as trial attorney took place at the local, state, and federal levels. He defended the shoemakers of Baltimore in their right to organize and strike against low wages—proof that in 1809 he was still an unusual Federalist, moved by the same concerns that had made him a friend to paper-money advocates twenty years before. When a large number of free Negroes began to concentrate in and around Baltimore, Martin defended the local constables and jailer, who had adopted a policy of confining those who appeared to be runaways or who lacked proper identification. Such a practice, Martin contended, was "necessary to public safety." Yet he also defended slaves and free persons of color who had been hastily charged with crimes, and he enforced contracts for manumission on condition of service performed. In his last term as attorney general, when confronted by abolitionists from Pennsylvania, Martin brought them to indictment and trial on a charge of inciting slaves to be discontented. Though the youthful Roger B. Taney got his abolitionist preacher client off with a warning, Martin took satisfaction at having discouraged future "visits" of the same kind.

His most famous cases, however, were before the U.S. Supreme Court. There he frequently used his authority as a member of the Constitutional Convention to embarrass justices like John Marshall. Before Marshall, sitting at the circuit level, Martin successfully handled the defense of Aaron Burr in a trial held in Richmond in 1807. In the process he revealed President Thomas Jefferson to be indifferent to the civil liberties of American citizens who were obstructing his will. In *Fletcher* v. *Peck* (1810), Martin maintained the continuing authority of British law in determining Georgia's legal right to the unsettled lands beyond her western boundaries before and during the Revolution. When the thirteen colonies had seceded from the British family of nations, Martin argued, they had carried with them the title to only such lands as were actually within their jurisdiction in 1776. His view was thus that the Yazoo lands in question had never been legally sold to Yankee speculators by the Georgia legislature and that therefore his client Fletcher had indeed been cheated when he made a purchase from the speculators.

Martin's most important case before the High Court was *McCulloch* v. *Maryland* (1819). In some respects it was the capstone of his career. In it he drove the Federalist justices to the wall and left them with nothing but an *ipse dixit* to sustain their defense of the federal powers. Of the reasoning of Daniel Webster and other attorneys for the government who were defending the second Bank of the United States against taxation by the state of Maryland, Martin observed, with reference to their use of the doctrine of implied powers:

It was maintained, by the enemies of the constitution, that it contained a vast variety of powers, lurking under the generality of its phraseology, which would prove highly dangerous to the liberties of the people, and the rights of the States, unless controlled by some declaratory amendment, which should negative their existence.

This apprehension was treated as a dream of distempered jealousy. The danger was denied to exist; but to provide an assurance against the possibility of its occurrence, the 10th Amendment was added to the Constitution. . . .

We are now called upon to apply that theory of interpretation which was then rejected by the friends of the new Constitution, and we are asked to engraft upon it powers of vast extent, which were disclaimed by them, and which, if they had been fairly avowed at the time, would have prevented its adoption.

In peroration, Luther Martin read aloud to the Court John Marshall's youthful promise given during the 1788 Virginia ratification convention that the Federalists understood that all powers not "expressly delegated" to the government of the United States are reserved to the states. Martin lost his case, but he surely won the argument.

Within less than a year Martin had suffered the paralytic stroke that deprived him of the power of speech. In the care of his friends, he survived until 1826. In respect for the magnitude of his achievements, the Maryland legislature passed a nonpareil act in February of 1822 that collected a license fee of five dollars from each member of the Maryland bar for the support of Luther Martin. The act was repealed in 1823, and Martin spent his final years in New York in the home of Aaron Burr. Martin's career greatly complicates the simplistic view that all the Antifederalists were democrats and prospective Jeffersonians. (See Paul S. Clarkson and R. Samuel Jett, *Luther Martin of Maryland* [Baltimore: Johns Hopkins University Press, 1970]; L. Marx Renzulli, Jr., *Maryland: The Federalist Years* [Rutherford, N.J.: Fairleigh Dickinson University Press, 1972]; Henry P. Goddard, *Luther Martin: The Federal Bulldog* [Baltimore: J. Murphy, 1887]; Norman K. Risjord, *Chesapeake Politics, 1781–1800* [New York: Columbia University Press, 1978]; Philip A. Crowl, *Maryland during and after the Revolution: A Political and Economic Study* [Baltimore: Johns Hopkins University Press, 1943] and his "Antifederalism in Maryland, 1787–1788," *William and Mary Quarterly* 4 [October 1947]: 446–449; Forrest McDonald, *E Pluribus Unum: The Formation of the American Republic, 1776–1790* [Indianapolis: Liberty Press, 1979], pp. 295–301; for a printing of Martin's 1788 pamphlet, *The Genuine Information*, see Max Farrand, ed., *The Records of the Federal Convention of 1787*, vol. 3 [New Haven, Conn.: Yale University Press, 1966], pp. 172–232, or Herbert J. Storing, ed., *The Complete Anti-Federalist*, vol. 2 [Chicago: University of Chicago Press, 1981]; Everett D. Obrecht, "The Influence of Luther Martin in the Making of the Constitution of the United States," *Maryland Historical Magazine* 27 [September 1932]: 173–190, and [December 1932]: 280–296.)

# JAMES McHENRY
November 16, 1753–May 3, 1816
Physician, soldier, statesman, and leader of Maryland
Federalists

*General Washington's secretary in the last years of the Revolution, and still his faithful retainer during the Constitutional Convention. A man of inherited wealth who did not practice his profession or follow any other calling apart from politics after independence was achieved. Son of Daniel and Agnes McHenry, he was born in Ballymena, County Antrim, Ireland. Educated in Dublin and, after his family's immigration to Baltimore in 1772, at the Newark Academy in Delaware. A student of medicine in Philadelphia under the redoubtable Dr. Benjamin Rush. A refined gentleman and a member of a prosperous family established in the importing business when the War for Independence broke out. Like most Ulster Presbyterians, inclined to resent British authority even before he found a good excuse to do so. McHenry volunteered for military service at Cambridge, Massachusetts, in 1775. After a time on the staff of the military hospital for the forces surrounding Boston, he was named surgeon for the Fifth Pennsylvania Battalion. He was captured in 1776 upon the fall of Fort Washington in New York, paroled in January of 1777, and exchanged in the following year. His probity and manners soon called him to the attention of the commanding general, at whose right hand he was from the spring months in Valley Forge until 1780, when he was detached to the staff of the Marquis de Lafayette. There he held the rank of major. He left service in 1781 when he was elected to the Maryland senate, where he sat for five years. From 1783 to 1785, he was a Maryland representative to the Confederation Congress and was elected to represent the commercial community of Baltimore in the Great Convention.*

James McHenry was in Philadelphia for only a few days before he was called back to Baltimore by the illness of his brother. He returned to share in the deliberations of the Framers on August 6, kept notes on what he observed and heard, both within and outside the Convention, and said little. However, his presence in Philadelphia put Maryland back in the Federalist column by canceling the Antifederalism of John Francis Mercer or Luther Martin. In the Convention, McHenry took his lead from Madison, Randolph, and George Washington, except for a little support given to George Mason against New England designs to control commerce. He was the delegate to the Convention who argued the case for the proposed Constitution before the Maryland legislature. His efforts were instrumental in gathering a pro-Constitution majority in Maryland's ratifying convention, where he also served. Subsequently he acted as a spokesman for the

Federalist cause in many of the struggles in Maryland during the early years of the republic. He was a member of the state assembly from 1789 to 1791, and once again a state senator from 1791 to 1796.

McHenry was one of those Federalists driven to support the idea of a stronger union and a government capable of using force to protect property and preserve the sanctity of contract as a result of popular unrest, mob spirit, and talk of "leveling" in his own city and state. He deplored the French Revolution and its American admirers. The Charles County debtors' riot of June 1786 and associated agitation among the lower orders in other sections of the state persuaded the merchants and great planters of Maryland to give up their characteristic suspicion of any plan for general government. Once committed to Federalism, McHenry stuck with it, later reinforced in his conviction by events such as the formation of the Democratic Societies in Baltimore and the riots of June 22, 1812. McHenry accepted the post of secretary of war in President Washington's cabinet in January of 1796 and continued in that office until May 1800, when President Adams called for his resignation. The charge against McHenry made by the Democratic-Republicans concerned his construction of a "standing army" prepared to negate the results of the next general election. The complaint of the Adams Federalists was disloyalty and collusion with Alexander Hamilton in the attempt to deny President Adams the nomination of his party for a second term. There was some truth in both accusations.

In the last years of his life, James McHenry was a private man, the ultraconservative patriarch of a dying party, who devoted his energies to the life of his church, to his family, and to a little writing. He was opposed to the War of 1812 but not politically active except as a counselor to younger men. Many of his disciples and their descendants later helped to form the Whig party in Maryland. (See Bernard C. Steiner, *The Life and Correspondence of James McHenry* [Cleveland: Burrows Brothers, 1907]; Manning J. Dauer, *The Adams Federalists* [Baltimore: Johns Hopkins University Press, 1968]; Philip A. Crowl, *Maryland during and after the Revolution* [Baltimore: Johns Hopkins University Press, 1943]; L. Marx Renzulli, Jr., *Maryland: The Federalist Years* [Rutherford, N.J.: Fairleigh Dickinson University Press, 1972]; Dorothy Brown, "Party Battles and Beginnings in Maryland" [Ph.D. dissertation, Georgetown University, 1962]; *A Biographical Dictionary of the Maryland Legislature, 1635–1789*, vol. 2 [Baltimore: Johns Hopkins University Press, 1985], pp. 588–590.)

# DANIEL OF ST. THOMAS JENIFER
1723–November 16, 1790
Politician, leader of the Revolution in Maryland, and perennial officeholder

*Named so curiously to distinguish him from other Daniel Jenifers. Always a friend to those in authority, at least until their power began to wane. Usually a high Federalist, taking his lead in the Convention from General Washington, James Madison, and the other Virginia nationalists. A convivial man, with an eye to the main chance. An unscrupulous, charming opportunist, a great host and giver of parties. A person of genuine social skill and aplomb, called upon throughout his life to perform in offices of trust. Son of Daniel Jenifer of Charles County and Elizabeth Hanson Jenifer. Born at Coates Retirement (Ellerslie), near Port Tobacco. Of English and Swedish descent. An educated man, particularly skilled in matters of finance. Wealthy, both by birth and by acquisition. Representative of Maryland's old aristocracy of tobacco, slaves, and great plantations.*

Daniel of St. Thomas Jenifer began his career of public service early in his life and was, by turns or simultaneously, justice of the peace, proprietor's agent and receiver general in charge of proprietary revenues, justice of Maryland's western circuit, member of the provincial court (1766) and, from 1773 until the end of British rule, member of the royal governor's council. He enjoyed the special favor of the last two Lord Proprietors of Maryland and sat on a boundary commission that settled disputes with Pennsylvania and Delaware. And he established a network of friendships and associations that made him one of the principal men in the colony.

For reasons made obvious in this summary of his good fortune as servant of the king, Jenifer was slow to embrace the banner of American independence. With other leaders of the "popular [i.e., aristocratically republican] party" in Maryland such as Samuel Chase, William Paca, Charles Carroll of Carrollton, and Charles Carroll, barrister, he was cautious in renouncing connection with the mother country and hoped for a reconciliation that would leave the state in their hands but under the nominal authority of the Crown. However, when the English moved toward enforcing their policy with the sword and declared the American colonies to be beyond the protection of the law, the Maryland gentry—and Jenifer with them—joined a shadow government and prepared to defend their community. From 1775 to 1777, Jenifer was the elected president of the Maryland Council of Safety. As an authority on this period of Maryland history has remarked, "Jenifer made the transition from courtier to rebel quite easily." But independence brought disorder in Maryland, disobedience to authority, threats to property, indifference to debt, and an effusion of paper money. The times forced the Maryland aristocracy to expedients that, with Jenifer included, they much disliked and that made Federalists of them, when the opportunity to be a Federalist arrived.

From 1777 to 1780, Jenifer served as president of the Maryland state senate. From 1778 to 1782, he had a seat in the Congress, where he continued the interest in supplies for the army and in western lands that he had shown in the politics of his own state. He speculated in confiscated Tory properties, became a close friend of General Washington, made his peace with former Loyalists who had avoided exile, and engrossed new and profitable offices, particularly as intendent of state revenue and financial manager of Maryland (1782–1785). He also improved his estate at Stepney, near Annapolis. He was a Maryland delegate to the Mount Vernon Conference of 1785 and by the time of the Philadelphia Convention, in view of his long experience in the political life of his state, an obvious choice as delegate from Maryland. During the Convention his presence was constant, his position constant, and his voice almost unheard. At sixty-four, he was one of the oldest men there. Within three years of his departure from Philadelphia he died at Annapolis, in quiet retirement. (See Ronald Hoffman, *A Spirit of Dissension: Economics, Politics, and the Revolution in Maryland* [Baltimore: Johns Hopkins University Press, 1973]; Robert G. Ferris, ed., *Signers of the Constitution* [Washington, D.C.: National Park Service, 1976], pp. 177–178; Philip A. Crowl, *Maryland during and after the Revolution* [Baltimore: Johns Hopkins University Press, 1943], pp. 28–29 and passim; Charles Albro Barker, *The Background of the Revolution in Maryland* [New Haven, Conn.: Yale University Press, 1940]; *A Biographical Dictionary of the Maryland Legislature, 1635–1789*, vol. 2 [Baltimore: Johns Hopkins University Press, 1985], pp. 485–486.)

# DANIEL CARROLL

July 22, 1730–May 7, 1796
Planter and member of the aristocratic political
establishment of Maryland

*According to his colleague William Pierce, "a man of large fortune and influence." Member of the collateral line of the tidewater clan of Carroll. A "law and order" Federalist, disgusted by the popular spirit abroad in the America of 1787. Interested in a sound currency and in preserving the value of property. Convinced that stability induced by a stronger central government might put an end to the disruptions of the times, arguing that most objections to the Constitution were "chiefly propagated in Maryland by men whose interests would be deeply affected by any change of government, especially for the better, and those to whose embarrassed circumstances regularity and order would be extremely inconvenient." Clearly the voice of authority within the Maryland delegation to the Great Convention. Born at Carroll Manor in Prince George's County. Son of Daniel Carroll (1696–1751) of Upper Marlboro, Maryland, and Eleanor Darnall Carroll (1704–1796). Brother of John Carroll, Archbishop of Baltimore (1735–1815). One of two Roman Catholic Framers. Like his Howard County and*

*Annapolis cousins, ostensibly descended from the kings of Ely ca. 1205. A man of quiet importance and "plain good sense."*

Daniel Carroll was, between 1742 and 1748, educated in Flanders by the Jesuits of St. Omers, and then by a "grand tour" of Europe. Returning from his travels, he married a cousin from the other side of the Carroll family and settled down to manage his inheritance, direct his slaves, and grow tobacco. Like many of his class in the Maryland of the 1770s, he was no violent proponent of revolution. Yet he served as a member of the state Council of Safety from 1777 to 1781, as a Maryland senator from 1781 to 1790, and as a delegate to the Congress from 1781 to 1783, where he signed the Articles of Confederation in the name of his friends in Annapolis. For a time he was the elected president of the Maryland senate. And during the war he played a part in gathering supplies for the American forces. He was chosen as a delegate to the Constitutional Convention because other Maryland leaders refused to accept appointment.

Daniel Carroll the Framer was essentially a private person; a shareholder (with George Washington) in the Patowmack Company, a project to extend the river with canals; a speculator in frontier lands; a Mason; and a generous supporter of his church. He was not ill at ease with his associates in the Constitutional Convention. Many of them he knew socially, particularly the important Virginians. Yet unlike a number of the Framers, he did not appear in Philadelphia in search of a role to play before the gallery of history. A mature and wealthy man, one of the senior members of the Convention, he was a median figure in its debates, standing halfway between the extremes of opinion present on the floor.

After his arrival on July 9, he was in almost continuous attendance and spoke on perhaps twenty different occasions. Carroll wanted a new constitution, not a revision of the Articles, and he wanted the government to have the power to tax the people directly. Yet he wished to deny to the new Congress the power to tax exports, to act without a large majority from most states as a quorum, and to create a powerful federal court. He wished the general government to pay the salaries of the members of Congress, lest the states bind it too closely. But, once the Constitution was in force, he opposed the doctrine of implied powers, favored the adoption of the Tenth Amendment as a check upon federal usurpations, and rejected the Bank of the United States as a northern plot. On the issue of equal representation in the Senate, he supported the position of Delaware, New Jersey, and Connecticut. And, though leaning a little in the direction of the nationalists in his political theory, he did not lean very far. Carroll hoped to see the Framers and the communities they represented work toward a civil agreement, a unanimity through concessions, remembering always that "experience overrules all other calculations."

Carroll was eloquent in his support of the instrument of government produced in Philadelphia. He defended the document before the Maryland legislature; wrote, as "A Friend of the Constitution," a reply to the Antifederalist Samuel Chase in the *Maryland Journal;* and conducted an energetic campaign through correspondence for ratification by his state. After the government was formed, he served from 1789 to 1791 as a Maryland member of the House of Representatives, where he supported the Bill of Rights, assumption of state debts, and the location of the national capital in his part of Maryland, on the banks of the Potomac. His friend President Washington then named him as one of the three commissioners to survey and define the District of Columbia, where he and his family owned land. Never a serious politician or a man hungry for major office, he died at his home at Rock Creek, Maryland, at the age of sixty-five. (See Sister Mary V. Geiger, *Daniel Carroll, A Framer of the Constitution* [Washington, D.C.: Catholic University Press of America, 1943]; Richard J. Purcell, "Daniel Carroll, Framer of the Constitution," *American Catholic Historical Society Records of Philadelphia* 52 [June 1941]: 65–87 and [September 1941]: 137–160; Philip A. Crowl, *Maryland during and after the Revolution* [Baltimore: Johns Hopkins University Press, 1943]; L. Marx Renzulli, Jr., *Maryland: The Federalist Years* [Rutherford, N.J.: Fairleigh Dickinson University Press, 1972]; Annabelle M. Melville, *John Carroll of Baltimore* [New York: Charles Scribner's Sons, 1955]; Charles Albro Barker, *The Background of the Revolution in Maryland* [New Haven, Conn.: Yale University Press, 1940]; Margaret C. S. Christman, *The First Federal Congress, 1789–1791* [Washington, D.C.: Smithsonian, 1989], pp. 246–249.)

# JOHN FRANCIS MERCER

May 17, 1759–August 30, 1821
Soldier, lawyer, and political leader in both Virginia
and Maryland

*Ardent Antifederalist. Fearful of granting power to a general government throughout his career. Connected with the Chase faction in Maryland following his service as member of the Continental Congress for Virginia. Inclined to regard even the Articles of Confederation as perhaps a threat to the sovereignty of the states. Outraged by an eleven-days' attendance at the Great Convention (August 6–August 17, 1787). Returned home convinced that the entire proceedings were an "aristocratic" or monarchist plot against the liberties of the people. Yet reluctant to allow the citizens of his state to vote on anything directly, or without a great restriction of the suffrage. Son of the illustrious Col. John Mercer of Marlborough in Stafford County, Virginia, and Ann Roy Mercer, the colonel's second wife. One of nineteen brothers and sisters, some of whom played impor-*

*tant roles in the history of their state. First educated at home, later at the College of William and Mary. Enlisted as lieutenant in the Third Virginia Regiment early in 1776. Promoted to captain the following year. Aide-de-camp to Gen. Charles Lee. Resigned from the service in 1779, after his commander was court-martialed following misconduct in the Battle of Monmouth. Returned to uniform in the fall of 1780 as lieutenant colonel of infantry under General Lawson. Served for a time in command of a unit of mounted dragoons with Lafayette. Commander of a corps of militia grenadiers in the Yorktown campaign.*

While still under arms, John Francis Mercer read law at Williamsburg with Gov. Thomas Jefferson. He practiced briefly at Fredericksburg, but for the remainder of his life he was chiefly occupied with politics and planting. He served in the Virginia House of Delegates in 1782, and again in 1785–1786. From 1783 to 1785 he sat in the Confederation Congress. Early in 1785 he married an heiress, Sophia Sprigg of Cedar Park, in Anne Arundel County, Maryland, and took up residence on her ancestral estate. After the habit of his family, Mercer was involved in speculation in western lands and thus linked to the "paper money" forces in his adopted state. Yet in 1787 he was a very wealthy young man, selected as a Maryland delegate to the Great Convention because many of the state's most eminent political figures refused to serve. But he was active and outspoken during his short stay in Philadelphia.

In 1783, while in the Congress, Mercer had declared, when an impost was proposed, that "if the Federal compact is such as has been represented [i.e., allowing for a power to collect customs tax], I will immediately withdraw from Congress and do everything in my power to destroy its existence." In precisely such a spirit did he appear briefly in the Constitutional Convention. His first share in the proceedings was a blunt statement that the plan under consideration was objectionable, followed by a statement that "it never could succeed." He mocked the solemn deliberations of his associates and scoffed, "It is a great mistake to suppose that the paper we propose will govern the United States."

The themes of his twenty or so speeches were force and influence: by one or by the other were men to be governed. If the tyranny of monarchy or of "high-toned government" by way of an aristocratic faction in the Congress (aristocracy here meaning men of privilege) were to be avoided, the executive would need the authority to hand out a few offices and thus create its own party in the national legislature. Otherwise the best men would never come away from the appointments they held in the states to serve the central government. Mercer also said a few words against a proposed tax on exports, and about rivalry between the sections. He attacked the idea of allowing the Supreme Court to review decisions of lower courts through constitutional construction. Mercer was negative and contentious on all counts. But it was to the theme of appointments that he returned on several occasions. Clearly the topic interested him. Perhaps Jefferson was correct in observing of Mercer, "Vanity and ambition seem to be the ruling passion of this young man and as his objects are impure, so are his means. Intrigue is a principal one on particular occasions as party attachment in the general."

After withdrawing from the Great Convention, Mercer returned to Maryland and fought the adoption of the new Constitution. He was a delegate to his state's ratification convention, spoke against adoption, and was sent by Antifederalists to Maryland's House of Delegates from 1788 to 1789 and from 1791 to 1792. In 1791 he took a seat in the U.S. House of Representatives, where, as a vehement opponent of Hamilton, he continued until 1794. As a Democratic-Republican Mercer returned to the Maryland legislature in 1800 and, after a somewhat embarrassing flight from a duel, was elected governor of the state in 1801. He was reelected in 1802 and later served three additional years in the House of Delegates. Like John Randolph of Roanoke, Mercer broke with his party on the question of war with England and disapproved of the French Revolution and the Emperor Napoleon. In his last years he lived quietly at Cedar Park. (See H. E. Buchholz, *Governors of Maryland from the Revolution to the Year 1908* [Baltimore: Williams and Wilkins, 1908]; L. Marx Renzulli, Jr., *Maryland: The Federalist Years* [Rutherford, N.J.: Fairleigh Dickinson University Press, 1972]; Jackson Turner Main, *Political Parties before the Constitution* [Chapel Hill: University of North Carolina Press, 1973]; Robert E. and B. Katherine Brown, *Virginia, 1705–1786: Democracy or Aristocracy?* [East Lansing: Michigan State University Press, 1964]; Dorothy Brown, "Party Battles and Beginnings in Maryland" [Ph.D. dissertation, Georgetown University, 1962]; Philip A. Crowl, *Maryland during and after the Revolution* [Baltimore: Johns Hopkins University Press, 1943], p. 112; Norman K. Risjord, *Chesapeake Politics, 1781–1800* [New York: Columbia University Press, 1978]; James Mercer Garnett, "John Francis Mercer," *Maryland Historical Magazine* 2 [September 1907]: 191–213; H. James Henderson, *Party Politics in the Continental Congress* [New York: McGraw-Hill, 1974]; Herbert J. Storing, ed., *The Complete Anti-Federalist*, vol. 5 [Chicago: University of Chicago Press, 1981], pp. 5–73 and 101–106; *A Biographical Dictionary of the Maryland Legislature, 1635–1789*, vol. 2 [Baltimore: Johns Hopkins University Press, 1985], pp. 594–595.)

# VIRGINIA

# GEORGE WASHINGTON

February 22, 1732–December 14, 1799
Planter, soldier, statesman, and first president
of the United States

*The moving force behind the Constitutional Convention, whose "presence propelled the meeting forward as his agreement to be there had insured that it would be held." In the struggle for ratification in the states, the one man whose support for the Constitution was indispensable to its adoption. For Americans of his generation, the summary figure, the man on the white horse who came in his own person to embody their sense of nationality. And for that portion of American history concluded with the War Between the States, the political icon against which the conduct of all public men might be measured. As early as 1775, recognized as the "pattern" for other Americans "to form themselves by." Persuaded by Madison, Randolph, and other friends to lend the personal prestige he had won in the Revolution to the labor of revising the Articles of Confederation, lest the honor he had achieved in arms be compromised by the political incapacity of the nation his military victories had produced. Of the opinion in 1786 and early 1787 that the republic was "fast verging to anarchy and confusion" and that "without some alteration in our political creed, the superstructure we had been seven years raising at the expense of so much blood and treasure must fall." The definitive military Federalist and full of doubts concerning democracy. Yet too much the soldier according to the Roman myth, the Cato Uticensis or Cincinnatus, to abandon the people in the chaos of popular tumult after he had led them to freedom in war. Acting a role throughout his adult life in keeping with a concept of public virtue not now readily understood and an essentially religious conviction that God would hold him accountable for the ultimate meaning of American independence as revealed in history.*

George Washington was born at Wakefield Plantation in Westmoreland County, Virginia, the son of Augustine Washington and his second wife, Mary Ball

Washington. He was descended from Lawrence Washington of Sulgrave, Northampton, England, and from many generations of solid yeomen and rustic gentry who produced finally the Reverend Lawrence Washington of Purleigh, Essex, whose son John emigrated to Virginia in 1657 or 1658 after his father had been deprived of his living by Puritans on charges of drunkenness and Anglicanism. Augustine Washington was the grandson of John Washington and the son of Lawrence Washington of Bridges Creek, Westmoreland County. He lived in Westmoreland until 1735, when he moved to other plantations on the Potomac and Rappahannock rivers. Augustine Washington was a man of monumental proportions, a figure of great energy, and an established member of the Virginia gentry. But his death in 1743 left his son George and the five younger children unfinished in their education and in a position of financial ambiguity. George Washington's elder half-brother, Lawrence, was his teacher and role model during his adolescent years. He may have had training in a local plantation school, and the boy did learn a good deal of mathematics, including geometry, trigonometry, and surveying. We know from his correspondence as a mature man that he was familiar with military history, that he read in biography, agricultural science, and in the standard classics of British letters familiar to a young gentleman of his era. And he had a special passion for the theater. Yet most of his formation came from a life out of doors, from hunting, farming, and travel and from the social life of his region.

The youthful Washington was a close friend of George William Fairfax, the son of William Fairfax, cousin and representative of the proprietary magnate, Thomas, Lord Fairfax, of Northern Virginia, a land baron on a grand scale. George's half-brother Lawrence was married to William Fairfax's daughter Anne. The two boys were sent to the Shenandoah Valley with Lord Fairfax's surveyor to examine some of his undeveloped lands that were being prepared for settlement. Young George learned the rudiments of surveying during that 1748 adventure and in the following year was appointed county surveyor for Culpeper County, Virginia. He also undertook for commission (approximately £1,500 in a two-year period) surveys in what are now Virginia and West Virginia. While a surveyor, he learned how to survive on the frontier and how to manage on his own. For the remainder of his life he continued to be greatly concerned with the development of the West, and he was directly familiar with conditions there to a degree not duplicated in the lives of the other Framers.

Lawrence Washington fell ill with tuberculosis in 1751–1752, and George accompanied him in his journey to the island of Barbados in the West Indies— George's only sea voyage and travel beyond the boundaries of what was to be the United States. But Lawrence's health did not improve in consequence of his stay in the tropics; he died in July of 1752, leaving to George a reversionary interest in Mount Vernon. With Lawrence's death, George Washington's hope of the English education his two older brothers had received was at an end. And for the moment at least, he gave up his dream of a British regular army commission such as

Lawrence had held. He did receive in his half-brother's place an appointment as military adjutant for the Southern District of Virginia and soon thereafter a similar appointment for his own region, the Northern Neck and Eastern Shore. Thanks to William Fairfax's suggestion, young Major Washington was chosen as emissary to the French posts on the Ohio frontier by Gov. Robert Dinwiddie, who had been ordered by George II to confront such encroachments. At twenty-one, Washington was given the difficult assignment of delivering to the French an ultimatum ordering them to leave English territory. The governor had attached an attendant mission of negotiation with the Six Nations—the Indian tribes in the area. Leaving in late November of 1753 with a small party, Washington encountered severe weather and French evasion, but he delivered Virginia's ultimatum. After treating with the Indians, he returned through trackless wilderness, swimming almost frozen rivers and displaying a hardihood that was to sustain him in later times of trial. His narrative of this adventure was printed by Governor Dinwiddie and widely read in England and America.

In 1754 Washington rose to the rank of lieutenant colonel and then colonel of the Virginia militia. On the governor's orders, he led a small force that sought to challenge French control of the Ohio River valley, but he met defeat at Fort Necessity in a battle that was a major cause of the French and Indian War. Confusion in questions of rank and authority brought on by Governor Dinwiddie and the pending arrival of British regulars compelled the youthful colonel to resign his commission late in 1754. But in 1755 he was back in service as colonel and aide to Gen. Edward Braddock. For his bravery and exemplary conduct at the Battle of the Monongahela he earned international fame and the restoration of his authority over Virginia's forces charged with defending that colony's frontier. There followed more disputes with British officers concerning precedence and embarrassing experiences in the struggle for command authority. Moreover, Washington's efforts were not backed by the authorities in Williamsburg. After traveling to Boston in 1756 to see Gov. William Shirley of Massachusetts (George II's commander in chief in North America) in order to determine the scope of his responsibility as commander of Virginia's troops, he was not given the status he desired. In 1757 he had an equally unsatisfactory encounter with Governor Shirley's successor, John Campbell, the earl of Loudoun. He was denied not only the necessary support for his campaign in the West but also the king's commission, which he so clearly had earned. Not surprisingly, late in 1758 Washington resigned his rank and retired to Mount Vernon, full of anger and disgust with colonial officials. On the occasion of this retreat from public responsibilities, the young colonel's officers praised him as mentor, the only man able to support "the military character of Virginia," a chieftain who could by example "inculcate those genuine sentiments of true honor and passion for glory from which the greatest military achievements have been derived."

This address to their former commander was prophetic. At twenty-six Washington seemed much older than his years and had established an international reputation. After Fort Necessity he had written his brother Jack, "I heard the bullets whistle, and, believe me, there is something charming in the sound." During General Braddock's retreat Washington had three horses shot from under him, and bullets had pierced almost every item of his clothing. Yet he came from that "inferno" with no mark on him. His action that day had astonished the old soldiers present, who agreed with the young colonel when he acknowledged "the miraculous care of Providence that protected me beyond all human expectation." On that field of battle, the "myth" of George Washington as an American Achilles was established—a myth that survived the quiet years that followed.

In January of 1759, Washington married Martha Dandridge Custis, the wealthy widow of Daniel Parke Custis, and shortly thereafter took his seat in the House of Burgesses for Frederick County. He received the thanks of the Virginia legislature for his military service and then settled in to a place on the back benches. He was also a justice of the peace and a member of the vestry for the local Anglican parish. He enlarged his house at Mount Vernon and improved his lands. During these domestic years the Washingtons traveled to Williamsburg, Annapolis, Alexandria, and other familiar places of resort, amusement, and social gathering within the confines of the closed world that had grown up around Chesapeake Bay. He had time for hunting, his favorite pastime, and for long political conversations with his learned and thoughtful neighbor, George Mason. He had power of attorney and authority to act as agent for the members of the Virginia regiment who had served under him in the effort to secure for them bounty lands in the West allotted in reward for their part in the French and Indian War. In that cause he made a canoe trip down the Ohio from Fort Pitt, far into the West, up the Great Kanawha in an attempt to locate the lands in question.

The neglectful or indifferent attitude of the British government toward this obligation, the questionable practices of his English factors, the business that came before his court in Alexandria, and the memory of indignities suffered during his military campaigns built up in Washington a hostility toward the English colonial system, which turned into overt antagonism with the passage of the Stamp Act. Washington was a proponent of the nonimportation agreements (as were most Virginians), which prohibited trade with the mother country until the revenue bills had been repealed by Parliament—whose members, according to the Virginia planter, had "no more right to put their hands into my pocket, without my consent, than I have to put my hands into yours for money."

After 1770 and the renewed resistance to encroachments by Parliament upon the inherited liberties of Englishmen in America, George Washington was not in the forefront of those who advocated violent resistance and entertained the possibility of independence. Before he could go as far as Patrick Henry, he would have to find evidence in British policy that America was being subjected to "a regular plan at the expense of law and justice to overthrow our rights and liberties." Yet by 1774 he recognized the tendency of the times to force the colonials into independence, once subjection had been identified as the only alternative to that last resort. Washington presided at Alexandria on July 18, 1774, in a meeting where the freeholders of his county adopted George Mason's Fairfax Resolves. It was Washington's opinion of the prospective struggle that "more blood will be spilt on this occasion, if the ministry are determined to push matters to the extremity, than history has yet furnished in the annals of North America."

He had hoped to see a rational division between the authority of the Crown and Parliament and the liberty of the subject. But he was not prepared to have that question settled by force, because for Washington liberty meant the self-determination of peoples. And Americans were no longer Englishmen in the same sense of those electors who governed themselves in selecting a House of Commons. He disliked the Boston Tea Party and disliked the idea of withholding payment of debt. But the passage of the Intolerable Acts and British occupation of Boston moved him to join other Virginia patriots at the first provincial convention or "revolutionary" legislature in the late summer of 1774 after the royal governor had dissolved the Virginia Assembly. A provisional government of Virginia was the result of these proceedings. By that government Washington was sent as one of Virginia's seven delegates to the First Continental Congress. In the Congress he grew impatient with petitions to George III, which he called "whining." "Something should be done," he ventured, "to avert the stroke and maintain the liberty which we have derived from our ancestors."

When returned to the Second Continental Congress in May of 1775, he appeared in Philadelphia in the blue-and-buff uniform of the Virginia militia. By that time he had become convinced that British policy "exhibited an unexampled testimony of the most despotic system of tyranny that was ever practiced in a free government." Its conduct was "subversive of the laws and Constitution of Great Britain itself." What was in question was the inherited legal rights of Englishmen residing in the North American colonies.

After Lexington and Concord, with an ill-organized and unruly army of New England militia besieging the British forces in Boston, and the willingness of Massachusetts' sister colonies to come to her aid still in doubt, it occurred to John and Samuel Adams that it might be wise to turn its hosts over to the Continental Congress and then ask for a southern general to command them. It is not certain that George Washington anticipated being given this assignment. Indeed, he announced himself to be unworthy of it. Yet when the call of duty came, it could not have been a complete surprise, for there had been much talk in Philadelphia of such a possibility. Certainly Washington looked the part of commander in chief—almost six feet, four inches tall, and about two hundred pounds, athletic, and with the eye and bearing of a general. At the time of his appointment Washington was the only member of the Continental army. Yet, according to James Thomas Flexner, "from the first moment of his command Washington was more than a military leader; he was the eagle, the standard, the flag, the living symbol of the cause."

Almost immediately following his receipt of command, Washington moved to organize and train the forces surrounding Boston, to gather and coordinate other American units placed under his authority, to dispatch officers for the command of independent operations, and to write Congress and the governors of the states, urging that they create what became the Continental Line—a corps of long-enlistment, regular regiments, a "standing army" that would not have to be replaced every few months. In the spring of 1776, Boston was liberated by guns brought overland from Fort Ticonderoga. But after that "victory" and the attendant British retreat to Halifax, Nova Scotia, Washington faced larger and larger invading armies, not mere garrisons. Until French reinforcements reached North America and French fleets operated along its coasts following recognition and a treaty of alliance with France in 1778, American strategy had to be defensive, with hope of an occasional victory brought about by English overconfidence or carelessness.

Such a victory came with the first British attack on Charleston—and again later, when Washington defeated the Hessians at Trenton and Gates isolated Sir John Burgoyne at Saratoga. The pattern for these unexpected triumphs had of course been set at Bunker Hill. But, as the British grew more respectful and more methodical, for the most part all the Americans could achieve against Lord Cornwallis, Sir Henry Clinton, and the brothers Howe was survival as a force in being. First, Washington was driven out of New York. Then, he was obliged to retire from New Jersey. After recovering a portion of the latter state in a brilliant campaign that turned on the frozen field of Princeton, he was compelled to retire to Pennsylvania and defend the seat of the government. The city slipped out of his hands at Brandywine Creek (September 11, 1777) and could not be recovered in the fog and mist of Germantown (October 3–4, 1777).

The turning point came during the following winter at Valley Forge. The "conspiracy" of Gen. Thomas Conway and a few members of the Congress came to nothing. Though the fortunes of Washington's army had reached their nadir, confidence in its commander continued as before. And thanks to Baron von Steuben's drill and other invisible evolutions of character, the force that emerged from that ordeal was ready to fight a long war and to battle any English army in their path. Supply procedures had been reorganized. French and Dutch money brought weapons and ammunition. Sir William Howe was relieved by Clinton, who retired toward New York. At Monmouth Court House, Washington fell upon him and fought an engagement that persuaded the British that conquest of the northern and middle states would require a great increase in their expeditionary forces. Soon there was a French garrison in New England under the Comte de Rochambeau and a French fleet at anchor in Boston harbor. The scene of the war shifted to the South, where Whitehall believed there was a chance of preserving at least some of the colonies.

Washington watched anxiously and sent troops and officers to forestall the disaster that seemed to be in prospect, particularly following the fall of

Charleston in 1780. But his old lieutenant, Gen. Nathanael Greene, ably supported by partisans and the long rifles of the southern frontier, proved equal to the task. Fighting for survival in the concluding stages of what was supposed to have been a final attempt at subjugation—having been depleted at King's Mountain and at Cowpens—Lord Cornwallis risked a desperate engagement with Greene at Guilford Court House, North Carolina, and then withdrew to the protection of British sea power in a fortified camp at Yorktown. The sea power did not appear, but Washington did. After a feint at New York, French and American forces under Rochambeau and Washington marched swiftly overland to the headwaters of the Chesapeake Bay and were then transported by boat to the Virginia tidewater, where they invested Cornwallis's position.

For all intents and purposes, the 1781 surrender of Lord Cornwallis's army, following a brief siege, marked the end of the Revolutionary War. For another year, Washington kept a force in the field and smaller units under arms until the Treaty of Paris was signed in 1783. Then, in keeping with his own notion of public virtue, the American Cincinnatus returned his commission to the Congress and retired to Mount Vernon to farm. In a letter to the Marquis de Lafayette, eschewing fame, power, and favor, in self-conscious fulfillment of his role, Washington declared: "I am become a private citizen on the banks of the Potomac, and under the shadow of my own vine and my own fig tree. . . . I am not only retired from all public employments, but I am retiring within myself, and shall be able to view the solitary walk and tread the paths of private life with heartfelt satisfaction. Envious of none, I am determined to be pleased with all, and this, my dear friend, being the order for my march, I will move gently down the stream of life until I sleep with my fathers." Had the citizen/soldier not understood the part he was playing in such traditional terms, he might well have converted his army into a source of political power. At Newburgh, New York, in February of 1783, the conditions had been ripe for a coup d'état. Washington's final service to the republic as commander in chief during the War for Independence was to quiet this unrest and give the Congress another chance to govern the country, now at peace, under the Articles of Confederation.

It was not, however, long after his return to private life that Washington began to talk and write among his friends concerning his dissatisfaction with the incapacity of the government under the Articles. Once out of uniform, he was free to speak his mind. Always from the example of his military experience, he called for a stronger central government, one that could defend itself and deserve the respect of nations. He despised the petty vanities of state officials who had been too jealous of their authority to let him defend the country, and he was mindful of the fact that the pattern of revolutions throughout history was that they ended in tyranny. What Americans needed was a constitution to replace the one they had lived under as Englishmen: a "liberal and energetic constitution, well guarded and closely watched to prevent encroachment [which] might restore us to respectability and consequence" and "establish the dominion of law over licentiousness."

Of the latter there was a good deal in the states—riot, a clamor for paper money, and a cry for equality, particularly in New England, which, according to the general, had gone too far toward "the levelling principles." In 1785 Washington hosted the Mount Vernon Conference, which settled disputes between Maryland and Virginia. That meeting led to the Annapolis Convention of 1786, which in turn called for the Great Convention, instead of contenting itself with drawing up commercial accords among the states. Washington was pleased by this activity, for he was alarmed by the reports of popular unrest in New England. He feared "some awful crisis" was in the offing and wrote of "combustibles in every state" waiting for the torch. He was not surprised that he was chosen to head the Virginia delegation in Philadelphia. Yet for a time, he was reluctant to commit himself to attend for fear of being caught up in an angry debate. His young friends prevailed upon him by telling him that the meeting would fail if he were not present.

When the Convention officially convened on May 25, 1787, on a motion of Robert Morris, seconded by John Rutledge, George Washington was elected unanimously to be its presiding officer. Though he spoke only once in the Convention, to recommend that each member of the House of Representatives be chosen from a district of thirty-thousand voters instead of forty thousand, it is difficult to overestimate Washington's influence on those proceedings. Most of the Framers either desired his good opinion or were restrained by the thought of his disapprobation. Moreover, he apparently did much to direct the proceedings through postadjournment persuasion in the social context of the City Tavern and various private homes. For Washington the entire Convention was part of an educational process, creating that community of interests to which it hoped to give law. Washington helped to draw up the Virginia Plan. Later he had to check James Madison and some of its other ardent advocates when they seemed likely to destroy the Convention rather than modify the model. In all disputes, Washington's response was like that of Benjamin Franklin's—sage and temperate. In some cases, a mere disapproving look from the chair may have been enough to turn the course of history. Furthermore, as Pierce Butler later reported, Washington "shaped" many delegates' "Ideas of the Powers to be given to a President" as "members cast their eyes towards General Washington" and consulted "their opinions of his Virtue." That most Americans knew George Washington would be the first president of the United States was of central importance in securing approval of the Constitution in the state ratification conventions, even as his support of the document had been a strong motive for many of the Framers who placed their signatures upon it on September 17, 1787.

Because of the delicacy of his situation as president of the Constitutional Convention and probable choice for the presidency of the United States, George Washington did little but urge forward his friends in the Federalists' campaign to win ratification. But after the process was complete and the electoral college was called upon to select a chief magistrate, Washington acquired some ironic distance from burdens yet to come and wrote to a friend, "My movements to the chair of government will be accompanied by feelings not unlike those of a culprit, who is going to the place of execution." In 1788 he was elected unanimously to fill, and in a sense to create, the office that he dreaded. Despite the overwhelming support and admiration of the American people, the task was as difficult as he had expected it to be.

Washington served two terms as president, from 1789 to 1797. During his first term he had to form a government on the basis of a general outline given in the Constitution. His second term was taken up by troubles with England and France and by the emergence of partisan politics, which he deplored. The great divisions of sentiment and principle, reflected in the Constitutional Convention itself, had by 1796 resulted in a contested election between Thomas Jefferson and John Adams over the right to be his successor. In office Washington was a moderate nationalist who did not think of the presidency as a source of innovation. He envisaged the government to be little more than a referee and expected American society, if "protected from disorder and attack, to prosper on its own." Hence, he favored the plan for a national bank and other elements of the financial system of his secretary of the Treasury, Alexander Hamilton, yet disapproved of Hamilton's plan for protective tariffs. Finally, he was the jealous guardian of the dignity and legitimate power of his limited central government, both in his own conduct and in his response to popular upheavals, such as the Whiskey Rebellion. When the time came for him to pass on his responsibilities to President John Adams, he did so with a sense of relief, leaving the country in his Farewell Address a final statement of his political philosophy.

In what scholars have called the Age of Democratic Revolutions, George Washington was an anachronism. There survives a famous story concerning a liberty Gouverneur Morris took with General Washington as part of a youthful wager and of the icy stare that Morris got for his trouble. Washington was no "man of the people" to be clapped on the shoulder. In moments of seriousness his formality was severe and aristocratic—the product of a code developed under the old regime in Virginia. Yet he was a republican, in the classical sense, and altogether in character when he declared, "The approbation and affection of a free people [are] the greatest of earthly rewards." There is no explaining his life without reference to an ancient concept of honor. As Donald Davidson has written, "Washington in his national aspect [as hero] represents the difficult Federal conception at a time when it was really Federal, not 'consolidated.'" In his old age Washington warned against the example of the French radicals, "the poison of their principles." And for American "Jacobins," he had even less patience. In 1798 President Adams called him back into uniform to face the possibility of a French invasion. Should Citizen Bonaparte bring his armies to Louisiana and threaten America's frontiers, Washington did not doubt the issue because, as he had observed some years before, "a sense of dedication to freedom . . . is natural to the American air."

Fearing not so much what external enemies might accomplish as what internal divisions might bring, still wondering if "mankind when left to themselves are unfit for their own government," yet hopeful that a few virtuous leaders might continue to set things right and give the people good counsel, the old soldier spent his final days in the labor he loved best, calling back to his standard the younger men who had served him so well. In his sixty-seventh year, while seeing after his estate, he caught a chill and died soon thereafter of respiratory complications. In his will, though he had condemned abolitionist activity as "inducing more evils than it could cure," and though he was a conventional Virginia planter in buying and selling such slaves as were required in order "to live up to his rank," Washington freed those slaves at Mount Vernon who were not part of the inheritance of his wife's grandchildren, and he made provision for their maintenance. Underneath the stoic reserve and great self-discipline, there was sentiment and a warm heart. It was not a marble figure who after the Revolution in the farewell to his officers in New York could barely speak and who embraced them all, one by one. The standing of George Washington's reputation as transformed by American myth is, on examination, in no way undeserved. (See J. C. Fitzgerald, ed., *The Writings of George Washington,* 39 vols. [Washington, D.C.: Government Printing Office, 1931–1944]; James T. Flexner, *George Washington,* 4 vols. [Boston: Little, Brown, 1965–1972]; Douglas Southall Freeman, *George Washington,* 7 vols. [New York: Scribner's, 1948–1957], vol. 7 by John A. Carroll and Mary W. Ashworth; Barry Schwartz, *George Washington: The Making of an American Symbol* [New York: Free Press, 1987]; John Ferling, *The First of Men: A Life of George Washington* [Knoxville: University of Tennessee Press, 1988]; Paul K. Longmore, *The Invention of George Washington* [Berkeley and Los Angeles: University of California Press, 1988]; Bernard Mayo, *Myths and Men: Patrick Henry, George Washington, Thomas Jefferson* [Athens: University of Georgia Press, 1959], pp. 25–48; Marcus Cunliffe, *George Washington, Man and Monument* [Boston: Little, Brown, 1958]; Forrest McDonald, *The Presidency of George Washington* [Lawrence: University Press of Kansas, 1973]; Glenn A. Phelps, *George Washington and American Constitutionalism* [Lawrence: University Press of Kansas, 1993]; John R. Alden, *George Washington: A Biography* [Baton Rouge: Louisiana State University Press, 1984]; Don C. Higginbotham, *George Washington and the American Military Tradition* [Athens: University of Georgia Press, 1985]; Edmund S. Morgan, *The Genius of George Washington* [New York: Norton, 1988]; Garry Wills, *Cincinnatus: George Washington and the Enlightenment* [Garden City, N.Y.: Doubleday, 1984]; Richard Norton Smith, *Patriarch: George Washington and the New American Nation* [New York: Houghton Mifflin, 1992]; Rosemarie Zagarri, ed., *David Humphreys' "Life of General Washington" with George Washington's "Remarks"* [Athens: University of Georgia Press, 1991];

W. B. Allen, "Washington and Franklin: Symbols or Lawmakers?" *Political Science Reviewer* 17 [Fall 1987]: 109–138; John Marshall, *Life of George Washington*, 5 vols. [Philadelphia: C. P. Wayne, 1804–1807]; Washington Irving, *The Life of George Washington*, 5 vols. [New York: G. P. Putnam's Sons, 1857].)

# JAMES MADISON
March 16, 1751–June 28, 1836
Political philosopher, planter, Virginia statesman,
and fourth president of the United States

*Though "little and ordinary" in his person (five feet, six inches) and soft in speech, the master spirit of the Great Convention, able (through a surrogate) to make his ideas the business of the house. Yet not precisely a measure of the kind of majority reflected in the Constitution. A protean figure, formed layer by layer out of the raw materials of temperament, reading, and experience. Yet, in retrospect, almost impossible to reconstruct. Described by a colleague as "a studious man . . . and [the] master of every public question that can arise, or he will spare no pains to become so." Quite properly denominated by Patrick Henry as a "theoretic statesman"—best suited, by his own account, to "the intellectual pleasures of the closet." Yet capable of political pragmatism, of legislative "management."*

*Described by the Spanish ambassador as "full of subterfuges, evasions and subtleties . . . devoid of that good faith which he always puts on display when speaking and writing" or, in the more colorful idiom of a frequent adversary, as a "cunning devil" driven by "deep and mischievous designs." Certain that the members of the Constitutional Convention were acting their parts "for the ages," on the stage of universal human history. Present in Philadelphia to earn for himself the everlasting fame of the lawgiver. Better prepared than any other Framer for this meeting. A great source of information on history and "political science," having composed detailed memoranda on the subject. Spoke 161 times, on almost every subject of importance discussed in the debates. Irritated and eventually depressed when the Convention did not go along with what he proposed. During the last three months of the Convention periodically stubborn and petulant—even to the point of putting the entire process at risk. Of necessity restrained by older and steadier hands. But, lacking support for the Constitution he had hoped to secure, later possessed of such good sense as to prefer another, less ambitious instrument of fundamental law, once it had been adopted.*

*Never so much a nationalist or centralizer as Gouverneur Morris, Hamilton, or James Wilson. A conscientious republican. Kept detailed records and preserved them for publication after his death. Not precisely the "Father of the*

*Constitution," but in his twenty-eight contributions to* The Federalist *one of its most important expositors. In his long public career able to test and modify his political theories many times. Always ready to follow "experience," which, according to his political preceptor David Hume, was a better guide than doctrinaire slogans. Therefore, frequently oversimplified by modern admirers.*

James Madison was born at Port Conway, Virginia, at the home of his maternal grandfather, Francis Conway, and was the oldest child of James Madison, a respected squire, and Nelly Conway Madison. The Madisons had first come to Virginia ca. 1652 and had risen to a modest but substantial condition by moving westward with the frontier. At his father's plantation, Montpelier, James grew up in the open-air, gregarious and hearty Piedmont society of Orange County, which was to be his emotional and moral locus, his base of power and point of reference for the next eighty-five years. Young James was taught to read and write by his paternal grandmother, Frances Taylor Madison, whose father had held original title to a 13,500-acre estate situated at the foot of the Blue Ridge. After some local tutoring, James Madison, in the company of other planters' sons such as John Tyler and John Taylor of Caroline, was sent at the age of eleven to the boarding school of the Reverend Donald Robertson, trained at Aberdeen and Edinburgh. There he studied for five years. For another three years he read with the Reverend Thomas Martin, the rector of his parish church, brother to the future Framer, Gov. Alexander Martin of North Carolina, and tutor to the younger Madison children. Martin was a recent graduate of the College of New Jersey and urged Colonel Madison to send his son there—and thus avoid the unhealthy climate of Williamsburg, the seat of the College of William and Mary. When James went north to the College of New Jersey (later Princeton) in 1769, the Virginia boy was unusually well prepared for higher education, especially in the classics.

Madison was extremely industrious while in residence at the College of New Jersey, completing the undergraduate curriculum in two years and then staying for another year of graduate studies—in Hebrew, ethics, and theology—with President John Witherspoon. Upon his return to Virginia in 1772, he continued to prepare for a career in the ministry but despaired of his health and fell into a serious depression during which he showed little interest in the things of this world, which "are useless in possessing after one has exchanged time for eternity." Eventually the youthful scholar, with the help of a loving family, overcame his melancholy and gave up the idea of life in the church. Madison had been so happy at Princeton that he was perhaps dispirited simply by removal from a congenial atmosphere. The life of the professor would have suited him well. But in any case the thoroughness of his education, particularly in history and political philosophy, would give him an advantage throughout his public life and mark him as one of the most thoughtful of the early American statesmen.

Moreover, Madison left the College of New Jersey a Whig. And a Whig he remained in the troubled times to come.

James Madison the younger was elected to the Orange County Committee of Safety in 1775. In the following year Colonel Madison, the leading citizen of his community, got his son elected to a seat in the Virginia convention that drafted a state constitution and to the first legislature convened under its authority. Madison's important contribution during these years of apprenticeship was some refinement of the language concerning religious freedom in George Mason's draft of the Virginia Declaration of Rights. (Madison had already, in the years of inactivity, proved himself to be a friend of toleration by defending the Baptists in his area against acts of petty persecution.) However, in 1777 the political career of this somewhat proud, prim, and distant young man almost came to an end. Despite their regard for James Madison the elder, the freeholders of Orange County refused to return his bookish and uncommunicative son to a place for which he made no suit. In retrospect Madison understood that his neighbors saw in his "extreme distaste" for "personal solicitation" only "a mean parsimony or proud disrespect." Usage required conviviality, a good portion of strong drink, easy circulation, and the direct appeal. In failing of election Madison learned that the political habits of Virginia were not to be despised by men who aspired to the public favor of its citizens. Of that truism he had to be reminded from time to time. But he never forgot that there were limits on his independence of judgment and his political style if he wished to accomplish anything at all. Though cool and reticent by nature, Madison eventually learned most of the social arts that are a necessary part of the science of politics in a republic.

In 1777, once again after some intervention by his devoted father, Madison was given a seat on the Virginia Council of State, where, under the direction of Governors Patrick Henry and Thomas Jefferson, he was responsible for the preparation of many state papers, thereby acquiring useful experience in the day-to-day operations of government. Madison served on the council until he was elected to represent Virginia in the Continental Congress for 1780. During his three years as a member of that body, he rapidly matured in his political thinking and developed a national point of view on many questions. As a member of Congress he distinguished himself in connection with such matters as trade, defense policy, war debt, foreign relations, the administration of western lands, and (especially) finance. No member of that assembly was a stronger supporter of the proposed impost or for plans to increase the powers of the Confederation to raise a revenue. In the view of the young delegate from the Piedmont, "imbecility" was threatening to "blast the glory of the Revolution." Virginia often refused to pay his salary, members from other states neglected to attend, and the Continental army seemed on the verge of collecting its pay with the sword. Madison was able to arrange for Virginia's cession of its western lands on terms agreeable to the state leadership in Richmond. In determining the proportion between population and taxation for the southern states, he persuaded his associates to accept the ratio of three-fifths in counting slaves, which later became the formula for representation under the Constitution. Much of the Congress came to notice the anomaly of so much thoroughness and application in a colleague so young and frail. It was their report that "sense, reading, address, and integrity" made the young legislator remarkably persuasive.

Yet this was the time of near-paralysis and failure for government under the Articles. Knowing what should be done and how to do it did not reconcile Madison to the frustrations of his situation as a congressional leader. Gladly he served on a committee to "prepare to invest congress . . . with full and explicit powers for effectually carrying into execution in the several states all acts or resolutions passed." With some of his friends he speculated about the "implied right of coercion" and of the need to "compel obedience." But the times were not yet right for the implementation of such doctrines. More economic confusion and a few riots and uprisings like the one Captain Shays would soon provide were a precondition for convincing the mutually suspicious leaders of the various states that a stronger government, one "not too democratic," would be required if the Union and the societies it protected were to survive. While awaiting the appearance of such "instructive" conditions, Madison returned home to Virginia and resumed his study of the "public" law, at which he had made some beginning as early as 1773.

Once restored to the comfortable ambience of Montpelier and his family, Madison did not completely eschew politics. In 1784 he was again elected to the Virginia House of Delegates. There, he was instrumental in bringing about a complete separation of church and state. He also did yeoman service in strengthening the basis of state finances. And most important, at the state level he continued to urge that action be taken to shore up the general government. He was a guiding force behind the Mount Vernon Conference (1785) and at the subsequent Annapolis Convention (1786), where with other "choice spirits" he planned the set of maneuvers that led to the Convention in Philadelphia the following May. During these years Madison established working relationships with General Washington and Colonel Hamilton of New York. In 1786 Madison was reelected to the Confederation Congress, where he took further steps in behalf of the Constitutional Convention.

Perhaps the best way to explain what James Madison hoped would be accomplished through a new constitution is to begin by describing the conditions he expected the improved government to correct. The most important problems of the Confederation were as follows: failure of the states to comply with requisitions; encroachments by the states on the authority of the general government, as in the case of Georgia's treaties with Indians; violations authorized by state legislatures of the law of nations and of treaties, as in the refusal of some Virginia planters to honor their debts in London and Glasgow; trespasses by the states upon the rights of their sister commonwealths, as in state duties on goods shipped through their ports but destined for merchants beyond their boundaries;

"want of concert in matters of common interest," such as international trade, naturalization, and grants of incorporation for national purposes. Madison's most serious concerns were the excesses of the state legislatures in issuing paper money and the contempt for the country created overseas by the powerless condition of the Congress. "The idea of erecting our national independence on the ruins of public faith and national honor," he insisted, "must be horrid to every mind which [has] retained either honesty or pride." These vices were "democratic" and resulted from the control of state governments by a "majority faction." A general government with a power to veto legislation in the states might readily correct these vices without sliding into despotism.

In aiming at his version of political justice, Madison spoke at times of individual and religious rights, and also of the "right of citizens to vote." A federal veto power over state laws would, he believed, work to secure such rights. What is noteworthy in this connection is that the Constitution as finally adopted included no such power of veto or "oversight." Neither did it transfer from the states the power to define the scope and number of "civil rights" belonging to their citizens. The exception to this generalization is a prohibition on theft by legislation with respect to paper money and the violation of contracts. Along with religious freedom and the suffrage, that prohibition in respect to property rights indicates most of what Madison had in mind when he talked about the "rights of men." *Inability* to secure the states against internal disorders, *inability* to check injustices spawned by the multiplicity and uncertainty of state laws, and *inability* to restrain the interest groups (agricultural, commercial, manufacturing) in their competition for influence were the glaring weaknesses of government by the Confederation. Much of what Madison proposed for inclusion in the Constitution follows directly from the critique in his memorandum, "Vices of the Political System of the United States." He did not intend for his ideas to be used to justify government activity aimed directly at changing the economic and social conditions of men, both within and without the social bond. He did not trust society in its relation to the state—at least where the small polis was concerned.

It was because of reservations concerning the "unreasonable" relationship of society to the homogeneous republic that Madison developed his theories of the "extended republic" and the "multiplicity of factions." But even though in 1787 in Philadelphia he did emphasize the unwholesome and centrifugal influence of the sovereign states on the development of an American political identity, Madison was always an advocate of specifically divided and balanced powers within the proposed federal structure. As he summarized the problem, "In framing a government which is to be administered by men over men, the great difficulty lies in this: you must first enable the government to control the governed; and in the next place oblige it to control itself." Trust in the power or watchfulness of the people would not be enough. "Auxiliary precautions" would be necessary. And the parts of the federal structure itself would restrain one another. They would pit the ambitions of one man against the ambitions of another, and of group against group. Domination would be impossible in a "large and various republic." Stability would result, allowing for development of a "third force," a group "disinterested" in its approach to national questions, devoted to the laws, and inclined to reverence them as they grew older and better established.

Madison looked with anxiety toward the subsequent history of the republic. And though such parts of the Constitution as were finally settled on by the majority of the Framers and also approved by James Madison were the uncontroversial components of his original political "model," Madison understood their long-range implications better than did most of his colleagues. "In framing a system which we wish to last for ages," observed the Virginia lawgiver, "we should not lose sight of the changes which ages will produce. An increase of population will of necessity increase the proportion of those who will labour under all the handicaps of life & secretly sigh for a more equal distribution of its blessings. These may in time outnumber those who are placed above the feelings of indigence. According to equal laws of suffrage, the power will slide into the hands of the former." Hence Madison wanted authority transferred from the states, which were subject to the politics of envy and resentment, into the hands of a not-too-consolidated government in which the powers were clearly distributed, "few and defined." Because contemporary experience connects enforced egalitarianism with the activities of the central authority and the sovereignty of the states with resistance to such measures, it is easy to overlook Madison's purpose in devising a federalism of his own. In his day it was the agency of the states that appeared to threaten property and the social order. In that context it was reasonable to advocate a stronger government to control the levelers, to intimidate mobs, not encourage them, to protect the institution of slavery and other property, not to undermine it.

Adrienne Koch has contended that Madison, in designing a Constitution, did not try to guarantee "too much" in the way of "rights." Out of prudence he said nothing about women or Negroes or suffrage. Another interpretation is, however, that he did not wish to establish too much of what modern civil libertarians describe as rights. The problem with much scholarship on this question is that it reads Madison's long-term objectives out of the idiom, the vehicle of his rhetoric, and thus overburdens what was, for the Framers, a convention of address. Madison hated sameness and uniformity in a way that made equality not merely unlikely but finally impossible. At the state level, where he knew it belonged, he accepted the conventional Virginia view that the right to vote belonged to freeholders; and later in his life he revised that formula by adding "housekeepers and heads of families." Furthermore, he made a part of his appeal for the Virginia Plan that it would offer security to the special interests of the southern states.

Madison was on the floor, speaking quietly and reasonably in behalf of his version of the Constitution on most of the days when the Great Convention was in session. Moreover, he served on the Committee of Style and the committee on postponed matters. Whenever some point of importance fell into dispute, he "took the lead," bringing to bear what William Pierce called "the most correct knowledge [of] . . . the affairs of the United States" to be found among the political leaders of his generation. But his colleagues did not always follow his lead. He fought that proposal which gave representation to the states by making them equals in the Senate. No one contended longer for proportional representation. He wanted the president to serve for seven years or an even longer term; and he opposed allowing the states any agency in electing the president. At every turn, he urged that Congress be given a veto over state laws. All these battles he lost. Furthermore, though he urged his proposals upon his fellow southerners as a protection of their regional interests (which he acknowledged at every opportunity), they would not agree with him concerning a tax on exports, a navigation law, or federal control of the militia. Even on regulations concerning executive authority to veto federal legislation, the number of votes in the Senate necessary to appoint judges, and the power for those judges in a council of revision designed to assist the president, Madison broke with most of his fellow southerners, while simultaneously announcing a firm devotion to their cause.

In Philadelphia Madison actually did all that he could to persuade the rest of the Framers to take power from the states. To that end he reviewed for the house his study of earlier confederations and conjured up specters of tyranny to frighten his associates into concurrence with the Virginia Plan. Once he was through, however, not even all the delegates from Virginia agreed that there was "less danger of encroachment from General Government than from State Governments." By Madison's own admission, the states were represented in the process settled upon for election of senators, in the selection of the president, and in the machinery for adopting, rejecting, and revising the Constitution. Yet much of the Constitution as finally approved suited Madison well: it rested on the people of the states, represented in their conventions, and it was not a "treaty" among legislatures. Moreover, through the federal chief executive, it acted upon the people. None of the components of the system would be too strong. Judges would at least require senatorial approval, and the president could be impeached or overridden. Even the "impetuous vortex" of "legislative supremacy" had been avoided by specific grants of power to the executive and judicial branches of government, by the reservation of powers to the states, and by the "defined and limited objects" of federal authority as specified by the instrument itself.

Though momentarily perplexed and angry, declaring on one occasion that "it was vain to purchase concord in the Convention on terms that would perpetuate discord," Madison finally accepted the inevitable and began to adjust his long-range planning to the advantages of the Constitution as it was going to read once completed. The basic maxim of his statecraft, that "all men having power ought to be distrusted," had been observed. According to Madison, such caution was important in establishing the new government and would be even more crucial in the years to come. Though senators would not serve nine years, they would at least serve six. The government would have an aristocratic element, and the president would be no mere cipher. Taxes would finally be collected and a defense maintained.

A national university to train leaders in a "national spirit" might have filled out the design further in the direction of adequacy, but the other Framers were unpersuaded of the advantages of a "national" education, as they had been with the other more ambitious elements in Madison's original plan. The basis for the lawgiver's hope would therefore have to continue to be people like his yeoman neighbors in Orange County: "Viewing the subject in its merits alone, the freeholders of the Country would be the safest depositories of Republican liberty. In future times a great majority of the people will not only be without land, but any other sort of property. These will either combine under the influence of their common situation; in which case, the rights of property and the public liberty will not be secure in their hands: or which is more probable, they will become the tools of opulence and ambition." There were clouds on the pastoral horizon— clouds that commerce and industry would not disperse. Establishing a government that for the people would seem habitual and that would command respect would therefore have to be done quickly and done well. On leaving Philadelphia, Madison hoped for the best, polished his *Notes*, and prepared to plead the case for a Constitution very different from the one he had expected to support.

In the Great Convention James Madison had insisted at one point that "the states never possessed the essential rights of sovereignty," and he had elsewhere added that "the people would not be less free as members of one great Republic than as members of thirteen small ones." By the time he collaborated with Hamilton and John Jay in producing *The Federalist*, his emphasis had already begun to change. Once the Constitution had been adopted by all of the states, it changed again—in the direction of his old adversaries, the Antifederalists. What is most interesting is the interval between Madison's emergence (ca. 1791) as party leader of the Democratic–Republicans and his advocacy in Philadelphia of the Virginia Plan: the period when he was a mild Federalist on at least partially Antifederalist grounds.

In his contributions to *The Federalist*, for the benefit of a New York audience, Madison made a few conventional noises about "energy" and "stability" in government. Moreover, he repeated his familiar objections to the Confederation's "imbecility" (which at the time meant weakness, not idiocy) and refuted the theoretical assumptions of such authorities as Montesquieu that only small republics could avoid being transformed into despotisms. But, as for instance in *Federalist* no. 39, he also added constructions of the operations of the Constitution that had not been part of his discourse in Philadelphia. The "jurisdiction" of the new government, he insisted, "extends to certain enumerated objects only, and leaves to the several States a residuary and inviolable sovereignty over all other objects." The Constitution provides for a regime "neither wholly federal, nor wholly national." The states in their capacity to approve or reject it were "distinct and independent." As Forrest McDonald has insisted, Madison's performance as Publius emphasizes the restraints built into the system, what it cannot do, rather than its potential for good works and creativity. The differences between his essays and Alexander Hamilton's foreshadowed their conflicts in the next fifteen years. Looking horizontally over the spread and disposition of the parts of the authority they were recommending, adverting to history and "political science," Madison emphasized its conformity to republican principles. Looking vertically up and down the federal "chain of command," speaking of economic concerns and of the administrative and judicial capacities of the new federal "engine," Hamilton viewed each grant of power as an opportunity.

Before the series had been completed, Madison was forced to hurry home to Virginia and stand for a seat in the Virginia ratification convention of June 1788. In Richmond, Madison carried much of the Federalist burden in the struggle against George Mason and Patrick Henry. Assisted by his "convert," Gov. Edmund Randolph, he went almost so far as to tell the Antifederalists that the Constitution was just what they had in mind: "The powers of the general government relate to external objects, and are but few." All their fears of centralized government were such as he himself would feel were the Constitution not so mild in its dealings with the liberties of citizens and the rights of the states. Stronger national authority was necessary to collect a tax, pay the public debts, and defend the frontiers. Currency had to be stabilized and popular cries for paper money restrained. The alternatives were defeat and utter chaos. Moreover, the South, if war came, would "need" the Union—particularly if its institutions were to survive the threat of "servile insurrection." Furthermore, there was the fugitive-slave clause of the Constitution, a guarantee never before available. No need to worry about the implied powers hidden behind language concerning the "general welfare" and "necessary and proper."

Madison complained of appeals to "apparent danger." The burden of proof for such contentions, he maintained, fell on his opponents, who were unjustly out to frighten Virginia into obduracy. As to the possible emancipation of slaves by federal action, there was "no power to warrant it." Concerning the federal judiciary he was equally encouraging: "The number of cases within the jurisdiction of these courts are very small . . . all controversies directly between citizen and citizen, will still remain with the local courts." The government was not "consolidated," nor should it be. The "watchfulness of the states"—their "extensive means of influence"—would protect its purity. Even the taxing power was finite: "I may say with truth, that there never was a more oeconomical government in any age or country; nor which will require fewer hands, or give less influence." Subsequent amendments to specify a few more limitations on the general government would do nicely. James Madison promised to support them. But previous amendments, such as Henry and Mason wished to make as a condition of ratification, would destroy the Union, and forfeit forever all the advantages the Constitution should bring.

The Federalists won this fight. Madison fell ill during the debates, and had to leave parts of the battle to other Federalists such as Edmund Randolph and Col. Henry Lee. In some cases this change was fortunate for the Federalist cause. Madison was not a powerful speaker and mainly impressed those already on his side or interested in close analysis. Even so, this was his most impressive public performance, under intense pressure. Madison won great respect for his efforts in the ratification convention, and he was later to declare that what was said there and in other such assemblies was the authoritative gloss on the fundamental law of the land. Thus the Constitution as Madison presented it in Richmond in June of 1788 had by his own announcement more authority than what he argued in Philadelphia and in *The Federalist*.

Patrick Henry denied Madison the seat in the original Senate that Madison so much desired and attempted to deny him also the opportunity of being elected to the House of Representatives. Yet despite a gerrymander and the formidable opposition of James Monroe, Madison won a House seat and was in New York when the members of the new government assembled. From 1789 through 1797, Madison was the leader of a southern bloc in the Congress. Moreover, he was instrumental in filling out the Constitution's skeletal framework by establishing the component parts of the government. Fulfilling his promise to the Virginia ratifying convention, Madison introduced and guided through the First Congress twelve amendments to the Constitution, ten of which became the Bill of Rights. Though they were not precisely what the Antifederalists had prescribed, they did much to pacify the friends of liberty who had originally opposed so drastic a change from the Articles of Confederation. For a time Madison continued to be of help to President Washington. But with his close friend Secretary of State Thomas Jefferson, he began to doubt the merit of certain measures undertaken at the suggestion of Alexander Hamilton, secretary of the Treasury. After declaring, "We are in the wilderness, without a single footstep to guide us," Madison settled on his choice of persona, as defender of the strict construction of the Constitution, and attacked Hamilton's plan for promoting manufactures, the Jay Treaty, and debt assumption because of its effect on the economy of the southern states. Concerning northern speculation in currency and land, he declared of the entire Federalist program that had Virginia Federalists foreseen its adoption, they would never have supported the Constitution's ratification.

During his four years out of office, Madison assisted his aging father in the operation of Montpelier and learned his role as husband to Dolley Payne Todd, whom he had married in September of 1794. These were also years of intense and partisan political activity and more of the kind of writing that he had done while party leader in the Congress. Madison was the author of the Virginia Resolutions of 1798, which called for state resistance to what he saw as unconstitutional acts of the Adams administration, and he was unquestionably a party to plans for more resistance had the Federalists moved to alter the political process by using the excuse of war or military necessity. In later years both Madison and his admirers would deny the reading of these events as a precedent for nullification or secession. Their explanation was disingenuous. Even in the Great Convention Madison had maintained, "The use of force against a state would probably be considered by the party attacked as a dissolution of all previous compacts by which it might be bound." Shooting, however, proved unnecessary, as Antifederalist rhetoric won for Jefferson the election of 1800.

If James Madison had been a good populist and disciple of Patrick Henry while out of power, he tended back toward federalism once restored to authority as secretary of state under President Thomas Jefferson. Madison was the principal adviser of the third president. In his official capacity he oversaw the Louisiana Purchase of 1803 and helped to win approval in Washington for this arguably unconstitutional bargain. He also counseled his friend Jefferson on party matters and arranged for the seizure of West Florida. In handling diplomacy with France, Spain, and England, Madison displayed considerable skill, but more craft than republican simplicity. However, he was unable to reconcile New England to the embargo instituted in response to English offenses against American ships, and he was unable to purchase Florida. On Jefferson's retirement in 1809, Madison ascended as heir presumptive to the presidency.

The central event of Madison's two terms as chief executive was the War of 1812. His conduct as wartime president was not above criticism, for he propelled the nation into mortal conflict without having made the necessary preparations. Hence it was no surprise that the first two years of the war did not go well for the United States. Moreover, many in America and in England believed that in joining the Emperor Napoleon as the enemy of England, the United States had made common cause with tyranny. Madison, in contrast, believed the war to be a necessary coda to the American Revolution, securing for the country its unquestioned place among the nations. With Bonaparte defeated, England turned in anger to administer a proper punishment on her "upstart relations." One British expedition burned Washington and another crossed from Canada into New York. Maine was under pressure, and New England prepared for secession. Then came a chain of American victories that no one could have expected. The English were driven back into Canada, defeated on the Great Lakes, and deprived of their control over the territories north of the Ohio River. More important, Gen. Andrew Jackson crushed their Indian allies in Alabama and drove back their army from the precincts of New Orleans. The young men in Washington had laughed at the indecisive "little commander-in-chief with his little round hat and huge cockade" as he visited the military departments attempting to restore morale. But with the Treaty of Ghent, which restored the status quo antebellum and finally gained the freedom of the seas, Madison had achieved his purposes and preserved his reputation for leadership and sagacity.

Other acts during Madison's presidency went against the announced principles of the party he had helped to create: the rechartering of the Bank of the United States, the creation of a military and naval establishment, and the Tariff Act of 1816. Yet in February of 1817, in his final act as president, Madison vetoed legislation providing for public works and internal improvements. The apparent violations of Democratic-Republican dogma were by implication justified by the experience of the war. Absolutely inactive government could not defend the country. American commerce and manufacturing had to be encouraged. But a teleocratic state was still foreign to Madison's political philosophy.

Upon leaving office in March of 1817, Madison retired to Montpelier, where he enjoyed entertaining visitors, polishing his *Notes of Debates in the Federal Convention of 1787* (which he had always planned for publication after his death), collecting his correspondence, and writing occasional comments on the political events of the day. In 1819 he became a member of the Board of Visitors for the University of Virginia, where from 1826 to 1834 he served as rector, following Jefferson. During the Missouri controversy of 1819–1820, southerners employed Madison to refute the "higher law" theories of Rufus King and the claim that the Fathers had meant to exclude slavery from all new states organized in the West. Later, during the nullification controversy, nationalists called upon Madison to deny the constitutional theories of John C. Calhoun. Madison consistently attacked abolitionists as unpatriotic and treated talk of peaceful secession or state resistance to "unjust" laws as illegal. The "right of revolution" was another matter but could be invoked only after great provocation. There were more than one hundred slaves at Montpelier, none of whom Madison freed. He disliked the "peculiar institution," was a gentle master, but could not imagine the free Negro as citizen.

No one recognized the frailty of the Union better than did its last surviving architect. And since his reputation as Founder and lawgiver would depend on its survival, he edited the history of his own previous activities just as he had edited his *Notes*—to shore it up a bit. In 1829, Madison was a delegate to the Virginia constitutional convention, where he acted the role of peacemaker and voted to sustain the great influence of the older slaveholding counties of his state. He died in his eighty-sixth year after remarking to the inquiry of his niece as to the final change in his condition, "Nothing more than a change of mind, my dear."

Of all the original generation of American statesmen and of all the Framers, James Madison is the most difficult to explain. Because his career was so long and so full of change, because he spoke with so many voices, he defies interpretation. Yet his republicanism was consistent and sincere, as was acknowledged by those who knew him well. (See Irving Brant, *James Madison*, 6 vols. [Indianapolis: Bobbs-Merrill, 1941–1961]; Ralph Ketcham, *James Madison: A Biography* [New York: Macmillan, 1971]; Alexander R. Landi, "The Politics of James Madison" [Ph.D. dissertation, University of Dallas, 1973]; Edward McNall Burns, *James Madison, Philosopher of the Constitution* [New York: Octagon Books, 1973]; Norman K. Risjord, *Chesapeake Politics, 1781–1800*

[New York: Columbia University Press, 1978]; George Carey, "Majority Tyranny and the Extended Republic Theory of James Madison," *Modern Age* 20 [Winter 1976]: 40–53; Adrienne Koch, *Jefferson and Madison: The Great Collaboration* [New York: Oxford University Press, 1964]; Neal Riemer, *James Madison* [New York: Washington Square, 1968]; Adrienne Koch, *Madison's "Advice to My Country"* [Princeton, N.J.: Princeton University Press, 1966]; Paul Eidelberg, *The Philosophy of the American Constitution: A Reinterpretation of the Intentions of the Founding Fathers* [New York: Free Press, 1968]; Virginia Moore, *The Madisons: A Biography* [New York: McGraw-Hill, 1979]; Adrienne Koch, *Power, Morals, and the Founding Fathers: Essays in the Interpretation of the American Enlightenment* [Ithaca, N.Y.: Cornell University Press, 1961]; Douglass Adair, "James Madison" and "That Politics May Be Reduced to a Science: David Hume, James Madison, and the Tenth Federalist," in *Fame and the Founding Fathers*, ed. H. Trevor Colbourn [New York: W. W. Norton, 1974], pp. 124–141 and 93–106; Gaillard Hunt, ed., *The Writings of James Madison*, 9 vols. [New York: G. P. Putnam's Sons, 1900]; M. E. Bradford, "Such a Government as the People Will Approve: The Great Convention as Comic Action," *St. Louis University Public Law Review* 4 [Spring 1987]: 215–228; Roy Branson, "James Madison and the Scottish Enlightenment," *Journal of the History of Ideas* 40 [April/June 1979]: 235–250; Henry Adams, *History of the United States during the Administrations of Jefferson and Madison*, 9 vols. [New York: Charles Scribner's Sons, 1889]; William T. Hutchinson et al., ed., *The Papers of James Madison*, 10 vols. [Chicago: University of Chicago Press, 1962–1977]; Robert A. Rutland et al., eds., *The Papers of James Madison*, vols. 11–17 [Charlottesville: University Press of Virginia, 1977–1991]; James H. Smylie, "Madison and Witherspoon: Theological Roots of American Political Thought," *Princeton University Library Chronicle* 12 [Spring 1961]: 118–132; Richard Buel, Jr., *Securing the Revolution: Ideology in American Politics, 1789–1815* [Ithaca, N.Y.: Cornell University Press, 1972]; William Lee Miller, *The Business of May Next: James Madison and the Founding* [Charlottesville and London: University Press of Virginia, 1992]; Jack N. Rakove, *James Madison and the Creation of the American Republic* [Glenview, Ill.: Scott, Foresman, 1990]; Drew R. McCoy, *The Last of the Fathers: James Madison and the Republican Legacy* [Cambridge: Cambridge University Press, 1989]; Robert A. Rutland, *James Madison: The Founding Father* [New York: Macmillan, 1987]; Robert Allen Rutland, *The Presidency of James Madison* [Lawrence: University Press of Kansas, 1990]; Lance Banning, "James Madison and the Dynamics of the Constitutional Convention," *Political Science Reviewer* 17 [1987]: 5–48; Lance Banning, "The Practicable Sphere of a Republic: James Madison, the Constitutional Convention, and the Emergence of Revolutionary Federalism," and Drew R. McCoy, "James Madison and Visions of American Nationality in the Confederation Period: A Regional Perspective," in *Beyond Confederation: Origins of the Constitution and American National Identity,* ed. Richard Beeman, Stephen Botein, and Edward C.

Carter II [Chapel Hill: University of North Carolina Press, 1987], pp. 162–187, 226–258; Harold S. Schultz, "James Madison: Father of the Constitution?" *Quarterly Journal of the Library of Congress* 37 [1980]: 215–222; John Agresto, "'A System without Precedent'—James Madison and the Revolution in Republican Liberty," *South Atlantic Quarterly* 82 [Spring 1983]: 129–144; symposium essays by Ralph Rossum, B. Nelson Ong, George Carey, Jonathan K. Van Patten, John S. Baker, Robert L. Cord, Paul Peterson, and Hrach Gregorian in "James Madison and the Constitution," *Benchmark* 3:1 and 2 [January–April 1987].)

# GEORGE MASON
December 11, 1725–October 7, 1792
Planter, political philosopher, and statesman

*One of the noblest and most disinterested of the many impressive figures responsible for Virginia's dominant role in the formation of the Union. When he arrived in Philadelphia, in some degree committed to the basic features of the Virginia Plan, which was later presented by Gov. Edmund Randolph for the delegation from his state. But before the Convention was over, the sternest opponent of the document produced by the deliberations: so outraged about what had been done that he declared, "I would have lost this hand before it should have marked my name to the new government." A staunch classical republican with "a temperament . . . like the younger Cato, constitutionally stern, firm and honest: . . . a most decided enemy to all constructive and implied powers." Fearful that the Constitution would deliver the southern states "bound hand & foot to the Eastern [northern] States, and enable them to exclaim, in the words of Cromwell . . . 'The Lord hath delivered them into our hands.'" Spoke 136 times and was present in every session. Angry with the course taken by the debates before they were over, insisting to his son, "I would not, upon pecuniary Motives, serve in this Convention for a thousand pounds a day." Yet stirred to a new-found zeal for battle against the adoption of the Constitution when he returned to Virginia. In his antifederalism a cause for the greatest concern among the proponents of the new system of government because of the magnitude of his reputation among American leaders, both in Virginia and throughout the country. Largely responsible for the proposal of a bill of rights by the First Congress of the United States.*

George Mason of Gunston Hall was the fourth of his name and line to occupy a position of importance in the northern neck of Virginia. He was a direct descendant of Col. George Mason of Worcestershire, England, a substantial yeoman with aristocratic connections in the Vale of Evesham, who in 1651 migrated to the Potomac River valley in Virginia after service at Worcester in the ill-fated army of King Charles II. The Masons prospered in Virginia, and by the time of the birth of the fourth George Mason held some five thousand acres at Dogue's Neck below Alexandria, plus sundry other plantations in Maryland and Virginia. George Mason IV was the son of George Mason III and Ann Thomson Mason. He was connected by marriage, business, political association, and friendship with the Mercers, the Lees, the Brents, the Fitzhughs, and other significant families. Upon his father's death in 1735 (by drowning during a storm), the George Mason who was to become a Framer fell under the guardianship of his mother, a capable woman, and his uncle by marriage, John Mercer of Marlborough, a distinguished attorney whose sizable library was to become young George's private college. Before the period of this tutelage, George Mason had some training in the local grammar schools and from private tutors. However, his most important teacher was his mother, from whom he learned the art of being the master of a great plantation and the necessity for personal management, planning, and careful accounts. Throughout his life, study was Mason's principal delight; he became one of Virginia's most learned men—particularly in constitutional questions. Indeed, his intellectual abilities were so marked that one of the most distinguished historians of the period of the American Revolution has maintained that Mason had a "talent that far outweighed Madison's."

In 1749 Mason became a justice of the Fairfax County Court. In the same year he was elected vestryman of Truro Parish, an office with considerable civic responsibilities. Also in 1749 he became a partner in the Ohio Company, and in April of 1750 he married Ann Eilbeck of Mattawoman—a neighbor from directly across the Potomac who brought him connections with important families in Charles County, Maryland. In 1755 Mason began work on the house that was to be symbolic of their lives, Gunston Hall, which was completed in 1758. Also in that year Mason was first elected by the freeholders of Fairfax County to the House of Burgesses, where he served until 1761. Even at that early age he found the ordinary moil and seethe of political life not to his taste—something to be endured only when the duty of a gentleman, his public virtue, required it of him.

The 1760s and the first four years of the following decade were for Mason a private time. Using the valetudinarian plea of chronic gout, the squire of Gunston Hall refused further public offices. Nevertheless, this was a busy period for him and not without political implications. The business of the Ohio Company did not prosper, since Indian policy issuing from Great Britain discouraged further white settlement beyond the mountains after the conclusion of the Seven Years' War. Yet under an earlier grant Mason claimed fifty thousand to sixty thousand acres in western Virginia and Kentucky, and he composed a learned annotation, "Extracts from the Virginia Charters, with Some Remarks upon Them" (1773), in defense of those claims. Earlier, upon the passage of the Stamp Act, Colonel Mason (who had acquired that rank for service as quartermaster in the war against the French) had published an open letter under the signature "A Virginia Planter" in the *London Public Ledger*, a letter that encouraged English merchants to correct the mistaken attitude of their government toward the colonies in North America. He grew irritated with the arrogance and the blunders of the king's ministers and after the adoption of the Townshend Duties favored and observed the terms of the "Association," an agreement of Virginians to boycott importation from the mother country. He was not yet very far toward revolution, and he scorned the idea of American independence. Much of his time in these years went toward the development of the social and economic institutions of his region. This was also a period of close association with his neighbor Col. George Washington, with whom he shared much of his thinking on political questions.

George Mason's political position as a conditionally loyal but profoundly uneasy subject of King George III places him in the camp of those apologists of American resistance who argued more from legal theory and precedent than from a definition of human nature. In his public letter "To the Committee of Merchants in London" he wrote, "We claim Nothing but the Liberty and Privileges of Englishmen, in the same degree, as if we had still continued among our brethren in Great Britain." To this he added the appeal of the common blood: "Let our fellow Subjects in Great Britain reflect that we are descended from the same Stock with themselves, nurtured in the same Principles of Freedom. . . . We are the same people with them in every respect, only not yet debauched by Wealth, Luxury, Venality and Corruption." In the same vein he advised his neighbors, "We must maintain the liberty which we have derived from our ancestors." To claim that British Americans would forfeit this heritage lightly was a lie of "ministerial" propaganda: "The wildest Chimera that ever disturbed a Madman's brain has not less Truth than this Opinion." Even so, "such another experiment as the Stamp-Act," he informed the merchants, "would produce a general Revolt in America."

The Townshend Duties were not quite so offensive as the Stamp Act, yet Mason responded to them as he had to the earlier provocation by drafting bills designed to muffle or circumvent their effect—bills presented to the House of Burgesses by Washington or some other member from the northern neck. And he urged his neighbors to become serious about enforcing the restrictions on trade to which they had agreed. He wrote essays in the press, then finally came to the opinion that there was a "premeditated design" and system "to introduce arbitrary government in America, to corrupt the relationship of the King and his British American subjects," and to "dissolve the original Compacts by which our Ancestors bound themselves and their Posterity to be dependent on the British Crown." At this point strictly constitutional arguments ceased to be of any avail. Reduced to "desperation," Americans had the right to act upon the principle of self-preservation and to appeal to the sword—the god of battles.

In the Fairfax Resolves (July 18, 1774), George Mason brought together these developments in his thought to produce one of the most significant political statements of the period preceding the American Revolution. It was not casually that he had observed of the ancient poets that "they have made a kind of Being of Necessity and tell us that the Gods themselves are inclined to yield to her." The circumstances surrounding the twenty-four Fairfax Resolves, which were adopted by the freeholders of that county in a meeting presided over by George Washington—and which became the mandate for the local committee of safety as well as an admonitory message to the proposed Continental Congress—were developments in New England, the Intolerable Acts, and the threat to the integrity of the other colonies posed by the British response to the Boston Tea Party. Mason wrote the resolutions knowing that war was almost inevitable. Yet he included in them expressions of thanks to the friends of America in the mother country. British history in the tradition of documents like the one in which he spoke continued to be part of his consciousness. But there was also something new—an insistence that Americans should act in concert, a tribute to Massachusetts for "acting in the Common Cause of all British America." The forms of remonstrance and petition were carefully observed, but the breath of life was not in them. Instead, at the heart of his message was the refusal to be treated like a conquered people and the suggestion of provision for military preparation. In this document Mason crossed over into the company of those Americans who were ready for independence if they could be free in no other way. Thus necessity and nature combined.

In 1775 and 1776, Mason was the representative from Fairfax County to the Virginia Convention—the ad hoc government of the state. He was forced to accept that assignment by the election of George Washington to the Continental Congress and by the consensus of his neighbors. Almost immediately he became a member of the committee of safety, which assumed the executive powers of the departed royal governor, Lord Dunmore. In 1776 Mason was the leading member of the special convention that drew up a constitution for the independent state of Virginia, and from 1776 through 1781 he sat in the Virginia legislature for Fairfax County. These were his most active political years.

Mason was himself the principal author of the Virginia Declaration of Rights, which laid a predicate for the Declaration of Independence adopted within the next three months. There were many competing versions of the original Virginia constitution; but, according to the participants, "that proposed by George Mason swallowed up all the rest." In the view of authorities on Mason's thought, the distinguishing characteristic of this document is its almost complete similarity to the old colonial government of Virginia under the British Crown, with a limited executive, an appointed council, and stringent property qualification for seats in both houses of the legislature. Mason's constitution is no democratic document but is, rather, republican in the classical sense. Its object was to restrict and distribute power, not to enforce an a priori ideological plan on Virginia society. Members of the council and governors could not serve consecutive terms. Governors and members of the council of state were chosen by the legislature, and senators by a college of electors. Mason wanted no permanent class of politicians or military officers. Gentlemen and freeholders should rule and defend the state, considering their time of service in various offices and ranks as the price of liberty—a duty, not an opportunity for advancement. As he had learned from Roman history, power is most safely entrusted to those who have something better to do and who prefer a private station.

Those who read the Virginia Declaration of Rights out of context are often misled by the statement of its first paragraph that "all men are by nature equally free and independent, and have certain inherent rights, of which, when they enter into a state of society, they cannot by any compact deprive or divest their posterity; namely, the enjoyment of life and liberty, with the means of acquiring and possessing property, and pursuing and obtaining happiness and safety." The record of the debates surrounding the adoption of this language indicates both how much and how little was intended by it. For one thing, slaves were specifically excluded from the protection of its sweeping generalization by the reference to a "state of society." The advocates of the Virginia Declaration, according to Edmund Randolph, included this phrase to reassure conservatives that they meant to foster no "civil convulsion" in the relation of the races. Indeed though Mason deplored the slave trade as harmful to Virginia, and was of the opinion that "every master of slaves is a petty tyrant," he opposed every threat to the "peculiar institution" and later sponsored legislation that made it difficult for his neighbors to free their slaves. Mason was certainly no egalitarian. In drafting "The Fairfax County Military Association," he wrote that "gentlemen and freeholders" were not the same, but together they made up a society. They were its "constituent members." The Marquis de Chastellux advised his fellow countrymen, following a 1780 visit to Virginia, to take American statements about the "rights of men" in this way and not as had the "half-philosophers . . . who have invariably mistaken the word *people* for mankind in general." The Virginia documents referred to planters and farmers who were freemen, participated in government, and owned slaves—both "citizens and masters" who "perfectly resemble the bulk of individuals who formed what were called *the people* in the ancient republics."

In 1777 Mason was named a member of the commission called upon to revise the laws of Virginia. In that company he urged the necessity of preserving the force of the English common law in Virginia's courts—just as he had insisted upon the necessity for a bill of rights to replace the English Declaration of Rights of 1689. He was active in promoting a sound currency and retirement of debt. He encouraged domestic manufacturing and trade with France. He took responsibility for organizing systems of supply for the Continental army, supported recruitment of troops, and drew up a realistic tax plan. With Patrick Henry, whom he valued as "the first man upon this continent, as well in abilities as public virtue," he secured the authorization for the 1779 expedition of George Rogers Clark to subdue British outposts along the Ohio. He labored to develop a consistent and defensible policy for the settlement of Virginia's frontier. Then he began to weary of the unpatriotic and trivial spirit so often present in the ordinary deliberations of the legislature. He was provoked by talk of repudiating legitimate debts to British merchants and by the mistreatment of former Loyalists who had done nothing to prevent American independence. Though no longer in the legislature, he exerted his influence behind the scenes. Despite his Anglican orthodoxy he joined James Madison in opposing a bill for state support of "Teachers of the Christian religion" and called for legal disestablishment and separation of church and state—a process left incomplete in the reforms of 1776, which went only so far as toleration.

Slowly Mason came to see the necessity for strengthening the general government into a power that could raise taxes and wage war. In 1785 he attended the Mount Vernon Conference, which settled disputes between Maryland and Virginia concerning the Potomac and Chesapeake Bay. In 1786 he agreed to return to the legislature and oppose proposals to issue paper money. He was proud of what had been achieved in the Revolution and wrote to his son, "Taking a retrospective view of what has passed, we seem to have been treading upon enchanted ground." To defend and to secure the miracle of liberty, he agreed to attend the Great Convention as one of the delegates from Virginia. He was prepared for a change, if the change was not too great.

George Mason went northward toward Philadelphia and the Constitutional Convention filled with a kind of enthusiasm for his task as Framer, and once there he was pleased to see that America had sent "her first characters" to serve in the labor of designing a new government. In the early weeks of the Convention he exhibited none of the "heterodoxy" against Federalist principles that Madison had predicted after an earlier conversation with him concerning the business at hand. But as the weeks drew out into months and after he had listened to the political theories of such nationalists as Hamilton, Wilson, and Gouverneur Morris, Mason took pause and began to raise questions about the intentions of his fellow Framers and the probable impact of their collusion on the liberties of his countrymen. He was not troubled by the necessity for compromise in giving equal representation to the states in the Senate. He stood by his agreement to the central features of the Virginia Plan. All that he required in addition were a few modifications in the direction of moderation. Though he feared that the New Englanders might overreact to popular upheavals such as Shays' Rebellion, he concurred with them that "we have been too democratic." He opposed the direct election of presidents and recommended a large property qualification for senators, but he could not tolerate the idea of creating a plutocracy through the instrument of law.

Mason was also uneasy when he heard talk about abolishing the states: "The State Legislatures also ought to have some means of defending themselves against encroachments of the National Government." The legislatures should elect senators. They should determine for themselves laws governing the suffrage within their boundaries. They should be left free to declare a moratorium on payment of debts in times of economic upheaval. They should be protected from harassment by the federal courts and from overregulation of their militia. In July Mason grew to be more and more testy and negative in his reaction to what the majority of the Framers seemed willing to accept. The presidency was too strong. A triple executive was more to his liking, with one member from the South, one from the Middle States, and one from New England. Or failing that, a kind of privy council of six (two from each section) to surround and protect the chief executive. It was not proper that the president should be reelected, that he should appoint federal judges, or that a law should require a three-fourths vote (as was agreed to at one stage of the proceedings) to override his veto. The idea of a power to tax the exports of the states filled him with alarm, as did the idea of a standing army. The amending process was too cumbersome and would lead to oppression. And most important, it was not safe for the South to agree to navigation acts passed by a mere majority, or for the states and the people at large to do without a bill of rights restricting the power of the "sovereign."

As the discussion moved toward consensus, Mason grew impatient and acerbic and in his role as *vir bonus*—the plain, blunt man—rumbled about the hunger for power that hides behind "pretty speeches Replete with Patriotism and moral cant." It was "a privilege of age" to "speak without reserve." On August 31, he announced that he expected to oppose this Constitution. He did not like the compromise between the Deep South and New England on the slave trade and navigation acts. He did not like the omission of sumptuary laws needed to improve the "manners" of the people. He had some experience in writing constitutions, had composed a bill of rights copied in many of the states, and knew better than to surrender the public liberty. There would have to be a second convention. Stockjobbers and placemen were not to be given the substance of his state. Mason was present to the end and almost immediately after the signing wrote his "Objections to This Constitution of Government," which was published in newspapers throughout the country and distributed as a handbill. Washington was furious, and Madison appalled. But many in the Old Dominion clearly agreed with what Richard Henry Lee had written to Mason after receiving a report on the Constitution from his old friend: "If it should be established, either a tyranny will result from it, or it will be prevented by a Civil war."

In his "Objections," Mason had sounded the tocsin for the battle to come. No declaration of rights, no guarantee of the common law, an imbalance among the branches of government, and a judicial system "so constructed and extended, as to absorb and destroy the judiciaries of the several States." Mason had wanted a new constitution, but not this Constitution. He expected the general government to protect self-contained and self-sustaining local communities. But he had learned from a lifetime of study and experience that others might well prefer Leviathan: "When we reflect upon the insidious art of wicked and designing men, the various and plausible pretenses for continuing and increasing the inordinate lust of power in the few, we shall no longer be surprised that freeborn man hath been enslaved, and that those very means which were contrived for his preservation have been perverted to his ruin."

In the Virginia ratification convention of June 1788, George Mason and Patrick Henry were the leaders of the Antifederalists. Mason, dressed in somber black, moved that the agenda provide for the consideration of the Constitution *seriatim*—section by section. Henry, on the other hand, ranged freely from fissure to fissure, flaw to flaw, weaving together a broad indictment of the whole. The two old-fashioned republicans had settled on this strategic division of responsibilities before they entered the hall, arm in arm. The Virginia convention was an adversarial proceeding, not a process of deliberation like the Constitutional Convention in Philadelphia. The two formidable orators and defenders of regional things had come to Richmond for a kind of vindication, for they had been subject to villainous abuse. Mason was called a "poor old man" who by reason of age had lost his wits. This argument was suggested in Mason's presence at the time of his election to the convention, and he replied to his inconsequential opponent: "Sir, when yours fail, nobody will ever discover it." Of Henry it was said that he wished to destroy the Union. His reply, foreshadowing arguments made by other southerners seventy years later, was that Union was to be valued only on certain terms. In the end, Henry and Mason were defeated, though a shift of four votes would have given them the victory. But in another sense, they won the day. For the issue in the convention came down finally to a choice between previous and subsequent amendments to the Constitution and to specifications concerning the proper understanding of the language of the document as it stood. Thanks to George Mason and Patrick Henry, Virginia spoke with a united voice in these regards.

George Mason attacked the handiwork of the Great Convention, still hoping to see "the beneficial parts of it retained." "Is it to be supposed," he asked, "that one National Government will suit so extensive a country, embracing so many climates, and containing inhabitants so very different in manners, habits, and customs?" Of the new government he maintained, its "power is calculated to annihilate totally the State Governments." If the "Sovereignty, Freedom and Independence" of each state are not guaranteed explicitly, no "inspiration" will be needed to predict what the taxing power, the appointive power, the judicial power, and a standing army can achieve. The Federalists did not trust their fellow citizens, even with the civil liberty guaranteed under the English Bill of Rights. Talk of disunionist objectives was a bugbear: "I have never in my whole life heard one single man deny the necessity and propriety of the union." The slave trade was an evil, but even worse was the absence from the Constitution of a guarantee "that will prevent the Northern and Eastern States from meddling with our whole property of that kind." Revision would require "a clause in the Constitution to secure us that property." The "necessary and proper" clause and the reference to "general welfare" were equally offensive. "Will powers remain to the States which are not expressly guarded and reserved?" Mason asked. "Artful sophistry and evasions" did not satisfy him. The Federalists were good at these, while they left the financial interests of their fellow Virginians open to "stockjobbers" and northern speculation. As to the judicial power, "There is no limitation. It goes to everything." It was an engine to bring on one great national consolidated government by slow and imperceptible stages. Hence, he preferred prior amendments or conditional ratification.

James Madison heard what was said, had a gastric attack, and denied that there was any "power . . . given to the general government to interpose with respect to property in slaves now held by the states." Edmund Randolph said the same. And John Marshall on the subject of the judicial power declared: "I hope no gentleman will think that a state will be called at the bar of the federal court. . . . It is not rational that the sovereign power shall be dragged before a court." Other Federalists rose to deny Mason's reading of the Constitution. Their assurances were sufficient to hold a few wavering votes in line, but not without subsequent amendments responsive to Mason's anxieties. George Wythe, Edmund Pendleton, and other moderate men had listened when Mason (borrowing from Saint Paul) had summarized, "They have done what they ought not to have done, and have left undone what they ought to have done." Amendments were drawn, and a conditional note was included in the instrument of ratification. Madison presented a version of them to the Congress of the United States in 1789. Mason was not entirely satisfied with Madison's version of Virginia's suggestions, but he acknowledged the improvement. With the additions of a stronger restraint on the judiciary, a clearer regulation of elections, a change in the size of the majority needed to pass navigation acts, and a presidential council which would exercise those "executive powers now vested in the Senate," he could at such a time "cheerfully put his hand and heart to the new government." These changes he was unable to secure.

One scholar has described George Mason in all his rectitude as the "veritable superego of Virginia politics"—the "conscience" of the Old Dominion. That he did not trust human nature so far as to give ambitious men great and unspecified powers is true. The proper conclusion of a revolution made against the abuse of authority was not to provide for a repetition of that abuse. Mason, like Patrick Henry, believed that the "genius" of a free society was best expressed through limited and time-tested institutions, working its way upward out of local communities represented by private and "independent" men. George Washington's charge against him, that he lacked the "manly candor" that would have permitted him to admit to "an error in his opinions," is lessened when one regards the whole pattern of Mason's life. In his last years he refused a Senate seat but visited with leading political figures on a regular basis as they passed through Alexandria and stopped at Gunston Hall. Amid his three-hundred slaves, his children, and his grandchildren, he presided like the patriarchs of old. He did not live to see the fulfillment of many of his darker prophecies, but he could write to his son, in some satisfaction, that his "conduct as a public man . . . has been such as will administer comfort to me when I shall most want it, and smooth the bed of death." Retirement and a private station were his preferences in any case. His political influence on his own period has for the most part been either distorted or grudgingly acknowledged, and his importance to the subsequent course of American politics has been generally overlooked. Yet Gen. Fitzhugh Lee wrote of him in the 1890s that George Mason was in large measure responsible for those features of the Constitution "which embrace the sovereignty of the states" and served as the intellectual preceptor of other southerners who withdrew from the Union in 1861. (See Robert A. Rutland, *George Mason, Reluctant Statesman* [Charlottesville: University Press of Virginia, 1963]; Helen Hill Miller, *George Mason, Gentleman Revolutionary* [Chapel Hill: University of North Carolina Press, 1975]; Pamela C. Copeland and Richard K. MacMaster, *The Five George Masons: Patriots and Planters of Virginia and Maryland* [Charlottesville: University Press of Virginia, 1975]; Duncan J. MacLeod, *Slavery, Race, and the American Revolution* [London: Cambridge University Press, 1974], pp. 38–39, 72–73, and passim; Edmund Randolph, *History of Virginia* [Charlottesville: University Press of Virginia, 1970]; Willi Paul Adams, *The First American Constitutions: Republican Ideology and the Making of the State Constitutions in the Revolutionary Era* [Chapel Hill: University of North Carolina Press, 1979]; Brent Tarter, "George Mason and the Conservation of Liberty," *Virginia Magazine of History and Biography* 99 [July 1991]: 279–304; Kate Mason Rowland, *The Life of George Mason, 1725–1792*, 2 vols. [New York: G. P. Putnam's Sons, 1892]; Marian Buckley Cox, *Glimpse of Glory: George Mason of Gunston Hall* [Richmond, Va.: Garrett & Massie, 1954]; Josephine F. Pacheco, ed., *The Legacy of George Mason* [Fairfax, Va.: George Mason University Press, 1983]; Robert A. Rutland, ed., *The Papers of George Mason*, 3 vols. [Chapel Hill: University of North Carolina Press, 1970]; Paul Eidelberg, *The Philosophy of the American Constitution: A Reinterpretation of the Intentions of the Founding Fathers* [New York: Free Press, 1968], pp. 53–56 and passim; Jack P. Greene, "Character, Persona, and Authority: A Study of Alternative Styles of Political Leadership in Revolutionary Virginia," in *The Revolutionary War in the South: Power, Conflict, and Leadership*, ed. Robert Higgins [Durham: Duke University Press, 1979], pp. 3–42.)

# GEORGE WYTHE

1726–June 8, 1806
Lawyer, jurist, professor, Virginia statesman, and signer of the Declaration of Independence

*One of the most distinguished men elected to be a delegate to the Constitutional Convention. Would most likely have exerted a considerable influence on the drafting of the Constitution had he not been called away from Philadelphia by illness in his family. Present in the Great Convention for only a few days, but present in spirit through his effect on two generations of political thought in Virginia. The unquestioned leader of the Virginia bar. A man of spotless reputation, called by many "the American Aristides." Mild Federalist, but closer in his basic attitudes to George Mason than to James Madison, James Wilson, or Gouverneur Morris. Devoted to the position that "not men but laws should be sovereign." An embodiment of the nomocratic, customary, and prescriptive tradition in English legal theory as it survived in America. Following the decision to seek independence, directly responsible for the preservation of the common law in Virginia as the leader of a committee (including Mason, Thomas Ludwell Lee, Edmund Pendleton, and his own former student, Thomas Jefferson) called upon to revise the Old Dominion's legal code. Coauthor of the instrument of ratification adopted by the Virginia Convention, which met to consider and judge the proposed U.S. Constitution in June of 1788.*

George Wythe was the second son of Thomas Wythe and Margaret Walker Wythe. His father was a member of the House of Burgesses, a man of property, and a great-grandson of Thomas Wythe, gentleman, who had immigrated to Virginia ca. 1680. For three generations George Wythe's progenitors had been, variously, justices of the Elizabeth City County courts, sheriffs, or members of the local vestry. His mother was the daughter of a wealthy Quaker and was the descendant of the learned and well-known Reverend George Keith. George Wythe was born at his father's plantation, Chesterville, on the Back River, Elizabeth City County, Virginia—a property that George inherited after the untimely death of his elder brother, Thomas, but then dissipated through youthful indiscretions. He was educated at home, chiefly by his accomplished mother, and at the College of William and Mary. Later he read law with his uncle by marriage, Stephen Dewey, and in 1746 was admitted to the Virginia bar in Prince George County. But most of the vast erudition for which in later years he was rightfully celebrated was a consequence of a lifetime's habit of disciplined private study.

Wythe established a legal practice in Spotsylvania County, where he married the sister of his partner, John Lewis. He made no name for himself until 1754, when he served briefly as attorney general of the colony, and 1755, when he was elected to the House of Burgesses for Williamsburg—where he had moved and where he thereafter made his home, at least until the capital of Virginia was moved to Richmond. In Williamsburg and in York and Elizabeth City counties, Wythe slowly established a reputation. He was admitted to practice before the general court and, with the arrival of Gov. Francis Fauquier (who became his close friend), grew rapidly into the polished figure of his mature years. William Small (professor of mathematics and natural philosophy at the College of William and Mary) and the youthful Thomas Jefferson (then a student at the college) completed with Wythe and Governor Fauquier a small and select circle of wits. From 1758 to 1761 Wythe represented the college in the House of Burgesses and from 1761 to 1768, Elizabeth City County. From 1769 to 1775 he was clerk of the House and a master of the office. In 1768 he was mayor of Williamsburg. In 1769 he became a member of the William and Mary board of visitors and was called upon to regularize and publish an edition of Virginia's colonial laws. He handled correspondence with Virginia's agent in London and in 1774 was elected member of the Virginia Committee of Safety, the rulers of his state for almost two years. Finally, in 1775 he was chosen by his fellow Virginians to be one of their delegates to the Continental Congress.

During the years of conflict with British authority that preceded the outbreak of the Revolution, George Wythe rose to be one of the most respected members of the Virginia bar and a leader of the state legislature. Apart from the practice of his profession, Wythe found time to devote to seeking learning for its own sake, and for the training of young men such as Jefferson in the mysteries of the English legal tradition "from doomsday down." The father of his second wife, planter and architect Richard Taliaferro, built for him a fine house on Palace Green in the little capital city, a place that became a center of political conversation and planning. In the House of Burgesses it was Wythe who was called upon to speak for his colleagues in drafting a petition to the Crown against the adoption of the Stamp Act. Wythe's argument concerning the claims of colonials upon their inherited rights as Englishmen was so forceful and provocative that his fellow legislators tempered his language. He was perhaps the first colonial in North America to call for the political independence of the colonies from the authority of Parliament, but within an English commonwealth of nations. Wythe was also early to recognize the necessity for a complete separation from Great Britain and for a regular army to give substance to the language of revolution.

During his brief term in the Continental Congress Wythe was a vigorous supporter of the position of Richard Henry Lee and of the party that had grown impatient with further efforts to compromise with England. After signing the Declaration, he returned to Virginia to work on the revision of the legal code, to serve as speaker of the House of Delegates (1777), and to design the Virginia state seal—the belligerent symbol of republican intransigence with the appropriate motto, *Sic Semper Tyrannis*, "thus ever to tyrants." In 1778 Wythe became one of the three original judges of the Virginia High Court of Chancery and in 1779 professor of law and police at William and Mary, the first American to hold such a position and the second or third in the English-speaking world. As professor, Wythe literally created an academic discipline, initiating such procedures as moot courts and mock legislatures to supplement conventional lectures and tutorials. Wythe trained the first lawyers formally educated in America—among them John Marshall, James Monroe, and Henry Clay—and gave to the entire southern bar a lasting impetus and direction. He continued in his professorship until his duties as judge required his relocation to Richmond in 1791. As chancellor (alone in this distinction for thirteen years, after the court of chancery was left with only one judge) and ex-officio member of the state superior court, he served until his death in 1806.

Chancellor Wythe came to Philadelphia for the Constitutional Convention on May 15 and departed, because of the mortal illness of his wife, on June 4. His only significant function during the Convention was in drawing up the rules that governed its operations. But he had a larger role to play in Virginia's pivotal ratification convention. Much of the time during those deliberations Wythe was called upon to chair a committee of the whole. But on June 24, 1788, he stepped aside from that post and moved for the adoption of the proposed Constitution, with recommended amendments attached. Wythe submitted a list of corrective alterations, an act that led the distinguished legal historian Charles Warren to describe him as "the father of the Bill of Rights." Wythe's personal authority with many in the Antifederalist camp allowed him to bring the business to a head in a way that warmer advocates of the proposed government could not. Most particularly because of the Antifederalist context within which he urged ratification, he could appear to speak for Virginia and not some distant abstraction. Wythe's plea for the Constitution was in keeping with his authority as master of the ancient law. Liberty, he argued, cannot exist outside of society. Theories concerning the aboriginal "rights of man" were not to his taste: "Experience . . . is the best guide." He admitted the imperfections of the document under discussion. Yet, the experience of Americans during and after the Revolution (a course he rehearsed) had demonstrated that a stronger government was necessary for the preservation of the various societies joined by the Union. That it was Wythe who called for the question was assuredly no accident. Of the Federalists, only he was safe against ad hominem attack. Concerning the disinterestedness of his motives not a word could be said.

In his last years George Wythe continued to occupy a position of honor in the Virginia courts, to run his own law school in Richmond, and to personify the public virtue of his state. A man of small physical stature, he seemed to shrink with the lengthening of years. Yet he kept his intellectual vigor and his curiosity. At seventy, he mastered the Hebrew language. He taught a special course in literature, ancient and modern, for the young people of his city. (And he learned to write with his left hand when the other was broken.)

Wythe deplored the efforts of the French to export their revolution to America. He disapproved of Jay's Treaty and of Hamilton's view of "implied powers." He presided over public meetings called to consider these developments. But he was most himself on the bench: "[If the whole legislature] should attempt to overleap the bounds, prescribed to them . . . , I in administering the public justice of the country, will meet the united powers at my seat in this tribunal; and pointing to the Constitution, will say to them, 'Here is the limit of your authority; and hither shall you go but no further.'" Such were his words in the case of *Commonwealth* v. *Caton*. Law should be sovereign, not men. Until the end, at eighty, he was jealous of the public liberty: always the man who had written (speaking for his neighbors), in limiting the scope of Virginia's approval of the

Constitution, "[We] declare and make known that the powers granted under the Constitution being derived from the people of the United States, may be resumed by them whenever the same shall be perverted to their injury or oppression and that every power not granted remains with them, and at their will." Wythe's mark on the life of the mind in the South was indelible. He was a source of continuity with the strict school of common-law jurisprudence. And his federalism was of a kind that would not preclude a southern secession in the decades yet to come, particularly if the fundamental rule of law seemed to be in doubt. (See Burke Davis, *A Williamsburg Galaxy* [Williamsburg, Va.: Colonial Williamsburg, 1968], pp. 149–157; Imogene Brown, *American Aristides: A Biography of George Wythe* [Rutherford, N.J.: Fairleigh Dickinson University Press, 1981]; William Clarkin, *Serene Patriot: A Life of George Wythe* [Albany, N.Y.: Alan Publications, 1970]; John Sanderson, *Biography of the Signers to the Declaration of Independence,* vol. 2 [Philadelphia: R. W. Pomeroy, 1822], pp. 157–180; W. Edwin Hemphill, "George Wythe, the Colonial Briton" [Ph. D. dissertation, University of Virginia, 1937]; David John Mays, *Edmund Pendleton, 1721–1803: A Biography,* 2 vols. [Cambridge, Mass.: Harvard University Press, 1952]; Hugh Blair Grigsby, *The History of the Virginia Convention of 1788* [New York: Da Capo Press, 1969]; Allan Dudley Jones, "The Character and Service of George Wythe," *Reports of the Virginia State Bar Association* 44 [1932]: 325–329; Oscar L. Shewmake, *George Wythe: Teacher, Lawyer, Jurist, Statesman* [Richmond, Va.: n.p., 1950]; Edwin Lee Shepard, "George Wythe," in *The Virginia Law Reports before 1880,* ed. W. H. Bryson [Charlottesville: University of Virginia Press, 1977], pp. 90–95.)

# JAMES MCCLURG
1746–July 9, 1823
Physician, banker, speculator, and minor politician

*As much out of his element in the Great Convention as any delegate to that assembly. Yet a man of fixed and decisive political opinions. A high Federalist, concerned with the security of large investments and fearful of social instability. Present in the Constitutional Convention because Washington and Madison (who arranged for his appointment when Patrick Henry and Richard Henry Lee refused to attend) could count on his support should Mason, Blair, and Randolph pull in another direction. A man of means, a holder of public securities, and a well-respected member of the medical profession.*

James McClurg was born near Hampton in Elizabeth City County, Virginia, where his father, Dr. Walter McClurg, was superintendent of Hampton Small Pox

Hospital and a very successful physician. After careful preparation in an atmosphere of privilege, young James attended the College of William and Mary, from which he was graduated in 1762 having made a good record. He then continued his studies in medicine at the University of Edinburgh, from which he received the M.D. in 1770. His thesis, "De Calore," was well respected; in 1772 he published a monograph, *Experiments upon the Human Bile and Reflections on the Biliary Secretions,* which was translated into many languages. At that time Edinburgh was perhaps the finest medical school in the world, and McClurg did additional postgraduate research in Paris and London.

In 1773 McClurg returned to Virginia, but he was not politically active before the Revolution. However, once the war broke out, he served as surgeon of the Virginia militia and as physician general and director of hospitals for the state. In 1779 he was appointed professor of anatomy and medicine at the College of William and Mary, but there is no clear record that he ever assumed the post. McClurg moved to Richmond when the capital of Virginia was relocated there. Eventually he was recognized as one of the leading physicians in his state and was elected president of the Virginia Medical Society in 1820 and 1821. Volume One of *The Philadelphia Journal of Medical and Physical Sciences* was dedicated to "the Elegant Scholar and Accomplished Physician, Dr. McClurg." He served one term as a member of the Virginia Council of State, and was in that office when selected to play a larger role in Philadelphia.

McClurg attended the Great Convention until the last week in July. He may have left when the Convention adjourned to let the Committee of Detail prepare a draft reflecting the agreements reached during that month. Madison wrote McClurg urging him to return, and their correspondence continued throughout the following weeks. While serving as a delegate, the Virginia physician urged that the proposed federal Congress be given a veto over legislation in the states. Perhaps at Madison's request, he made one other significant motion. On July 17, he recommended that the president be elected to serve "on good behavior"—for life, unless his impeachment seemed necessary. In effect, this resolution would have produced "an elective monarchy." The suggestion was not well received, since in the matter of executive authority, as in much else, McClurg was too much the "high-toned" Federalist for his colleagues. Indeed, he went so far as to raise the question of the president's need for a military force—militia or a standing army—to enforce his will. No more explosive issue came before the Convention.

On McClurg's return to Virginia, he reported to Madison that the Constitution would be supported in the "towns" and by "the friends of Order." He referred to Pennsylvania accounts of a "tendency of Insurrection" in Virginia and grumbled of "continued depravations of manners" and threats to suspend payment of debts. He deplored the popular leaders of his state. His view of the proposed federal authority was that it was necessary to prevent "anarchy and civil convulsions."

During Washington's administration, James McClurg became one of the original directors of the Bank of the United States. There is some evidence that he was proposed as a successor to Thomas Jefferson as secretary of state. Yet he was put aside as he had been when Madison had mentioned him for an equivalent assignment under the Articles—"because he was subject to a charge of speculation"—and the post went to his friend Edmund Randolph. For a time he continued on the Council of State, and he was three times mayor of Richmond (1797, 1800, 1803). It was agreed by all his acquaintances that no more loyal Federalist was to be found in Richmond. In the history of southern politics, he is to be remembered as an evidence of Madison's skill in political tactics and as a great anomaly. (See Robert M. Slaughter, "James McClurg," in *American Medical Biographies,* ed. Howard A. Kelly and W. L. Burrage [Baltimore: Norman, Remington, 1920], pp. 731–732; W. B. Blanton, *Medicine in Virginia in the Eighteenth Century* [Richmond, Va.: William Byrd Press, 1931], pp. 328–335; Forrest McDonald, *We the People: The Economic Origins of the Constitution* [Chicago: University of Chicago Press, 1958], pp. 73, 88–89; and Robert A. Rutland et al., ed., *The Papers of James Madison,* vol. 10 [Chicago: University of Chicago Press, 1977], pp. 120, 134–135, 154–155, 157, 161–162, 165–166, and 233–234.)

# JOHN BLAIR, JR.

1732–August 31, 1800
Lawyer, jurist, and political leader of the Revolution
in Virginia

*A Federalist by way of prudence. From the early days of the Revolution, in search for some authority to replace the Crown. Uncertain in his approach to independence from Great Britain, holding on to the hope of some continuing formal connection as long as he could. Also uncertain in his approach to the creation of a stronger federal government. Chosen as a delegate to the Great Convention to represent the Virginia establishment, as one of the old "ruling class," and for his learning in the law. But not always willing to vote with Washington, Madison, and McClurg, nor to support every particular in the Virginia Plan as presented by Gov. Edmund Randolph. A highly respected figure, though he never spoke in any of the sessions of the Convention.*

John Blair was born at Williamsburg, the son of John Blair and Mary Monro Blair, the daughter of the Reverend John and Christian Monro. He was the grandson of Archibald Blair, an Edinburgh-trained physician, and great-nephew of James ("Commissary") Blair, Virginia deputy of the bishop of London, founder of the College of William and Mary, and the leading citizen of the colony in his time. John Blair, Sr., was acting governor of Virginia (in 1758 and again in 1768), deputy auditor general (1728–1732), auditor general (1732–1771), member of the House of Burgesses (1734–1741), clerk of the council (1741–1743), and a member of that body until 1770, when forced to resign by the infirmities of great age. From 1763 he was a member of the Virginia Committee of Correspondence and a Whig legalist who doubted the power of Parliament to place an internal tax upon Virginians.

John Blair, Jr., grew up in an atmosphere of privilege and intense political concern—a very conservative atmosphere. He was educated at the College of William and Mary and in the Middle Temple (1755–1756), where he was a protégé of his father's old friend, Gov. Robert Dinwiddie.

Upon his return to Virginia, young Blair established a successful practice of law in Williamsburg and appeared before the general court, "where he enjoyed a respectable share of the business before that tribunal." From 1766 to 1770 he sat in the House of Burgesses as the representative of the College of William and Mary, in which role he acquired a reputation for conservatism, gentleness, and gravity. Moreover, even in those years he exhibited "that strict attention to his dress which was the characteristic of the colonial regime; . . . [a quality] he preserved to the last." He opposed Patrick Henry's Stamp Act Resolves of 1765, but he signed the Virginia Association of June 22, 1770, which called for a boycott on the importation of British goods until the Townshend Duties were repealed, and he endorsed the Association of May 1774, calling for a meeting of the colonies in a Continental Congress. Yet he continued to maintain that peaceful means of protesting the policies of the British government should be explored in all detail before harsher measures were applied. He was a member of the Privy Council from 1776 to 1778 and was a member of Virginia's constitutional convention of 1776, where he served on the committee called upon to draft a plan of government. In 1778, Blair was elected by a joint vote of the two houses of the Virginia legislature as a judge of the general court, of which body he was chosen chief justice in 1779.

Blair faithfully attended almost every session of the Great Convention, even though he kept silent outside the Virginia caucus. He opposed control of money bills by the House of Representatives and, along with his fellow Virginians (except Madison), reacted with alarm at the idea of an export tax. He agreed with George Mason that the election of the executive should be in the charge of the state legislatures. For a time he favored a plural executive. He had doubts about the document finally produced, yet he voted for the Constitution since he was convinced that further indecision would bring chaos and ruin. Blair was also a Federalist delegate to the 1788 Virginia ratification convention, where he was once again quiet but supported the motion for approval.

He was a planter and slaveholder as well as a judge. But his real life was in the courts, and there he was not reluctant to speak his mind. In 1780, he became a judge on the Virginia High Court of Chancery and a member of the court of appeals. In 1782 he took part in the celebrated case of *The Commonwealth of Virginia* v. *Caton et al.,* in which he and George Wythe declared (but did not exercise) the power of their court to rule an act of the Virginia legislature unconstitutional. In 1787, he participated in the case of *Commonwealth* v. *Posey,* in which the applicability of English law and precedent to American court decisions was upheld. After the passage of the Judiciary Act of 1789, President Washington appointed Blair an associate justice of the U.S. Supreme Court, a post in which Blair served until 1796. As a member of the High Court, Blair continued to be a strong Federalist; in *Chisholm* v. *Georgia* (1793), he maintained that there was a federal jurisdiction in disputes between citizens living in one state and governments of other member states. (The impingement on state sovereignty embodied in this ruling was explicitly rebuked in the adoption of the Eleventh Amendment to the Constitution.) However, unlike some of his associates in this decision, Blair did not fall back on "implied" powers or deny the sovereignty of the states in many questions.

The burden of riding the circuit disposed Blair to retire from the Supreme Court. He spent his last four years at home in Williamsburg, where he is buried in the graveyard of Bruton Parish Church, near the place where he had worshipped since the days of his youth. (See J. Elliott Drinard, "John Blair, Jr., 1732–1800," *Reports of the Virginia State Bar Association* 39 [1927]: 436–449; Fred L. Israel, "John Blair, Jr.," in *The Justices of the United States Supreme Court, 1789–1969: Their Lives and Major Opinions,* vol. 1, ed. Israel and Leon Friedman [New York: R. R. Bowker/Chelsea House, 1969], pp. 109–115; Robert G. Ferris, ed., *Signers of the Constitution* [Washington, D.C.: National Park Service, 1976], pp. 145–146; Frederick Horner, *History of the Blair, Banister, and Braxton Families* [Philadelphia: J. B. Lippincott, 1898]; Forrest McDonald, *We the People: The Economic Origins of the Constitution* [Chicago: University of Chicago Press, 1958], pp. 74, 86 ff.)

# EDMUND RANDOLPH

August 10, 1753–September 12, 1813
Lawyer, political leader of Virginia, and American
statesman

*By turns, both Federalist and Antifederalist—the former by reason of temperamental caution and circumstance, the latter by conviction. In the context of the Constitutional Convention, perhaps most properly described as an enthusiastic advocate of a very limited federal union: an instrument of government stronger than the Articles of Confederation but much milder than what the Convention produced. According to his biographer, John J. Reardon, animated by "the idea of a national government neither dependent on nor destructive of the authority of the state governments." Yet shocking to high Federalists when he "strongly implied that he considered the preservation of the ultimate power of the states more important than the Union itself." In the Great Convention, a troubled figure. In even greater difficulty during the Virginia ratification convention of June 1788. Driven to support the proposed Constitution by fear of the alternative to adoption (as he understood that dark prospect)—or by his desire for the good opinion of the leaders of his state. Called a "trimmer" by many, and described as "the Benedict Arnold of Virginia" by his old ally, George Mason. The Framer whose introduction of a revised plan of government determined the shape of the entire Constitutional Convention, whose motion (much revised) produced the resulting Constitution, who then scrupled to sign it, and who later was responsible for defending it in Richmond when it was considered by representatives of the people of his state.*

*A Federalist per se only for a constitution never written, but a supporter of the document produced in Philadelphia because the other horn of the dilemma (riot, disunion, "democratic licentiousness") looked even more dangerous to the good of the country. A vigorous advocate for a bill of rights containing explicit limits on the power of the federal courts and of the other branches of the general government, especially with regard to the states. The uncertain and ambiguous heir to one of Virginia's most honored names, an aristocratic republican who hoped to preserve the kind of society in which the Randolphs had played so great a role. Brought up in an atmosphere of privilege balanced with responsibility to do public service and practice law. Later, in a partisan political arena, the victim of his own habitual search for a "middle way" and for the grounds of consensus.*

Edmund Jenings Randolph was born at Tazewell Hall, near Williamsburg. He was the son of John Randolph, clerk of the House of Burgesses and the Crown's attorney general, and Ariana Jenings Randolph, daughter of the attorney general of Maryland. Randolph's uncle (and role model) was the vast and jovial Peyton Randolph, a prominent public figure in the Virginia of his day and (at various times) attorney general and speaker of the House of Burgesses. Edmund's grandfather was Sir John Randolph, the first native Virginian to be knighted—a man of considerable distinction who held most of the offices that in due course came to his sons and grandson. Sir John's grandfather, the founder of the dynasty, was the fabled William Randolph of "Turkey Island." In a deferential society, where names had a negotiable value, Edmund Randolph started life with a genuine advantage.

Though by the times prevented from following the family pattern with a period in the Middle Temple, young Edmund was educated at the College of William and Mary and in the law offices of his father. However, the onset of the American Revolution greatly complicated the established way of life for Edmund Randolph. When prospects pointed toward armed conflict with Great Britain, John Randolph would not lift his hand against his sovereign. Therefore, upon the disestablishment of Virginia's colonial government, he removed to England, selling all his property, and refusing to act for either side. Peyton Randolph, who had made Edmund his heir, was cautious and measured in his reactions to offensive conduct by Crown and Parliament. But in the end he sided with his neighbors—and his nephew Edmund with him. However, Peyton Randolph died in 1775, while acting as president for the Continental Congress. At that time, Edmund Randolph, who was serving as aide-de-camp to Gen. George Washington, was forced to return to Virginia, and without the comforting auspices of family, to organize a life of his own. No wonder that he could say, "I am a child of the Revolution." Yet he remained at the same time a Randolph, a man of the old prescription in important respects.

Upon his return to Williamsburg, Edmund Randolph was elected by his neighbors to the Virginia constitutional convention of 1776, the youngest member of that body at the age of twenty-three. At this time he became engaged to Elizabeth Nicholas, the daughter of Robert Carter Nicholas, also a member of the convention. Randolph sat on a great many committees. Because he had earlier spent some months as judge on a court of admiralty, he was called upon for information regarding the handling of Tory property. Edmund Pendleton, who was presiding, also assigned him to a grand committee, which prepared a declaration of rights and a general plan of state government. Another committee acting in this same convention sent instructions for independence to Virginia delegates at the Continental Congress meeting in Philadelphia.

In the Virginia convention, Randolph behaved in keeping with his upbringing and connections. Both he and his future father-in-law were made uneasy by talk of "equality" in a slaveholding state, though George Mason assured the house that only citizens were covered by such language. There was a general fear that they had acted with "too great an indifference to futurity." Randolph did nothing to assert himself or to presume upon the "old lions" who had enjoyed power in the time of his father and uncle and who were accustomed to ruling the state. Equal or not, no reapportionment for the frontier counties was attempted. And, according to Randolph, it was agreed "that every body and individual came into the Revolution with their rights and was to continue to enjoy them as they existed under the former government."

Under the new state government, Randolph was appointed attorney general of Virginia—a post he held for ten years. In 1779 and again in 1781 and 1782, he was elected to the Congress, where he became a friend of James Madison, who had served with him in the Virginia constitutional convention. His first term in Congress was uneventful, and he soon returned to Virginia. For a time he was mayor of Williamsburg and clerk of the House of Delegates. Moreover, he practiced a little law on his own, because the business of attorney general did not fully occupy his time—or fill his purse. But when he went back to Philadelphia, British armies were moving in and out of Virginia, and he was convinced of the priority of national concerns. He also recognized the opportunity for service in the formation of national policy. In these months in Congress, Randolph's awareness of the necessity for a stronger general government, with real powers, grew rapidly, and he supported an amendment to the Articles that would have empowered Congress to collect a duty on imports, though he questioned the power of Congress to charter the Bank of North America. With Madison, he served on a committee asked to draw up a plan for strengthening the government. He appealed to the states, in the name of the Congress, to send their overdue payments to the treasury for military supplies. After 1782, Randolph was a moderate nationalist—though he had no desire to see the states reduced to insignificance.

Back in Virginia during the years following his service in the Congress, Randolph played his part in a concerted effort to strengthen the Union. But, at the same time, he came to believe, after watching postwar Virginia, that a well-ordered state government could, in most respects, take care of its own. In 1786, at the age of thirty-three, he was elected governor of Virginia. From that position of authority he assisted in arranging the September 1786 Annapolis Convention, for which, as a member, he wrote the first draft of an appeal to the states—an appeal that led to the Constitutional Convention of the following May. Randolph had the major role in selecting the Virginia delegates to the Philadelphia meeting, was personally responsible for persuading his old commander in chief, General Washington, to attend, and was present himself to speak "officially" for the Old Dominion. The strategy followed by the Virginia delegation as a whole was well considered. They decided during private deliberations that the best course was to have Governor Randolph, well spoken and a fine figure of a man, move the consideration of a plan of government essentially the handiwork of James Madison. (Madison held no great office and was not a powerful speaker or, at this point in his career, a person of presence.) Those delegates of "associated republics" (as Randolph called them) who were met in this Convention would need a little goading. It would be good to have a state governor remind them of their present need for "sufficient checks against the democracy"—debtors, mobs, and men like Captain Shays. A constitution could be a law to restrain feckless majorities, to forbid the making of "wanton laws," and to overawe the anarchic and silence the perverse. Therefore, on May 29, once the Great Convention had been properly organized, Edmund Randolph rose and proposed a formula for a completely new government, not a revision of the Articles.

After giving the Convention a definition of its "business," Governor Randolph was quiet for some time, speaking only to refute emphatically charges that he intended to threaten the integrity of the states. The purpose of union would be to protect the states from popular tumult within and from foreign enemies without. Then he began to get restless. He did not like the compromise on representation in the Senate. He wanted a plural executive to secure the interests of the sections. He insisted on a two-thirds vote of both houses of the proposed congress for laws regulating commerce. He was irritated by northern unwillingness to count three-fifths of the slaves as a security for the "peculiar institution." Moreover, apportionment should be attached to a census required by the fundamental law, otherwise the legislature might feel free to perpetuate itself. And he insisted on a clear specification of all federal powers, with a statement attached declaring that only those stated powers had been granted by the sovereign states. Finally, limitations on the authority of the federal judiciary should be written into the Constitution. On September 10, 1787, Randolph announced that without these and other changes in the document as proposed, and without provision for a second convention following recommendations for amendments from the states, he would not be a party to the business now almost complete. With Elbridge Gerry of Massachusetts and George Mason of his own state, Randolph attended the entire Constitutional Convention and refused to sign the proposed instrument of government. According to his apology, he could not endorse a plan that would "end in Tyranny."

This resolve on Randolph's part to stand against the majority of the most distinguished political company ever assembled in America did not survive his return to Virginia. And from the moment of his first vacillation back toward the Federalists, his career spiraled slowly downward toward ignominy. First, once back in Virginia, Randolph saw that the reception of the Constitution was mixed, that states were ratifying, and that more debate over what it should include would not produce a larger consensus. He saw also that the Union might divide into smaller confederacies and that it would be "expedient" to ratify and then revise. Therefore, Randolph began to rumor that his failure to sign did not necessarily mean opposition to ratification. He was uncertain as to how he might vote on the question, but he did not let the Antifederalists know how he was leaning. After all, he had written a pamphlet criticizing the Constitution, and he had been elected by people who did not care for it. Randolph delayed important communications between the states—particularly with New York, whose governor was against ratification. This strategy prevented the attachment of the prior amendments he supposedly favored. Then, in Richmond, he surprised all Virginia by supporting unconditional ratification. No wonder that Patrick Henry reflected on Randolph's character in the ratification debates. No wonder that George Washington made Randolph the first attorney general of the United States. No wonder that Randolph prospered greatly. And no surprise that Thomas Jefferson called him "the poorest chameleon I ever saw, having no colour of his own, and reflecting that nearest him."

But Edmund Randolph was still unable to settle into a consistent position after leading the Federalists in the debates at the ratification convention. Some elements in his view of the Union would never satisfy certain members of that party. He defined the federal power in reference to its limitations, not its scope: it contained no authority over the "existing state of slavery," no sanction for sponsorship of "internal improvements," or for chartering a bank. Indeed, no Virginian present in the Great Convention had "the smallest suspicion of the abolition of slavery" by any federal action or of any other innovation not based on "powers expressly given." As for the general-welfare clause, the "sweeping clause," it could refer to nothing but a limitation on the power to tax—not to a license to enact legislation that might seem useful. Even when the Bill of Rights passed the Congress and came to be considered by the Virginia legislature, Randolph continued to complain that the powers reserved to the states by the Ninth and Tenth Amendments were not named *seriatim* and the powers given the federal government likewise made specific. Randolph could not accept that he was defending the position of the "other side." A world divided into permanent political parties, where politicians made lasting commitments, was not to his taste. Nor could he comprehend why his political habits angered the leaders of the early republic. Yet even when he followed influence or bowed to a drift in popular sentiment, Randolph persisted in searching for a "middle way."

As the first attorney general of the United States, Randolph tried not to take a position in the quarrel between Thomas Jefferson and Alexander Hamilton. His ostensible objective was to serve George Washington—to be above faction. Yet he opposed the plan for the Bank of the United States as unconstitutional, opposed other parts of the Hamiltonian system, and wrote essays in the press defending Jefferson's foreign policy. And when Jefferson resigned, the Sage of Monticello persuaded President Washington to make Randolph his successor as secretary of state. From January 1794 until August 1795, Randolph occupied a position of genuine power. In meetings of the cabinet, he continued to dispute with the high Federalists. Randolph was for the most part a successful secretary of state. He moved Spain toward the Treaty of San Lorenzo, which opened New Orleans and the Mississippi to the commerce of the West. He gave good direction to John Jay, chief justice of the U.S. Supreme Court, who had been sent to England to negotiate a treaty arranging for improved commercial relations and resolving certain disputes. But Jay's Treaty, drawn largely to Hamilton's specifications, created a partisan cry of outrage among Republicans throughout the United States. The Federalists, for their part, were angry with Randolph for agreeing with critics of the treaty. Their hostility found an instrument to serve their purpose in dispatches from Genet's replacement in North America, Joseph Fauchet, that were captured by the British and turned over to the friends of England in the United States. These dispatches contained reports of the French diplomat's conversations with Secretary Randolph—reports that suggested the secretary had been improperly confidential and had asked Fauchet for loans for certain American merchants who favored close ties with France. The dispatches were shown to President Washington, who angrily demanded an explanation.

Randolph resigned under a cloud of suspicion of dishonesty and disloyalty. Thus, at the age of forty-two, his public career was at an end. Randolph prepared and published in his own defense *A Vindication of Mr. Randolph's Resignation* (1795), but it convinced almost no one. On the whole, James Madison's judgment of the episode stands up rather well: "His greatest enemies will not easily persuade themselves that he [Randolph] was under a corrupt influence of France and his best friend can't save him from the self-condemnation of his political career as explained by himself."

Randolph returned to Richmond, and in the remaining eighteen years of his life engaged in a successful practice of law. He had little to do with politics in his retirement, though he was plagued by charges that he was responsible for a $49,154.89 shortage in the accounts for diplomatic and consular funds of the Department of State. Eventually the claim was paid, though the Treasury Department later added to it more than $60,000 of compound interest. Sixty-five years after Randolph's death, the attacks on his probity were refuted and withdrawn.

Randolph approved of the Virginia and Kentucky Resolutions of 1798, but he spoke of secession as a constitutional last resort. For the instruction of young men, he sometimes reminisced about his days in the Great Convention. But the important work of his old age was a history of Virginia through the Revolution— a work not published until 1970. The theme of this labor of love was the character of Virginia public leadership produced through negotiated consensus, a species of leadership made possible by English gentlemen who joined no party and who put the good of the patria above their own careers. (See John J. Reardon, *Edmund Randolph: A Biography* [New York: Macmillan, 1975]; M. D. Conway, *Omitted Chapters of History Disclosed in the Life and Papers of Edmund Randolph* [New York: G. P. Putnam's Sons, 1888]; Forrest McDonald, *E Pluribus Unum: The Formation of the American Republic, 1776–1790* [Indianapolis: Liberty Press, 1979], pp. 339–340 and passim; Norman K. Risjord, *Chesapeake Politics, 1781–1800* [New York: Columbia University Press, 1978]; Edmund Randolph, *History of Virginia*, edited and with an introduction by Arthur H. Shaffer [Charlottesville: University Press of Virginia, 1970]; Charles F. Hobson, "The Early Career of Edmund Randolph, 1753–1789" [Ph.D. dissertation, Emory University, 1971]; Keith B. Berwick, "Moderates in Crisis: The Trials of Leadership in Revolutionary Virginia" [Ph.D. dissertation, University of Chicago, 1959]; H. J. Eckenrode, *The Randolphs: The Story of a Virginia Family* [Indianapolis: Bobbs-Merrill, 1946]; Irving Brant, "Edmund Randolph, Not Guilty," *William and Mary Quarterly* 7 [April 1950]: 180–198.)

# North Carolina

# William Richardson Davie
June 20, 1756–November 29, 1820
Lawyer, planter, statesman, military hero

*With Charles Cotesworth Pinckney, one of the mildest of southern Federalists, though ever faithful to that creed. Forced to see the necessity for an effective central government by his service as commissary general for North Carolina and the armies of Gen. Nathanael Greene. Son of Archibald and Mary Richardson Davie. Born at Whitehaven in Egremont Parish, County Cumberland, England. Of distinguished Scottish ancestry in both the paternal and maternal lines. Migrated with his family to the Waxhaw settlement in South Carolina. Educated at Queen's Museum, Charlotte, North Carolina, and at the College of New Jersey, where he took a B.A. with the class of 1776. Began the study of law under Judge Spruce Macay at Salisbury, North Carolina, but interrupted his studies to enlist in the patriot cause in 1777. Served under Gen. Allen Jones of the Halifax District Militia, later his father-in-law. Was successively lieutenant, captain, and major of cavalry. Wounded while leading a charge at Stono, near Charleston, in 1779. After recovery, commander of a legion of Carolina irregulars, which he raised with his own funds. Following Camden, as colonel of his partisans, one of the major obstacles to British conquest of the South, especially distinguished by his check of Cornwallis at Charlotte Court House in September of 1780. For the remainder of the war, as commissary general for Greene, part of the inner council of staff officers who planned the defeat of the British armies in the South. At the end of the war, one of the most popular men in the Carolinas. Tall and of a commanding presence, gifted in speech, and connected by marriage with powerful people in his state. Admitted to the North Carolina bar in 1780 and active in his profession during the following two decades.*

In the Great Convention, William Richardson Davie spoke infrequently but much to the point. He favored a union "partly federal, partly national," in which local prejudices and interests "could not be denied to exist" and had a right to representation. He spoke bluntly of northern unwillingness to allow the South political representation for its slaves and declared, "if the Eastern States meant therefore to exclude them . . . the business was at an end." Originally he had preferred that the Senate be weighted to represent wealth and property. But he changed his position after listening to the arguments of the delegates from the smaller states and helped swing the members from North Carolina behind the compromise for the equality of the states in the upper house of Congress. Davie left the Constitutional Convention late in August, convinced that most of the great questions had been decided. With James Iredell, he led the fight for ratification in North Carolina. During the first ratification convention at Hillsborough, Davie carried much of the debate for the Federalist cause and, though defeated, laid a groundwork for final approval in a second convention held at Fayetteville on November 16–21, 1789. His publication of the debates of the first convention of July 1788 and his efforts in the composition of pamphlet literature and in the formation of a pro-Constitution political organization were recognized as having been instrumental in bringing North Carolina into the Union.

From 1786 to 1798, Davie sat in the lower house of the North Carolina legislature, the House of Commons. He was active in behalf of the establishment and administration of the University of North Carolina, selected its faculty, and drew up its curriculum. He was responsible for ordering the revision and codification of the laws of his state, arranged for cession of Tennessee to the Union, was chairman of North Carolina's boundary commission, and commanded the state's militia. In 1798, he was elected governor of North Carolina by a legislature dominated by a large majority of Jeffersonians—a measure of his popularity. President Adams appointed Davie brigadier general in the regular army during the mobilization against France and in 1799 sent him as part of a peace commission to Paris, where he was instrumental in negotiating the Treaty of Mortefontaine in 1800.

General Davie returned from his diplomatic adventure to a North Carolina with a changing political atmosphere. The Democratic-Republicans had achieved as part of the "Revolution of 1800" an internal transformation of the state; and for the rest of his life, Davie, by reason of the firmness of his convictions, was a private citizen of little political influence. He failed in 1803 in his efforts to win a seat in the House of Representatives and disgusted with politics retired two years later to his plantation at Tivoli, in Lancaster County, South Carolina, to his books and to his passion for scientific farming. Davie hated Jacobins and electoral condescension. In reaction to the French Revolution, he recommended for the federal service only officers "untainted in any manner by French politics or principles." He was opposed to the War of 1812 because he believed it was motivated by domestic politics and because he regarded England in its struggle with Napoleon as the defender of the "civilized community of man." Indeed, he looked forward to the extermination of the French emperor and his revolutionary armies, adding, "These mad men possess nothing upon which you can certainly calculate, no moral principle, no fixed political data: they seem to have no system but anarchy, no plan but plunder."

Davie refused all appointment under the Democratic–Republicans. Yet he recommended against support for Aaron Burr as an alternative to Jefferson. Though consistent in his federalism, he was always a Federalist of the southern variety. When New England threatened secession in 1814, he maintained that option had been left to the states in the Philadelphia Convention. And he rejoiced in the triumph of American arms at New Orleans. Furthermore, when his friend Justice James Iredell dissented from the decision of a northern Federalist majority of the High Court in the case of *Chisholm* v. *Georgia*, Davie concurred vehemently, observing that Justice James Wilson's argument from the "spirit of the Constitution" and the implied powers read like a "rhapsody" or a radical poem, but not like law. Iredell in his dissent had held that the states were "sovereign as to all powers not expressly delegated to the Federal Government by the Constitution." Davie concluded, in support of his old companion, that there could be no limit to a government if it were free to set aside the law whenever it found "moral" excuse for such innovations. He had never been a supporter of that teleocratic kind of Federalism. Instead, he was one of those aristocratic Old Whigs who gave to the nation its original political configuration and impetus. (See Blackwell P. Robinson, *William R. Davie* [Chapel Hill: University of North Carolina Press, 1957]; Jackson Turner Main, *Political Parties before the Constitution* [Chapel Hill: University of North Carolina Press, 1973], pp. 311–317; Lisle A. Rose, *Prologue to Democracy: The Federalists in the South, 1789–1800* [Lexington: University of Kentucky Press, 1968]; James H. Broussard, *The Southern Federalists, 1800–1816* [Baton Rouge: Louisiana State University Press, 1978]; Blackwell P. Robinson, ed., *The Revolutionary War Sketches of William R. Davie* [Raleigh: North Carolina Department of Cultural Resources, Division of Archives and History, 1976]; Louise Irby Trenholme, *The Ratification of the Federal Constitution in North Carolina* [New York: AMS Press, 1967]; J. G. de Roulhac Hamilton, ed., *William Richardson Davie: A Memoir, Followed by His Letters, with Notes by Kemp P. Battle* [Chapel Hill: University of North Carolina Press, 1907]; Richard A. Harrison, *Princetonians: 1776–1783* [Princeton, N.J.: Princeton University Press, 1981], pp. 25–30; Blackwell P. Robinson, "William Richardson Davie," in *Dictionary of North Carolina Biography*, vol. 2, ed. William S. Powell [Chapel Hill: University of North Carolina Press, 1986], pp. 28–29.)

# HUGH WILLIAMSON
December 5, 1735–May 22, 1819
Preacher, physician, land speculator, scientist, and
North Carolina politician

*A mild, reasonable Federalist, looking toward a system that would "secure the existence of state governments" in a union of "equally sovereign" states. Unwill-*

*ing to surrender to the federal power the authority to "restrain the States from Regulating their internal police." With the oath required of state officers to support the Constitution, suggested "that a reciprocal oath should be required from the National officers, to support the Governments of the States." Moved to enthusiasm for a strengthening of the central government by his large holdings in western lands, his commercial experience, and his service in positions of responsibility during the Revolution. In the company of the Framers, a curious figure, a "projector," as Swift uses that term. Like a character in a whimsical English novel in the number of his identities and careers. During the period of the Great Convention, a southerner, but a resident of Pennsylvania and New York for most of his life. Nonetheless, a faithful and effective representative of his Tarheel constituency during that fateful summer in Philadelphia.*

Hugh Williamson was born at West Nottingham, Pennsylvania, into a Scotch-Irish family. His father, John W. Williamson, came from Dublin to the Quaker colony in 1730 and, sometime during the following year, married Mary Davison, whose family had migrated from County Derry, Ireland. Hugh was the eldest child of this union. He was educated in local and Delaware preparatory schools and in the College of Philadelphia, from which he was graduated in 1757. He had been destined by his parents for a career in the ministry. But after two years' delay in settling his father's estate and following theological training in Connecticut, Williamson gave up the idea of a life in the service of the church and returned to his alma mater as a professor of mathematics. He was, however, licensed to preach by the Presbyterians and held some services at the behest of his mentor, Dr. Samuel Finley, and the Presbytery of Philadelphia. In 1764, Williamson turned away from teaching and mathematics as he had from divinity, and began the study of medicine in Edinburgh, London, and Utrecht, where he submitted a thesis and took an M.D. degree in 1766. For some years thereafter, he practiced his profession in Philadelphia, but he found it a strain on his composure and slowly withdrew in search of a fourth vocation. Business came next, and he persisted in it rather well.

Even so, abstruse researches and the pleasures of science continued to occupy much of his time. In 1768, Williamson was made a member of the American Philosophical Society. In 1769 he served on a commission appointed to observe the transits of Venus and Mercury. He read a paper on the subject of climate in North America—an essay that finally resulted in his celebrated *Observations on the Climate in Different Parts of America* (1811) and in an honorary LL.D. from the University of Leyden. His astronomical observations bore fruit in an original theory concerning the life of superior beings beyond this earth, which appears in "An Essay on Comets," printed in the first volume of *The Transactions of the American Philosophical Society*. In the company of the Framers, he was clearly a virtuoso.

With the onset of the American Revolution, Hugh Williamson began to pay attention to the world of politics. In 1772, trade carried him to the West Indies on a journey also designed to raise funds for an academy at Newark, Delaware. The latter purpose carried him to England, where he became a close friend of Benjamin Franklin and participated in some of his electrical experiments. Williamson read a paper of his own, on eels, before the Royal Society—a paper that appears in the *Transactions* for 1775. As a philosopher, he moved with ease in the highest circles and received a contribution from George III himself. He wrote a public letter to Lord Mansfield, *The Plea of the Colonies,* which appeared as a pamphlet—a letter in which he insisted that Americans wanted only "a reconciliation . . . on constitutional principles," not (as Mansfield had maintained) "absolute independence." Williamson played his first direct role in politics during this English visit; he advised certain members of the Privy Council (in February of 1774) that there would be civil war if they did not change their policies. On a visit to an office where colonial papers were stored, he pretended to be an official and made away with letters to the ministry from two prominent Tories, Governor Hutchinson and Lieutenant Governor Oliver of Massachusetts—letters that he turned over to Dr. Franklin, who dispatched them to America. Their arrival in New England inflamed the situation to a point that the regular governments of those colonies could not continue to function and only force could rule.

In 1776, Williamson was in Holland, and after hearing of the Declaration of Independence he sailed for home, carrying American dispatches. When the British captured his ship, he escaped by rowing a small boat to shore near the Delaware capes. Soon thereafter he relocated to Charleston, South Carolina, where he practiced medicine and carried on some trading in association with a younger brother. Then he shifted his base of operations to Edenton, North Carolina, where he continued in the same occupations. At this time, his business was with the French West Indies, business that the British blockade made impossible to conduct from Philadelphia or Baltimore. Thus, in effect, Adm. Richard Howe made Hugh Williamson a North Carolinian. For more than twenty years he kept that identity and made of it a source of significant influence over the national destiny.

Once established in the South, Williamson, on the basis of his good reputation as a physician, was appointed surgeon general of North Carolina. He served at the Battle of Camden, South Carolina, and did distinguished work on both sides of the line, among British and American forces. He went freely back and forth and had real success with the wounded and in promoting smallpox inoculation. For a North Carolina garrison facing the British in southern Virginia, Williamson so carefully arranged the housing, dress, diet, and drainage of its camp that it had an exceptional record for good health under circumstances that ordinarily produced great losses. Soon he was so popular as to be elected to the state House of Commons for Edenton in 1782. In the same year he was elected by the North Carolina legislature as one of its delegates to the Confederation Congress. He served for three years before returning to the local House of Commons. He was once again elected to the Congress in 1787 and was given a seat in the Constitutional Convention by a general consensus concerning his merits as a statesman and legislator.

Williamson as North Carolina politician was clearly a representative for commercial and speculative interests. He was a mercantilist, an enemy of paper money, an active merchant, and the holder of more than seventy thousand acres of frontier land. In 1783 he had voted to exclude slavery from the territories because "slaves are an encumbrance to society." Yet he had no passion on this subject. And in 1784 he was ready for another southern slaveholding state to come into the Confederation when Vermont won admission—in order to "preserve the Balance." Indeed, by 1787 Williamson had absorbed much of the spirit of North Carolina particularism into his political thought and was assuredly no Philadelphia Federalist in disguise during the deliberations of the Great Convention.

In the conversations and debates of the Framers, Hugh Williamson was quite outspoken. He was the most articulate of the members from North Carolina—at times almost too articulate. He often repeated earlier motions, and he suggested numerous minor revisions in the proposals of other delegates, particularly regarding the definition of the presidency. Williamson's most important decision during the Convention was to support equality in the voting strength of the states in the Senate. He opposed Madison's federal veto power over state legislation, and he opposed a power to tax exports or an authority to pass navigation acts with less than a majority of two-thirds. He did not want the Constitution to prohibit the importation of slaves, since it was "more in favor of humanity, from a view of all circumstances" to let the Deep South continue the trade and join the Union. In general he was "less afraid of too few than of too many laws."

Williamson warned the Convention against the danger to "the Southn. Interest" that could come from giving to the North a majority in the Congress with the means of perpetuating that advantage. He wanted members of the electoral college paid from national funds, members of Congress paid by their states, and no internal tariffs between the states. When tempers flared, he counseled moderation; when debate on the size and makeup of the proposed Senate had exhausted its purpose, he insisted, in the name of realism, that "[unless] we concede on both sides, our business must be at an end." Williamson did not wish the chief executive to be given too much authority; his preference was for a triple executive, with one member from New England, one from the Middle States, and one from the South. Failing to secure that arrangement, he preferred that the president be elected by the state legislatures. Williamson, according to his first biographer, was not thought to be very "democratic," though he had humor and could be spirited and magnetic. He often appeared to be haughty, and some of his oratory seemed overblown and florid to the other

Framers and those who had heard him in the Confederation Congress. But, all pedantry aside, he was clear about one thing—he wished to get for North Carolina all the seats in the new Congress that he could persuade his colleagues to give.

Though he worried about its future consequences (he expected that the nation would eventually drift into monarchy), Williamson was a vigorous supporter of the Constitution once it had been completed. After the Convention, he went directly to the Confederation Congress in New York, where he continued to sit until government under the Articles officially expired. Then he served as the unofficial North Carolina ambassador to the government that eleven states agreed to in 1788 when they accepted the Constitution. But he did get back to Edenton and to his political base in the South in time to sit as a delegate in his state's second ratification convention, held in Fayetteville in November 1789—and to make the motion that finally brought the state under the Constitution. He reassured his neighbors that the federal courts would not intrude in state matters. He presented the document as no threat to the integrity of the states or to the liberty of their citizens. Indeed, he praised it highly as a marvel of political sagacity.

Once North Carolina became a member of the Union, it immediately picked Hugh Williamson as one of its members in the House of Representatives. He completed his political service to his adopted state with two terms in Congress, 1789–1793. He disliked the attitude of the Northeast toward the navigation of the Mississippi and its importance to western commerce. He voted for a whiskey excise (because he was a prohibitionist) but opposed the bill for a Bank of the United States. And when Congress considered subsidies and special considerations for New England enterprises, Williamson sounded a warning: "I wish the Union may be perpetual [but] the remedy is plain" for the South, should the power of government be used to rob it by "unequal taxes." In other words, he considered secession as a legitimate possibility if the South did not enjoy those protections in the Union that it had been led to expect.

In 1793 Williamson settled permanently in New York, where he had married into an old Tory family. He had long since become a man of means and won respect as a savant. As he had been a trustee of the University of North Carolina, he became a trustee of the University of the State of New York and of the College of Physicians and Surgeons. He was a founder of the Literary and Philosophical Society of New York and a prominent member of the New York Historical Society. He continued with his scientific work and publications, including a history of North Carolina. At the age of eighty-three, he died in New York City and was buried at Trinity Church. (See David Hosack, *A Biographical Memoir of Hugh Williamson* [New York: C. S. Van Winkle, 1920]; Louise Irby Trenholme, *The Ratification of the Federal Constitution in North Carolina* [New York: AMS Press, 1967], pp. 74–77, 79–80, and passim; Fletcher M. Green, *The Role of the Yankee in the Old South* [Athens: University of Georgia Press, 1972], pp. 9–10;

Delbert H. Gilpatrick, "Contemporary Opinion of Hugh Williamson, *North Carolina Historical Review* 17 [January 1940]: 26–36; John Washington Neal, "Life and Public Service of Hugh Williamson," *Historical Papers Published by the Trinity College Historical Society,* series 13 [1919]: 63–115; Louis W. Potts, "Hugh Williamson: The Poor Man's Franklin and the National Domain," *North Carolina Historical Review* 64 [October 1987]: 371–393; Helen Jenkins, "The Versatile Dr. Hugh Williamson, 1735–1789" [M.A. thesis, University of North Carolina, 1950]; Forrest McDonald, *We the People: The Economic Origins of the Constitution* [Chicago: University of Chicago Press, 1958], pp. 75–76; Hugh Williamson, *The History of North Carolina,* 2 vols. [Philadelphia: Thomas Dobson, 1812]; Margaret C. S. Christman, *The First Federal Congress, 1789–1791* [Washington, D.C.: Smithsonian, 1989], pp. 348–350.)

# RICHARD DOBBS SPAIGHT
March 25, 1758–September 6, 1802
Soldier, planter, statesman, and political leader of
North Carolina

*In 1787 moved to favor a stronger legal union by experience in arms and state government and by service in the Confederation Congress. In the company of the Framers a strong Federalist, but soon after the adoption of the Constitution greatly changed in his opinion of the value of consolidated federal authority. Before the Great Convention, made impatient with the states by their failure to support the Revolution and their subsequent unwillingness to support national functions under the Articles. After the new government was in place, soon angry with northern Federalists because of what he perceived as their economic exploitation of the South and their tendency to make of authority an end in itself. Devoted to the idea of a "union of sovereign states preserving their civil liberties and connected together by such ties as to preserve permanent and effective government," though he doubted the possibility of such balance. Of the opinion that those gathered with him in Philadelphia had assembled to produce "a system not described, . . . that has not Occurred in the History of men." Though moderate in his politics, a Hotspur, and quick to take offense at all things personal. Confident of his own abilities and of the propriety of his employment in posts of responsibility.*

Richard Dobbs Spaight was born in New Bern, North Carolina, the son of Richard Spaight, an Irish gentleman, and Elizabeth Wilson Spaight. His father was a retainer of his kinsman, the royal governor Arthur Dobbs, and a member of the colonial council, secretary of the colony, and paymaster of the local forces during the French and Indian War. Richard Dobbs Spaight was orphaned at the age of eight and educated in Ireland, among relatives, and at the University of Glasgow, in accordance with the arrangements of his guardian and great-uncle, Governor Dobbs. In 1778, upon completion of that schooling, he returned to North Carolina and promptly accepted a commission in the local militia. In 1780, Spaight fought at the Battle of Camden as an aide to Maj. Gen. Richard Caswell. He was later promoted to lieutenant colonel, commandant of artillery, but left active duty in 1781 upon his election to the North Carolina House of Commons for New Bern and Craven County.

Spaight served two years (1781–1783) in his first appearance in the legislature, then a two-year tour in the Confederation Congress (1783–1785), and thereafter returned to the North Carolina House of Commons, of which he was the elected speaker in 1785. In the Congress Spaight served on a committee to organize a government for the territories in the West. He was one of the southerners opposed to prohibitions against the spread of slavery along the frontier and was quick to anger at the shortcomings of his "tightfisted and unpatriotic" northern colleagues, sometimes offering to prove his point on the field of honor. Returning to the state legislature by his own choice, from 1785 to 1787 Spaight exercised a considerable influence for a person of his years. In state politics, in an investigation of state judges, he proved to be a strict constructionist, hostile to judicial activism and usurpation by review. In 1787, the North Carolina General Assembly elected him as one of its representatives in the Constitutional Convention scheduled to meet in Philadelphia.

In the Great Convention Richard Dobbs Spaight attended every session and was more of a nationalist than the rest of the delegation from his state. He did not approve of equal representation for the states in the Senate. In his report to the North Carolina legislature, he rejoiced in the northern agreement to a strong fugitive-slave clause and had no fear of navigation acts passed by a simple majority, since the "Northern Brethren" needed some inducement to cooperation. At one point he even favored a suffrage based on the number of "white inhabitants." Yet he leaned toward the thinking of the Antifederalists in supporting the election of senators by the state legislatures and a two-thirds vote for the ratification of treaties. He favored seven-year terms for senators and for the president and had some doubt about the value of electors chosen by the various state legislatures. Yet, in his view, the advantage of having senators elected in that fashion was in the check to "consolidation" they would provide.

In the July 1788 North Carolina ratification convention held at Hillsborough, Spaight was a strong and frequently heard voice speaking in behalf of the new instrument of government. His construction of the document produced in Philadelphia allowed him to assure his neighbors that it would not destroy the states or put them under the power of a hostile northern majority. He assured his fellow Carolinians that federal courts, under the Constitution, would not have jurisdiction over state concerns or attempt to apply the Constitution to state and local (or personal) activities. He agreed with William Richardson Davie that North Carolina's fear of consolidation was a "bugbear" but was, with the other Federalists present in this assembly, unable to persuade the majority to vote for approval. Spaight did not attend the later convention held in Fayetteville in November 1789, which finally ratified the Constitution.

From 1787 through the following four years, Spaight was often in poor health, and for a time he left the United States to recuperate in the West Indies. In 1787, when his name was proposed for chief executive of his state, he received only moderate support. And in 1789 he withdrew his name as a candidate for one of North Carolina's original seats in the Senate. But after his return from the Indies, he became (in 1792) North Carolina's first native-born governor, in which office he served three one-year terms. In 1798, he was chosen to be a member of the House of Representatives from North Carolina, where, after reelection, he sat until 1801. In Congress he joined the Democratic-Republicans (with whom he had long been affiliated), advocated repeal of the Alien and Sedition Acts, and opposed the impeachment of his colleague in the Great Convention, Sen. William Blount of Tennessee. In the disputed presidential election of 1800, Spaight voted consistently for Thomas Jefferson. Upon his return to North Carolina, he was elected to the lower house of the legislature in 1801 and to the upper chamber in the following year. This election of 1802 was hotly contested by John Stanly, a Federalist, who so thoroughly offended Spaight that the former governor described his rival as "a liar and a scoundrel" and offered him "satisfaction." The result of these sharp words was a duel. On the fourth exchange between the bitter adversaries, Spaight fell mortally wounded. Ordinarily one fire would have been enough for honor, but Stanly had called Spaight a "dodger," an insult the older man could not endure. Spaight, dead at the age of forty-four, was buried at his estate, Clermont, near New Bern.

Spaight's change from Federalist to Jeffersonian may have cost him his life, but it was symptomatic of what was happening among the political leaders of the South who did not for long remain within Washington's party once the general had retired from office. In his private life Spaight was typical of his class, quiet and responsible. He was a devout Episcopalian and a vigorous supporter of education, having served as one of the original trustees of the University of North Carolina and as a member of the governing board of the local academy. Though a wealthy man (having more than one hundred slaves and many plantations), Spaight for the most part left his private business in other hands, and devoted his life to the public service for which he had been prepared since childhood. His son, Richard Dobbs Spaight, Jr., was, in his footsteps, elected governor of North Carolina in 1834. (See Alexander B. Andrews, "Richard Dobbs Spaight," *North Carolina Historical Review* 1 [April 1924]: 97–120; John H. Wheeler, *Sketch of the Life of Richard Dobbs Spaight of North Carolina* [Baltimore: William K. Boyle, 1880]; Robert G. Ferris, ed., *Signers of the Constitution* [Washington,

D.C.: National Park Service, 1976], pp. 212–213; H. James Henderson, *Party Politics in the Continental Congress* [New York: McGraw-Hill, 1974]; Louise Irby Trenholme, *The Ratification of the Federal Constitution in North Carolina* [New York: AMS Press, 1967]; an entry on Richard Dobbs Spaight by Gertrude S. Carraway will appear in the forthcoming *Dictionary of North Carolina Biography*, ed. William S. Powell [Chapel Hill: University of North Carolina Press].)

# WILLIAM BLOUNT
March 26, 1749–March 21, 1800
Planter, merchant, land speculator, and political leader
of North Carolina and Tennessee

*A reluctant Framer who, though in favor of a stronger national government, feared the political repercussions of being involved in creating one and doubted that North Carolina would approve of any large-scale revision of the Articles of Confederation. Great-grandson of Sir Thomas Blount, who had settled on Pamlico Sound in North Carolina ca. 1662. Son of Jacob Blount, grandson of Thomas, and Barbara Gray Blount. Born on his grandfather's plantation at Rosefield, in Bertie County. Of distinguished lineage, Anglo-Norman and Scottish, with quarterings reaching as far back as the Conquest, and connected by kinship to important families in both Virginia and his own state. Educated at home, and in the business of his father, which was principally politics and trading in land.*

William Blount, along with the other "Tar River" Blounts, took the patriot side in the American Revolution. In 1776 he was enlisted as paymaster in the North Carolina forces, and from that time onward his life was spent in the public arena. From 1780 to 1784, he was a member of the lower house of the North Carolina legislature, where he served as speaker. From 1788 to 1790 he sat in the upper house of the same assembly. He was twice appointed member for his state in the Confederation Congress, first from 1782 to 1783 and again in 1786–1787. He was serving in the Congress when, at the age of thirty-eight, he was asked by North Carolina to represent it in the Philadelphia Convention.

Blount said almost nothing in the debates at the Convention, was late arriving to the sessions, and was then absent from them for almost a month on business in the Congress. Before the call had gone out for a convention, Blount had expressed the opinion that the Union might break up into two or three lesser confederations. He did not have a "long view" of the proceedings he so neglected. Furthermore, he was among the aristocratic republicans who had been alarmed by a rising popular spirit in the western counties of North Carolina and the other states. But his reaction to these developments differed from those of similar men who shared in his concern. His family had learned a salutary lesson from the 1770–1771 Regulator movement in the Carolinas. To preserve cohesion and the authority of its leaders, a deferential society required that concessions work both ways, up and down. Moreover, the Blounts of Blount Hall had always been interested in the development of the West. Their fortune was, even after 120 years, still to be made there, if anywhere. For, as Blount recognized, the movement of power and wealth tended in that direction. A strong federal authority would increase the value of Blount holdings in what was soon to be Tennessee. Yet William Blount, if he hoped to make his way, could not afford to make Governor Tryon's mistakes and offend the backcountry. Therefore, he signed the Constitution only to "attest the fact that the plan was the unanimous act of the States," not to express his approval of the document.

Blount was not surprised by North Carolina's original refusal to ratify. He was, moreover, very cautious about the kind of support he gave the Federalist cause and waited until the instrument of government had been ratified in all the other states, except Rhode Island, before he took any public stand. His term as state senator produced a Caswell-Blount resolution calling for a second convention, which easily passed both houses of the legislature. And he sat as a delegate from Tennessee County—in the transmontane west—during the Fayetteville deliberations, which finally brought North Carolina into the already functioning federal Union. But Blount was denied the reward for Federalist loyalty he most desired, a seat in the new Senate, which went to Benjamin Hawkins.

Therefore, after helping arrange the cession of North Carolina's western lands to the United States, Blount in 1790 moved to Tennessee, settling first at Rocky Mount and then in Knoxville. Once there, he sought and received from the national government appointment as governor for the territory south of the Ohio River, an office he filled tactfully and skillfully in dealing with Indians and frontiersmen until Tennessee became a state in 1796. He presided over the constitutional convention for the new state and was elected one of its original senators. Blount as territorial governor and senator continued in his land speculations and at one time held title to or options on more than a million acres. But by this time he had left the Federalist camp and joined with the Jeffersonians, chiefly because of their promise not to neglect the West. Then his paper empire collapsed. Notes were called in, and the Federalists took advantage of Blount's foolish involvement in a plan to give Spanish Florida and Louisiana to England, expelling him from the Senate and thus embarrassing his party. Efforts to impeach or punish him further failed, and upon Blount's return to Tennessee, he found that his popularity there was undiminished, as was proved by his election in 1798 to the state senate and by his elevation to the speakership of that body. Though disgusted by "Jacobins" and the leveling doctrines of the French, he had the kind of popular touch that was to be a characteristic of southern leaders in the generations to come. Certainly his political career would have continued had it not been cut short by his death at the age of fifty. (See William H. Masterson, *William Blount* [Baton Rouge: Louisiana State University Press, 1954]; Thomas Perkins Abernethy, *From Frontier to Plantation in Tennessee* [Chapel Hill: University of North Carolina Press, 1932]; Alice B. Keith, "William Blount in North Carolina Politics, 1781–1789," in *Studies in Southern History,* ed. Carlyle S. Herson [Chapel Hill: University of North Carolina Press, 1957], pp. 47–61; Louise Irby Trenholme, *The Ratification of the Federal Constitution in North Carolina* [New York: AMS Press, 1967].)

# ALEXANDER MARTIN

1740–November 2, 1807
Merchant, lawyer, planter, soldier, and political leader
during the Revolution, under the Articles, and after
the adoption of the U.S. Constitution

*The voice of the Carolina Piedmont in the Great Convention. A moderate in the context of the politics of his state, with some reputation as a "trimmer." In Philadelphia, a man of no settled convictions, but "suspicious of the ultranationalism of the Convention." Less a Federalist than any other member of the North Carolina delegation. Left Philadelphia in late August doubting the value of the constitution that was emerging, but changed his opinion within a few months of his return to the Salisbury/Guilford County region of North Carolina, which was his base of power. Not a man to lead when others were loath to follow.*

Alexander Martin was Scotch-Irish, born in Hunterdon County, New Jersey, the son of the Reverend Hugh Martin, originally of County Tyrone, Ireland, and Jane Martin. The Martins were Presbyterians. They had five sons, four of whom immigrated to North Carolina; the fifth settled in Virginia. Alexander Martin, the eldest, was educated at the College of New Jersey, from which he was graduated in 1756, at the age of sixteen, and from which he received an M.A. three years later. Young Martin then moved to Virginia and thereafter to the village of Salisbury, North Carolina, where he set up as a merchant. He became a justice of the peace in 1764, king's deputy attorney in 1766, and judge of the King's Bench for the Rowan County Court of Oyer and Terminer from 1774 to 1775. Martin's legal practice was small, but at times dangerous to his safety. In 1770–1771, as commissioner of Salisbury and officer of the court at Hillsborough, he was confronted by Regulators, forced to sign an agreement concerning his fees, and beaten by the mob. Yet he urged conciliation of his angry neighbors in writing Governor Tryon, who rebuked him for this interference.

Under the royal governor, Martin served in the North Carolina House of Commons (1773–1774) for Guilford County, where he had moved after the unpleasantness at Salisbury, and in the Second and Third Provincial Congresses (1775), which had been assembled ex officio to administer the business of the colony as it moved toward independence. Like many of his origins, Martin came from a family already impatient with the policies of the English government before arrival in the New World. He took the side of the protesting Americans or patriots from the first and was appointed lieutenant colonel of the Second North Carolina Continental Regiment in September of 1775. He served in the "Snow Campaign" against the South Carolina Loyalists ("Scovellites") and was at Moore's Creek Bridge in February of 1776 and at the defense of Charleston the following June. After being promoted to colonel of his regiment, he marched it northward to join Washington's army, where he saw action at Chad's Ford and elsewhere. On October 4, 1777, he participated in the Battle of Germantown. Here, however, Washington's efforts to surprise and overwhelm the English army only recently settled in Philadelphia were frustrated by weather, disobedience, and poor communications. Martin meandered during this engagement, wandering sometimes in the fog. He was charged with cowardice, subjected to a court-martial, and found "not guilty," but not so completely exonerated as to be of further use to the service. He resigned his commission on November 22, 1777, returned to North Carolina, and was almost immediately elected to represent Guilford County in the state senate.

Martin was a member of the upper house of the North Carolina Assembly from 1778 to 1782 and during 1787–1788. He was the speaker of the senate during those years except for the term of 1778–1779. In 1781, he became acting governor when Gov. Thomas Burke was captured by local Loyalists. For a time in the early months of 1782, Burke was restored to his office, but Martin succeeded him and continued as governor from 1782 to 1785. Martin was successful in securing support among the citizens of western North Carolina; he left office only because the law restricted his tenure to three out of any six years. He was a weak governor; indeed, as a state senator he exercised almost as much authority as he had as chief executive, serving in 1780 with John Penn and Oroondates Davis on a board of war and in 1781 on an equivalent council extraordinary with Gov. Richard Caswell and Allen Jones. These special boards attempted to transact the military business of the state during the period of its greatest danger. Martin led them in this effort.

As governor he proposed a plural religious establishment, a moderate and conciliatory policy toward Loyalists, better treatment for Indians and for the frontier, and a careful approach to the cession of North Carolina's lands beyond the mountains to the authority of the Confederation Congress. Though he did not push, he did advise. There was some consistency in his view of the proper order of government in North Carolina, and some willingness to see power applied when nothing but the application of power would suffice. But in general Alexander Martin was a champion of limited government, a man who pledged on his first election as governor of North Carolina that "the sole object of my administration shall be to maintain and defend the Sovereign Independent power of this State." It was thus difficult for him to play the Federalist, though he sometimes tried.

Governor Martin made no speeches or motions in the Constitutional Convention. He seconded three proposals, one of which sought merely to add another seat for North Carolina in the original House of Representatives. He supported the effort to give equal voice to each of the states in the Senate. Hugh Williamson spoke of this near-silence as the conduct of a man who had "exhausted his fund" of leadership. The trouble was that Martin had come north to see "thirteen Independent Sovereignties" made a nation, while at the same time "preserving the particular Interest of the Individual States." Such was not the business he found in Philadelphia. But he had recognized the need for a united policy on trade and military matters and for a national revenue even while serving as an Antifederalist leader in North Carolina. Moreover, he was a member of the Society of Cincinnati, which was almost synonymous with Federalism. Therefore, he decided to give the proposed reform in government a chance, offered to go as a Federalist to the North Carolina ratification convention to be held in Hillsborough in July of 1788—offered and was defeated by his old friend, Dr. David Caldwell.

Yet in the same year Martin was elected again to the state senate. In the following year he was elected as North Carolina's first governor under the Constitution—which had finally been adopted by a second ratifying convention in November of 1789. He served three additional terms in the office, making him the most reelected governor in the history of his state. The Federalists helped to put Martin back in power. But the policies of Alexander Hamilton had him by 1790 once more in the other camp. He complained of federal "interference" and "intrusion," of "extravagance" and "mindless folly." He wrote, asking a member of Congress, "Will not the Central Government quickly bear down the State Government?" Of the high Federalists he observed, "They should establish the new government on the affections of the people and not exercise powers that appear to be doubtful." He took alarm at talk of "implied powers." And, when elected by the Antifederalists as U.S. senator at the end of his long tenure as governor, he renewed his old pledge to preserve inviolate the individuality and internal sovereignty of the state.

As senator from North Carolina he kept this pledge until the end of his term, supporting economy, opposing Jay's Treaty (for its failure to recover confiscated slaves), opposing expansion of the military establishment, new federal courts, and a growing civil list. Yet after the French insult to the delegation of Pinckney, Gerry, and Marshall, Martin anticipated a shift in sentiment. He already deplored the French Revolution; how could he be expected to tolerate the Jacobins, their heirs in the Directory, or their American friends after what the Regulators had done to him? Hence, Martin made a political mistake and voted for the Alien and Sedition Acts. After a half-hearted effort to win reelection, he returned to his home at Danbury, to his comfort, his books, and his family—his mother, brothers, and their numerous children. There had been too much wild talk, too many noisy radicals. Now there was time for poetry (Martin wrote conventional eighteenth-century verse), for promotion of the University of North Carolina (of which he had been a trustee since 1790), and for a final appearance in the assembly (1804–1805, including another turn as speaker of the senate). In a long poem about Columbus, he looked forward to the future of the country, symbolized by the national capital being built in the District of Columbia:

> Thy worth a grateful nation there shall own,
> In fair Columbia's plain thy name revise
> Long dormant—where another Rome shall rise
> With her broad Capitol near Tyber's stream.

At the time of his death in 1807, Alexander Martin had spent more than thirty-five years in the service of his state. In 1793, Princeton awarded him an LL.D. He seems, when compared to the decisive men who joined him in Philadelphia during the summer of 1787, an uncertain figure; yet in his uncertainties he was a forecast of American politics to come. (See Richard Walser, "Alexander Martin, Poet," *Early American Literature* 6 [Spring 1971]: 55–61; Robert M. Douglas, "Alexander Martin," in *Biographical History of North Carolina: From Colonial Times to the Present,* ed. Samuel A. Ashe et al., vol. 3 [Greensboro, N.C.: Charles L. Van Noppen, 1905], pp. 274–280; Louise Irby Trenholme, *The Ratification of the Federal Constitution in North Carolina* [New York: AMS Press, 1967]; Francis Nash, *Presentation of Portrait of Governor Alexander Martin to the State of North Carolina* [Raleigh, N.C.: North Carolina Society of the Sons of the Revolution, 1909]; Elizabeth Winston Yates, "The Public Career of Alexander Martin" [M.A. thesis, University of North Carolina, 1943]; Charles D. Rodenbough, "Alexander Martin," in *Dictionary of North Carolina Biography,* vol. 4, ed. William S. Powell [Chapel Hill: University of North Carolina Press, 1991], pp. 222–224.)

# SOUTH CAROLINA

# JOHN RUTLEDGE

September, 1739–July 18, 1800
Lawyer, jurist, and patriarchal chieftain of the people
of South Carolina during the Revolution

*After the war, called by them (with affection) "Dictator John," in memory of the*
*two years (February 3, 1780–January 29, 1782) when he held absolute sway over*
*the fortunes of a people who had given him something like the old Roman office.*
*For fifteen years following independence, the most respected man in his state.*
*The southern Framer most instrumental in bringing about amity between the*
*sections during the Great Convention. An Old Whig, a man of the ancient*
*prescription, and far removed from allegiance to the abstractions of natural*
*rights. A "nabob," with the habit of command and no patience for effrontery, of*
*either the intellectual or the personal variety. Yet a man of tact and judgment.*
*One of the men who would have to approve of the Constitution if the firmer union*
*was to be accomplished. A Federalist only if the established regime of South*
*Carolina could find a source of strength and security in that camp. A man of*
*great property, but in 1787, like most Carolina planters, short of funds. An exotic*
*experience for New England delegates to the Constitutional Convention. A figure*
*of reference in any history of southern political thought.*

John Rutledge was born in Charles Town, the son of Dr. John Rutledge, a
physician, and Sarah Hext Rutledge, the only daughter of the wealthy Col. Hugh
Hext. John Rutledge's uncle (and eventually his role model) was Andrew
Rutledge, speaker of the Commons House of Assembly and leader of the South
Carolina bar. Both the father and the uncle were graduates of Trinity College,
Dublin, Ireland, the sons of a French and Scotch-Irish farmer of County Tyrone.
Though always at the center of a large family (he had six brothers and sisters),
John Rutledge lost both his father (1750) and his uncle (1755) while still a boy. He
was educated by his father, by the Episcopal minister of Christ Church Parish,

and by Dr. David Rhind, a respected tutor. Later he read law with James Parsons, also speaker of the house. In 1757, he journeyed to Great Britain, where, according to the pattern with South Carolinians of his class, he studied in the Middle Temple, and was called to the English bar in 1760, trying and winning two cases in London courts before his return home. Within two years of his first appearance in the courts of South Carolina, Rutledge had become one of the three most successful attorneys in the province. In 1761, he was elected to the Commons House from Christ Church Parish and continued to carry out that assignment until, during the Revolution, he rose to be the president and governor of an independent and sovereign state.

As an attorney, Rutledge earned an average of perhaps £9,000 a year between 1762 and 1774. While still a young man, he was the acknowledged measure of propriety in his world, the spokesman of a closed, conservative order that set a high premium on eloquence, skill in debate, knowledge of the inherited law, and personal honor. Rutledge was involved in all manner of commercial business for the great merchants of his commercial city. Yet his political activity was also constant. In 1764, he was royal attorney general for the colony. In 1765, he was a South Carolina delegate to the Stamp Act Congress in New York, where he chaired a committee that petitioned the House of Lords for redress. He drew up a remonstrance for the local legislature against abuses of office by the royal governor, Thomas Boone. In 1774 he was the first man selected to speak for South Carolina in the Continental Congress.

John Rutledge approached a final division between the North American colonies and their mother country with hesitancy and many reservations. In the First and Second Continental Congresses, Rutledge insisted that Americans not press their case with appeals to theories concerning the rights of man, but draw their arguments instead from the English constitution and their "inherited rights." He opposed moves toward independence so long as there seemed hope of reconciliation. In March of 1776, Rutledge became the first president of the Republic of South Carolina, under a constitution he himself had helped to draft when government under a committee of public safety no longer seemed sufficient. Yet on taking office, he described the authority with which he would rule as temporary, operative until "an accommodation of the unhappy differences between Great Britain and America can be obtained." John Rutledge concurred with his brother Edward (who signed the Declaration of Independence) that the identity of South Carolina would be in more danger if subject to the government of New England than it was from the fleets and armies of King George III: "I dread their low cunning and . . . leveling Principles." Yet after Charleston was attacked in June of 1776, the Rutledge brothers accepted the necessity of formal independence for the organization and prosecution of a war effort, since outright submission was the alternative. Later, John Rutledge vetoed the proposed constitution of 1778 and resigned his office because it was too much like the New England instruments of government—and because it would make accommodation with Great Britain impossible. In other words, though a leader of the rebellion, he continued to look backward toward a still-English, self-governing America.

The British conquest of Charleston and the low country in 1780 turned his thinking in a new direction, toward a recognition of South Carolina's vulnerability and of its future role as part of an American nation. Yet as he fled Charleston, governor again, he was still a defender of the old regime, not a democrat and not a revolutionary by disposition or local practice. Where he was, in his saddle, was now "the seat of government," and he, in effect, the state of South Carolina—the entire state, which signified the up-country as much as it did Charleston and its environs. On the men of the Piedmont, the frontier, and the remote sections of the state Rutledge was forced to depend. They assisted him in restoring self-government to South Carolina. And "Dictator John" did not forget, once the fighting was done. War fostered unity in South Carolina of a kind never known in colonial times. Or at least unity among various kinds of patriots. After 1782, the backcountry was never again without influence in South Carolina politics.

To rescue South Carolina, after organizing the militia, Rutledge rushed north for assistance. The devastation of British rule had cured him of Anglophilia. In North Carolina he got men and a base of operation. From Congress he got (after an interruption called Horatio Gates) Gen. Nathanael Greene. Rutledge was tireless and omnipresent in prosecuting the war. After Cornwallis left the state, Charleston was finally evacuated. Meanwhile, Rutledge had called an election and assembled a new legislature at Jacksonborough. It passed statutes providing for confiscation and amercement of Loyalist properties and banishment of Loyalists. The outgoing governor had already pardoned repentant Loyalists, punished some of the worst offenders, and pacified the most troubled areas. But the new laws probably prevented even harsher measures. Moreover, they were soon modified. Payment of debts was suspended, and indigo was made negotiable currency. Then, with satisfaction and general congratulations, John Rutledge gave up the staff of office and retired to the house as a member for St. Andrew's Parish. His difficult trial as leader of South Carolina was now in the past, but he had a major role yet to play in the larger arena of national politics.

In 1782 and 1783, Rutledge returned to the Congress as a representative of his state. He declined a position on the national court set up under the Articles and declined to serve as minister to the Netherlands. Instead, he focused on judicial duties in South Carolina. In 1784 he was appointed chief judge of a state court of chancery. From 1784 through 1790 he also held a seat in the legislature. When the Constitutional Convention was called for in Philadelphia in May of 1787, it was inevitable that he would lead the delegation sent from his state. He, Charles Cotesworth Pinckney, Charles Pinckney, and Pierce Butler preconsulted concerning what position they would assume during the debates and (apart from some deviations by young Pinckney) managed to act in concert most of the time—according to a design drawn by John Rutledge.

During the Constitutional Convention Rutledge behaved as a man conscious of the power in his hands. He spoke often, briefly, and pointedly. And he chaired the committee that drafted the original version of the Constitution, once the major differences that divided the house had been adjusted: the Committee of Detail. It was Rutledge who introduced into the document language that describes it as "the supreme law of the land"—a cautionary expression designed to restrain the lawless, but not the high Federalism some imagine it to be. Like his brother Edward, John recognized the peril carried in an authority for "destroying Provincial Distinctions and of making every thing of the minute kind bend to what they [Puritans and centralizers] call the good of the whole." Therefore he insisted that James Wilson's detailed description of the judicial powers be reduced to a simple jurisdiction over cases relating to the concerns that were truly federal in their implications. He opposed Madison's proposal to give Congress a veto over state legislation, and he opposed a provision for lower federal courts, under the Supreme Court. Just the opposite of judicial activism is what John Rutledge expected to foster with his "Supremacy Clause." As he saw matters, the problem in 1787 was that the Supreme Court and the Constitution might be allowed no authority whatsoever if such authority were claimed in explicit terms. Besides, he was a man of law and wanted a "government of laws," particularly as a check on "democratic power," which "however unexceptional [it] may first appear, . . . in its effects [continues to be] arbitrary, severe, and destructive."

Rutledge had absolutely no patience with antislavery rhetoric applied to the advantage of northern political and economic power. "Religion and humanity," said he, "had nothing to do with this question—Interest alone is the governing principle with Nations." He threw down the challenge: "The true question at present is whether the Southn. States shall or shall not be parties to the Union." On almost every important issue to divide the Convention, Rutledge insisted that discussions should begin with a recognition of political reality already in place, that the delegates should be "guided . . . by long experience." The small states would have an equal voice in the Senate, or they would have it under the Articles. The South would either hold slaves on the present basis, or under the new Constitution. No nation was being invented, since a nation was already in existence. Only "fools" would give up the slave trade, as South Carolina was being asked to do, or neglect to insist upon counting their slaves for purposes of representation. Only hypocrites would pretend to be excited about a "moral issue" when actually in the midst of a power play—for their own profit attempting to decrease the voting strength of a partner in a matter of mutual concern. "Property was certainly the principal object of Society" and, instead of numbers, should be the basis of representation. Let seats in the House of Representatives be distributed according to the contribution paid into the national treasury by each state. Let members of the House of Representatives be elected by the state legislatures, and let senators serve without pay. By these means property could be protected, and the stability of government ensured. South Carolina did not elect a legislature on the basis of population alone, since that procedure would not reflect "the sense of the whole community." Rutledge capped his argument: "If this Convention had been chosen by the people in districts it is not supposed that such proper characters would have been preferred."

Rutledge recommended good salaries for federal judges and the election of the president by Congress. He held that the historic rights of Englishmen had, as a result of the Revolution, their repositories in the states and that they did not require federal reaffirmation by a remote authority, since that arrangement had caused the trouble in the first place. He favored wealth as a condition of service for representatives, senators, and the president. He hoped to see the powers of Congress specified, rejected any tax on exports, criticized the notion that elected officials might hold appointed posts, urged the quiet members of the Convention to speak up, and, finally, complained that the proceedings had grown tedious and overly particular. After taking the measure of his associates, he decided to bring the question to a head and, through an agreement with the members from Connecticut, closed the conversation concerning slavery, the slave trade, and political representation—thereby opening the way to a resolution of many other divisions. What Roger Sherman and Oliver Ellsworth desired was a security for Connecticut's claims in the Western Reserve in Ohio, either in the Senate or in the Supreme Court. What Rutledge needed was an increase in the number of slaves sufficient to develop the open lands of the Southwest and to replace those removed by the British during their occupation. Out of this accommodation of finite needs rose a temporary spirit of accommodation.

After bringing in the August 6 report of the Committee of Detail—a draft of the Constitution shaped by the skill of his hand—most of the work of Rutledge as Framer was complete. On his return to South Carolina, he informed the low country that the northerners had behaved well and that, on balance, his neighbors should approve the Constitution. He had, at least with reference to his own state, been quite correct in recommending that no elaborate apologia be attached to the proposed Constitution when it was transmitted for approval. In 1784, when a tavern keeper had insulted one of the Rutledge household slaves, the South Carolina legislature had defined it to be a crime, punishable by exile, to offend John Rutledge. And Carolinians told with affection and amusement the story of Chancellor Rutledge's coming late to the bench, at 10:45, and declaring, "When this court sits is ten o'clock, and no other hour." In such a context, Rutledge could scarcely be refused ratification, especially since the gentry agreed with him in this case. Though much of South Carolina disapproved of the Constitution, with regard to its merits, many of its citizens voted for it as a gesture of confidence in John Rutledge.

Once the new government was organized, President Washington called

Rutledge from his post as chancellor of the southern district of South Carolina to be associate justice of the U.S. Supreme Court. Rutledge accepted the assignment, met with the Court in 1790, and rode with certain of his colleagues on the southern circuit. No cases were argued before the Court in 1790 through August 1791, and Rutledge resigned to become chief justice of the South Carolina Court of Common Pleas, where he made his reputation for both justice and severity. In 1795, when Chief Justice John Jay resigned from the Supreme Court, Rutledge was openly eager to be appointed in his place and was given it by his old friend. He presided over one term of the Court, but his temporary appointment was not confirmed by the Federalist Senate—in part because of exaggerated rumors concerning the instability of his mind, but chiefly because he had led an attack on Jay's Treaty in a South Carolina public meeting. In a state of depression at this rebuff, Rutledge withdrew from public life. Respect for this undervalued Father of the republic remained unchanged in his own city. In 1798 and 1799, he served final terms in the assembly. His disposition improved. He practiced a little law and visited his friends. At the age of sixty he died at the home of his son-in-law, the Episcopal bishop of South Carolina, the Reverend Dr. Robert Smith. He was buried in St. Michael's churchyard, under the most modest of inscriptions.

John Rutledge has been, in the history of his reputation, a neglected Framer. Like John Dickinson of Delaware, he has received little emphasis in the scholarship because his career does not support the now accepted theories of the origins of the American regime. (See Richard Barry, *Mr. Rutledge of South Carolina* [New York: Books for Libraries Press, 1971]; Forrest McDonald, *E Pluribus Unum: The Formation of the American Republic, 1776–1790* [Indianapolis: Liberty Press, 1979], pp. 289–290 and passim; Leon Friedman, "John Rutledge," in *The Justices of the United States Supreme Court, 1789–1969: Their Lives and Major Opinions*, vol. 1, ed. Leon Friedman and Fred L. Israel [New York: R. R. Bowker/Chelsea House, 1969], pp. 33–49; Charles Gregg Singer, *South Carolina in the Confederation* [Philadelphia: Porcupine Press, 1976]; Margaret B. MacMillan, *The War Governors in the American Revolution* [New York: Columbia University Press, 1943]; Ernest M. Lander, Jr., "The South Carolinians at the Philadelphia Convention, 1787," *South Carolina Historical Magazine* 57 [June 1956]: 134–155; George C. Rogers, *Evolution of a Federalist: William Loughton Smith of Charleston, 1758–1812* [Columbia: University of South Carolina Press, 1962], pp. 112–188 and passim; Allan Nevins, *The American States during and after the Revolution* [New York: Macmillan, 1924]; John Drayton, *Memoirs of the American Revolution, From Its Commencement to the Year 1776, Inclusive; As Relating to the State of South-Carolina*, 2 vols. [Charleston: A. E. Miller, 1821]; Lisle A. Rose, *Prologue to Democracy: The Federalists in the South, 1789–1800* [Lexington: University of Kentucky Press, 1968]; Jerome Nadelhaft, "The Revolutionary Era in South Carolina" [Ph.D. dissertation, University of Wisconsin, 1965]; Raymond G. Starr, "The Conservative Revolution: South Carolina's Public Affairs, 1775–1790" [Ph.D. dissertation, University of Texas, 1964]; S. Sidney Ulmer, "The South Carolina Delegates to the Constitutional Convention of 1787: An Analytical Study" [Ph.D. dissertation, Duke University, 1966]; Edward McCrady, *The History of South Carolina in the Revolution*, 2 vols. [New York: Macmillan, 1901 and 1902]; Robert W. Barnwell, "Rutledge, 'The Dictator,'" *Journal of Southern History* 7 [May 1941]: 215–224; Hoyt P. Canady, *Gentlemen of the Bar: Lawyers in Colonial South Carolina* [New York: Garland, 1987].)

# CHARLES COTESWORTH PINCKNEY

February 1746–August 16, 1825
Soldier, statesman, lawyer, and planter

*Federalist candidate for the presidency in 1804 and 1808, and for the vice-presidency as running mate for John Adams in 1800. Member for South Carolina in the Constitutional Convention of 1787, and one of its leading spirits; indubitably an aristocrat, a Carolina "nabob" who, with John Rutledge and John Dickinson, bespoke an American flowering of the Old Whig tradition of liberty through inherited, ancient law. Already the second man of his state when the Convention assembled. What he said during its debates was received by his associates as the considered opinion of the lower South and was weighed accordingly. Brought up in a milieu that connected property, education, and public service. He practiced a quiet virtue that required he efface himself and represent the corporate things.*

Charles Cotesworth Pinckney was the son of Charles Pinckney, Esq. (1699–1758), chief justice of South Carolina, and Eliza Lucas Pinckney (1722–1793), perhaps the most gifted woman to live in the colony during its development as an English possession. His grandfather was Thomas Pinckney (1666–1705), the founder of the line. And his elder cousin was Charles Pinckney II, a legal and political force in prerevolutionary South Carolina. The boy grew to manhood in an atmosphere where privilege was balanced by duty, within the expectation that he would fulfill an inherited role. Charles Cotesworth Pinckney was educated at Westminster School, at Oxford (where he studied with Sir William Blackstone), and in the Middle Temple. In France he was instructed in botany, chemistry, and military science to complete his preparation. Thanks to his mother's skill as a planter, he returned to his homeland as a man of great property, personally acquainted with the leaders of British and French society, and as a qualified member of the English bar, after one round on the circuit. Nonetheless, he was from his earliest youth modest and gentle in manner, gracious in all circumstances and conditions. Throughout his life, he attempted to perform a part assigned to him in his father's will: "to prove . . . of service and advantage to his country, [and] an honour to his stock and kindred." From his first appearance in the South Carolina Commons House of Assembly in 1769, his was, in the words of his biographer, the politics of "experience" and prescription, not of private fancy or speculation. Said another way, he was never a man to surprise his friends.

Pinckney brought to the Constitutional Convention no draft of a new compact, as did his youthful cousin Charles Pinckney III, but only his conviction, shaped in the crucible of the Revolution, that the United States should not fight another war without the concentrated strength necessary to defend itself, and the related conviction that a national policy concerning foreign trade, currency, and finance was needed to relieve the burden of debt that weighed upon South Carolina and the other states. He was, in other words, a moderate military Federalist, a soldier politician, in whom the lawyer had been submerged by the exigencies of war. In Philadelphia he spoke plainly and displayed for effect none of his considerable erudition. Neither did he claim any special authority from the distinction of his name. Instead he went to the heart of whatever question was before the house and in the debates continued in an effort begun when, in 1775, he sat in the provisional provincial congress and put on a uniform to assist in organizing the defenses of the southern coast. As he had written a friend during the Revolution, "The freedom and independence of my country are the gods of my idolatry."

A Pinckney (Picquigny) had been among the barons who forced King John to sign the Great Charter. And, in South Carolina, a Pinckney had, for three generations, stood ready to protect "the inherited rights of Englishmen." The defense of the patrimony had always presupposed the possibility of a final recourse to arbitration by the sword and did so especially when Americans were threatened by Parliament's determination to bind them "in all cases whatsoever." In 1787, no new objectives animated the Pinckneys and the other Carolina gentry attending the Convention, even though the times called for extraordinary measures, a revision of the Articles, and the application of talents rarely employed on the field of arms. Out of the resources of their common identity, a set of political reflexes tried and proven, they did their work on the spot. And Charles Cotesworth Pinckney articulated the predominant pragmatism of their approach.

Pinckney, as a junior officer, saw service in the first attack on Charles Town, in the first attempt to recover Georgia from British occupation, in the Florida campaign of 1778, and as an aide on the staff of General Washington during the battles of Brandywine and Germantown. He was captured with his city in 1780 and exchanged, after resisting considerable British pressure to defect. He rejoined the army in 1783 and was commissioned a brigadier general before his discharge from active duty. Later, at George Washington's behest, President John Adams promoted him to major general, during the 1798 preparations for war with France. In all these martial adventures, Pinckney answered to his personal sense of honor, expressed the outrage of his family at the Crown's replacement of Carolina worthies (like his father) by mere "placemen," and made use of the military training he had received at the royal military academy at Caen. Most important, he learned from his life as a soldier that South Carolina would not be secure on its own, in isolation, outside a union of the former colonies and a close cooperation among them. And he brought this lesson back to the politics of his state, even before he took off the uniform of the Continental Line.

After the Revolution, Pinckney was active in rebuilding the lower South, had a secure and almost permanent place in the South Carolina legislature, and developed a successful practice at law. Some years he made more than £5,000 in his profession. Most legislation and a state constitution passed under his shaping hand. In many respects his word was *the* authority in the low country—his, and that of the Rutledge brothers, to whom he was connected by marriage. After the establishment of the national government, Pinckney stayed at home in Carolina. From 1790 to 1796, he sat in the state senate, saw to his crops, and gave constant support to the Episcopal Church. He was a large and genial man, a social being and the acknowledged head of a large family of kin and connection. At his plantation, Belmont, he entertained the local aristocracy and important visitors to his region. But a few important parts of his adult life had to be played out a long way from Charleston, if Charleston was to be well served.

The political rule of thumb observed by Charles Cotesworth Pinckney in the Great Convention was stated succinctly in a letter to his old friend Gen. Andrew Pickens: "The great art of government is not to govern too much." Like his brother-in-law, Gov. Edward Rutledge, he was uneasy about the probable effects of political combinations with New England and its "leveling principles." At the beginning of the debates he announced his uncertainty about how much revision of the Articles could be attempted under the mandate most of the delegates had received from their states. He was consistent in maintaining that they could only "recommend" to the states, not conclude. But he developed a confidence in his colleagues as the days of deliberation ran into weeks and months. He was favorably impressed by the generous spirit of some of his northern counterparts—as he had been during the war. He accepted the three-fifths rule on representation of slaves, the twenty-year extension of the slave trade, the prohibition of taxes on exports, and the unanimous agreement of all present that the Constitution provided no authority to touch slavery in the states that chose to have it.

This government, he believed, would be limited enough to reflect what Americans, by way of the Revolution, had become. Too, it would protect the special interests of the South. For parts of this network of compromise he made the necessary motions himself. Indeed, he liked the Constitution so well when it reached its final form that during the Convention's last days he pledged publicly to fight for its approval in South Carolina. He kept that pledge, acting as a leading supporter of ratification during the debates in the legislature of his state and in the special convention of May 1788, called to pass judgment on the new organic law. It is possible that, without Charles Cotesworth Pinckney, no Constitution could have been agreed upon in Philadelphia or approved in the lower South.

General Pinckney was offered many posts of responsibility under the government he had helped to create—a seat on the Supreme Court and a variety of offices in Washington's cabinet. He refused these honors without hesitation. Only in the case of a special diplomatic posting as emissary to France in 1796 did Pinckney accept a nonmilitary assignment from the national government. Because the French did not perceive him to be a friend of their revolutionary movement, he was not recognized by the Directory as Minister James Monroe's successor; and, after threats, he was forced to flee to Holland. In 1797, President John Adams named him, with John Marshall and Elbridge Gerry, as a member of a mission to Paris, in the hope of reducing tensions between the two republics. The results of this embassy were not favorable. French demands for a loan and a bribe brought from Pinckney an outraged "No! No! Not a sixpence!" And brought him home a hero to enjoy his moment of national fame.

In the South, the Federalist party declined into insignificance after the election of 1800. Charles Cotesworth Pinckney was loyal to it, but he did not complain at the conduct of Jefferson and his Virginia successors, except perhaps for their foreign policy toward France. For Pinckney was never in agreement with the "commercial" Federalists and their energetic government, was opposed to the Alien and Sedition laws, and turned against the French Revolution after the Terror began and the Jacobins came to power. He did not care for the intemperance of Jeffersonian politics, and he hoped the United States would avoid the examples of ideological excess he had seen in France. Yet there is no Framer who kept further away from the extreme reaches of democratic thought. Indeed, during the South Carolina ratification debates, Pinckney had warned his fellow southerners against any clamor for a federal bill of rights because it might contain language about natural equality. On this subject he was never confused. He wanted the senators to serve without pay and congressmen to be elected by the various state legislatures. There is no evidence that he ever feared his slaves, yet neither was his conscience troubled by his possession of them.

Pinckney enjoyed his later years. He was, in 1805, elected president general of the Society of the Cincinnati. And to the end of his life he functioned as patriarchal leader of the bar and oracle in his city and state, trusted and admired. He embodied the best qualities of a special civilization and left to Carolina as his legacy the example of a prudent and ample spirit, a civility rare in any time and place. (See Marvin R. Zahniser, *Charles Cotesworth Pinckney, Founding Father* [Chapel Hill: University of North Carolina Press, 1967]; Frances Leigh Williams, *A Founding Family: The Pinckneys of South Carolina* [New York: Harcourt Brace Jovanovich, 1978]; Ernest M. Lander, Jr., "The South Carolinians at the

Philadelphia Convention, 1787," *South Carolina Historical Magazine* 57 [June 1956]: 134–155; George C. Rogers, Jr., "South Carolina Ratifies the Federal Constitution," *South Carolina Historical Association Proceedings* [1961]: 41–61, and *Charleston in the Age of the Pinckneys* [Norman: University of Oklahoma Press, 1969]; Charles Gregg Singer, *South Carolina in the Confederation* [Philadelphia: Porcupine Press, 1976]; James H. Broussard, *The Southern Federalists, 1800–1816* [Baton Rouge: Louisiana State University Press, 1978]; Lisle A. Rose, *Prologue to Democracy: The Federalists in the South, 1789–1800* [Lexington: University of Kentucky Press, 1968]; Hoyt P. Canady, *Gentlemen of the Bar: Lawyers in Colonial South Carolina* [New York: Garland, 1987]; Robert M. Weir, "South Carolinians and the Adoption of the United States Constitution," *South Carolina Historical Magazine* 89 [April 1988]: 73–89.)

# PIERCE BUTLER
July 11, 1744–February 15, 1822
Soldier, statesmen, and political leader

*An aristocrat, a "man of family," by either the English or the American definition. Wealthy, and of considerable influence in his adopted state. Yet, like so many Carolina and other southern public men who came after him, a gentleman with a genuine popular flair, with a considerable following among plain men "up the country." A minimal Federalist, and never a regular member of the party that came to bear that name. But, because of the South's military and economic experience during and after the Revolution, ready to support a strengthening of the general government even before he was elected to a seat in the Great Convention. Not, however, prepared to accept any proposal that might threaten the future integrity or the continued existence of the regime he had been chosen to represent in Philadelphia. Even though he "considered the interests" of the eastern and southern states "to be as different as the interests of Russia and Turkey," determined to serve both his region and the republic, if he could. Born in County Carlow, Ireland, the second son of Sir Richard Butler, fifth baronet Cloughgrenan, and Lady Henrietta Percy Butler, daughter of Sir Henry Percy of Seskin, County Wicklow. Descended on one side from the Duke of Ormonde. Father in Parliament 1729–1761. After the fashion of younger sons, sought his fortune in a military vocation. Following some training in the law, entered commissioned service in 1765 in His Majesty's Twenty-Ninth Regiment of Foot. Posted to Canada, where he rose to the rank of major. Resigned from the British service in 1773, after marrying Mary Middleton, an heiress and daughter of the late Col. Thomas Middleton, planter and commander of the South Carolina militia. Immediately identified with the ruling gentry of the low country. A supporter of South Carolina's struggle to resist British authority from the moment of his settling there.*

Pierce Butler was appointed adjutant general of his state in February of 1779, having been elected to a seat in the legislature in the previous year. Into the cause of the Revolution he poured money and goods as well as his personal security. His opinion in military matters was consulted with great respect. He was active in the 1780 defense of Charleston but, upon the fall of the city, fled the state with his family to avoid capture by British troops. After some time in North Carolina and in Philadelphia, Butler returned home to resume his political career and to restore his plantation in Prince William's Parish. He served in the legislature throughout the following years and took part in the leadership of the democratic forces from the western counties of the state. Financed by a large personal loan negotiated in Amsterdam, he recovered his fortune, pushed for reform in the pattern of representation in the South Carolina legislature, and supported relocation of the state capital to Columbia. Somewhat hypersensitive in dealings with men of his class, Butler was often at odds with important figures among the ruling gentry. Throughout his life he was a man of independent views. Yet, from planting and some trade, hard work, and shrewd speculation, he came to be worth more than one million dollars and to own many plantations and hundreds of slaves. In 1787, he was a logical choice for a place in the South Carolina delegation to the Confederation Congress and the Constitutional Convention.

In the Convention, Butler (always addressed as "the Major") spoke on at least fifty occasions. And the mode of his discourse was usually impressive—cautious, prudent, and full of the information provided by a cosmopolitan experience. Agreeing to a firmer connection to the northern states was difficult for this Carolina nabob. From his first coming to the New World as a soldier of King George III, Butler had acquired a distaste for New England manners and New England ideas. Nor did most of the middle colonies suit him any better. As early as 1782, he had concluded from observing sectional tensions in the Confederation Congress that the northern politicians meant to control the Union and to acquire influence and authority over the future development and internal life of the southern states. To this he would never agree, nor to granting any power, or prospect of power, over slavery in the states. From early in the Convention it was Butler who, against "innovations" and "running into an extreme," invoked the authority of Plutarch's Solon, "who gave the Athenians not the best Govt. he could devise; but the best they wd. receive." No root-and-branch "founding" would be allowed, only a building upon orders and institutions already in place and worthy of preservation.

Of the Framers, none was more suspicious of the dangers to liberty in an elaborate system of federal courts, empowered with authority over questions of constitutional interpretation, than was Pierce Butler, or more determined that the national legislature represent and protect property instead of some general notion of individual rights. Butler wanted members of Congress tied to the states by the manner of their election—in the various legislatures—and, particularly in the case of senators, by the source of their salaries. He spoke openly of the possibility of future revolts following "encroachments" upon the states; opposed giving Congress veto power over laws made in the states; and called for sharp, enumerated restrictions upon the scope and authority of the proposed Senate and House of Representatives. Philosophically, Butler held moderate views on the justification of slavery. Usually he defended the institution with only the argument from circumstance. But with his insistence that the South be made, by the Constitution, forever secure against any possibility of an outside attack upon the "peculiar institution," he was absolutely firm and definitive: "The security the Southn. States want is that their negroes may not be taken from them." Butler was also the author of the fugitive-slave clause in Article 4 of the Constitution and of a proposal that slaves be counted equally with freemen in the census.

In the Convention Pierce Butler showed apprehension that too energetic a government was being made: a government with too many judicial powers, too many legislative powers, and an executive branch that might spawn a "Cromwell or a Catiline." Yet for the sake of economic stability and national defense, he signed the document on which most of his associates were finally agreed. The nation was growing to the south and west. There was a balance of powers that recalled the English constitution. In South Carolina, when the legislature debated the proposed instrument of government, Butler advised his neighbors to approve it and hope for the best.

As one of South Carolina's original senators (1789–1796), Butler supported the enactment of Hamilton's financial plan, but he steadily retreated from his nationalism and spent most of his time in opposition to the government. In his view the Judiciary Act went too far, the Tariff Bill of 1789 was a threat to southern prosperity, and Jay's Treaty was an abomination. More and more he outraged Charleston Federalists. And, with Charles Pinckney III, he was instrumental in bringing about Jefferson's victory in the presidential contest for South Carolina's electors in 1800. As a Democratic-Republican Butler returned briefly to public life by replacing in the Senate, from 1803 to 1804, John E. Calhoun, who had died in office. But, like John Randolph of Roanoke and the strict Republicans of the *Tertium Quid* he found Jefferson in office too much like a Federalist in disguise. In disgust he eschewed further involvement in politics, confining his irritation with the government he now regretted having helped create to private correspondence with such friends as James Monroe. But while still in office, Butler had specified what he had intended in his original approval of the Constitution when he denounced John Marshall's decision in *Marbury* v. *Madison*:

> The right of the Court to give opinions on laws or Acts of the Legislative body extends no further than to explain the true Construction, intent and meaning of the Laws as they may affect the concerns

between Man and Man. . . . If Courts had authority to say what power shall be law, their power would be greater than the Sovereignty of the Country and no Legislature would be needed . . . an absurdity too great to be Admitted.

He also insisted that "the powers of the General Government are [in the Constitution] so defined as not to destroy the Sovereignty of the Individual States."

In his old age Butler presided in splendor at Hampton Point on St. Simon's Island and in his home in Philadelphia. For a time he was director of the Second Bank of the United States. And, even though it put his property in peril, he was a warm advocate of war with Great Britain in 1812. He died in Pennsylvania at the age of seventy-seven. (See Lewright B. Sikes, *The Public Life of Pierce Butler, South Carolina Statesman* [Washington, D.C.: University Press of America, 1979]; Sidney Ulmer, "The Role of Pierce Butler in the Constitutional Convention," *Review of Politics* 22 [July 1960]: 360–374; George C. Rogers, *Evolution of a Federalist: William Loughton Smith of Charleston, 1758–1812* [Columbia: University of South Carolina Press, 1962]; John H. Wolfe, *Jeffersonian Democracy in South Carolina* [Chapel Hill: University of North Carolina Press, 1940]; Raymond G. Starr, "The Conservative Revolution: South Carolina's Public Affairs: 1775–1790" [Ph.D. dissertation, University of Texas, 1964]; Ernest M. Lander, Jr., "The South Carolinians at the Philadelphia Convention, 1787," *South Carolina Historical Magazine* 57 [June 1956]: 134–155; Malcolm Bell, Jr., *Major Butler's Legacy: Five Generations of a Slaveholding Family* [Athens: University of Georgia Press, 1987]; James H. Hutson, "Pierce Butler's Records of the Federal Constitutional Convention," *Quarterly Journal of the Library of Congress* 37 [April 1980]: 64–73; Francis Coghlan, "Pierce Butler, 1744–1822: First Senator from South Carolina," *South Carolina Historical Magazine* 78 [April 1977]: 104–119; N. Louise Bailey and Elizabeth Ivey Cooper, eds., *Biographical Directory of the South Carolina House of Representatives*, vol. 3 [Columbia: University of South Carolina Press, 1981], pp. 108–114; articles by Robert W. Weir, M. E. Bradford, and Robert E. Shalhope in "South Carolina and the U.S. Constitution: The First of Two Special Issues," *South Carolina Historical Magazine* 89 [April 1988]: 73–113.)

# CHARLES PINCKNEY
October 26, 1757–October 29, 1824
Planter, lawyer, soldier, and statesman

*One of the youngest of the Framers, and the liveliest member of a sober tribe. Grandson of William Pinckney (1704–1766), commissary general of South Caro-*

*lina and one of three sons born to the founder of the dynasty, Thomas Pinckney of County Durham. Son of Charles Pinckney II (1731–1782), who was counted among the leading citizens of Carolina in the years preceding and immediately following independence, but who sought the king's protection after 1780. Charles Pinckney III, loyal to the Revolution and unforgiving of the apostasy of his father. Spent the remainder of his life being more visibly loyal to South Carolina, the nation, and the values of his class than anyone could rightfully expect him to be, in order to live down the shame of his father's public disgrace.*

In his time, Charles Pinckney III held most of the offices of trust in the gift of his society. Educated at home, and early in the public life, he was by turns a member of the South Carolina legislature, a governor of his state, representative to the Confederation Congress, U.S. senator and U.S. representative under the Constitution. He was mentioned as a potential president of the republic and served a term as its minister to Spain. Within a few years of the Philadelphia deliberations, he had, like most of the southerners originally involved in writing and ratifying a federal instrument, left the party of central authority and energetic government. In 1800, working against his distinguished second-cousins, Thomas and Charles Cotesworth Pinckney, he helped deliver South Carolina to Jefferson. Soon he was the acknowledged leader of the Democratic-Republicans in the lower South. In that role he became a favorite of the Carolina up-country and built a mansion just outside Columbia, which became a center of political activity. In his remaining years, his was a part that he enjoyed playing, in that he always sought the center of the stage and habitually saw his own function as heroic, even when partisan enthusiasm for his side of the political drama sometimes injured his reputation as a gentleman. To his Federalist contemporaries, he was "Blackguard Charlie," though their language was, on the whole, too severe.

From the time of his election to the Confederation Congress in 1784, Charles Pinckney III was an enthusiastic advocate of a stronger and more binding replacement for the Articles of Confederation. In 1787 he arrived in Philadelphia with a draft version of a new compact. Some of his proposals were embodied in the final version of the Constitution as adopted in 1788, but the draft itself died in committee. Pinckney's ideas for a government are somewhat difficult to reassemble from the arguments and votes that he contributed to the proceedings in Independence Hall. He supported both a federal veto over state legislation and a restriction upon the legislative powers of Congress to change state laws and institutions. He spoke of equality as a "leading feature of the United States" and of slavery as a positive good that required no moral apology. His draft of a bill of rights contained no philosophical preamble. He praised the constitution of Great Britain as the "best . . . in existence." And his proposals for a large property qualification for holders of high national office belied his occasional democratic posturings.

A wealthy man who ultimately owned hundreds of slaves, Pinckney was basically an aristocrat who was willing to trust his less fortunate neighbors so long as they did not seem to threaten the world he and they had fought to preserve. It was to secure the fruits of the Revolution that Pinckney sought a more democratic constitution for his state, opposed the Jay Treaty because it neglected the West, called for the opening of the Mississippi territory to slavery, and acted as a mild centralist in the Great Convention: a military Federalist who had been impressed by the incapacity, during the British conquest of the state, of South Carolina on its own and of the Continental Congress to offer it effectual support.

In February 1820, Pinckney made a definitive comment on his personal performance as Framer and short-term Federalist. The setting for these remarks was the debate over the admission of Missouri as a state. He specified in unmistakable terms that a government capable of doing more in the domestic sphere than raising taxes and maintaining a military establishment, a government empowered to reform the moral shortcomings of its component parts on the basis of abstract normative propositions or a general theory of human nature, was not what he had in mind. Argued Pinckney, had there been any "intention . . . to touch slavery, no Constitution would have been achieved." Hence, according to the compact, the right to own slaves ought to be "sacredly preserved." For, "if you say there shall be no slavery, may you not say there shall be no marriage?" Charles Pinckney III was a nationalist, but in a very limited sense. He died in November of 1824 while serving as spokesman for the aristocracy that he had so much offended as a young man. (See Frances Leigh Williams, *A Founding Family: The Pinckneys of South Carolina* [New York: Harcourt Brace Jovanovich, 1978]; Mark D. Kaplanoff, "Charles Pinckney and the American Republican Tradition," in *Intellectual Life in Antebellum Charleston,* ed. Michael O'Brien and David Moltke Hansen [Knoxville: University of Tennessee Press, 1986], pp. 85–122; Andrew J. Bethea, *The Contribution of Charles Pinckney to the Formation of the American Union* [Richmond, Va.: Garrett and Massie, 1937]; J. Harold Easterby, "Charles Pinckney," in *Dictionary of American Biography,* 20 vols. [New York: Charles Scribner's Sons, 1928–1936], 14: 611–614; N. Louise Bailey and Elizabeth Ivey Cooper, eds., *Biographical Directory of the South Carolina House of Representatives,* vol. 3 [Columbia: University of South Carolina Press, 1981], pp. 555–560; W. S. Elliott, "Founders of the American Union: Charles Pinckney of South Carolina," *DeBow's Review* 1 [April 1866]: 372–378; Charles C. Nott, *The Mystery of the Pinckney Draft* [New York: Century, 1908]; S. Sidney Ulmer, "The South Carolina Delegates to the Constitutional Convention of 1787: An Analytical Study" [Ph.D. dissertation, Duke University, 1966]; Ernest M. Lander, Jr., "The South Carolinians at the Philadelphia Convention, 1787," *South Carolina Historical Magazine* 57 [June 1956]: 134–155; M. E. Bradford, "Preserving the Birthright: The Intention of South Carolina in Adopting the U.S. Constitution," *South Carolina Historical Magazine* 89 [April 1988]: 90–101.)

# GEORGIA

# ABRAHAM BALDWIN
November 22, 1754–March 4, 1807
Lawyer, statesman, educator, and clergyman

*The archetypal southern Yankee. A great force for reconciliation between the sections in the Constitutional Convention. Instrumental in effecting the compromises on slavery and on equality of representation in the Senate that made possible a final agreement among most of the delegates present. A moderate Federalist, brought by the experience of the Revolution and the situation of Georgia after its conclusion to recognize the need for a stronger central government. But after 1789 never a Federalist, per se, of any of the recognized varieties. Son of Michael and Lucy Dudley Baldwin. Born in North Guilford, Connecticut. Father a blacksmith who moved to New Haven in order to improve the opportunities of his children. Graduated from Yale College in 1772. After further study, licensed to preach by the established church in 1775. For four years tutor on the faculty of his alma mater. Renowned for his piety, learning, and skill with students. Resigned in June of 1779 to devote himself to his duties as a chaplain in the American army. Called to the professorship of divinity at Yale in 1781 upon the death of Napthali Daggett, but declined. After his military service was at an end, entered the study of law. Made a member of the Connecticut bar in April of 1783.*

Abraham Baldwin did not make his career in his home state. Instead, he joined a large company of New England's ambitious young men who, after independence was achieved, sought their fortunes in the developing regions of the South, particularly in Georgia, where they rose to positions of great importance. In January of 1784, the general assembly of Georgia granted Baldwin's petition to practice in its courts. In the next year he was granted lands in Wilkes County and elected to represent it in the House of Assembly. From that point he climbed quickly. Because of his energy, prudence, and application, he was called upon to perform tasks not of interest to less literate men. Baldwin was sent to represent Georgia in the Confederation Congress from 1785 to 1789. Meanwhile, on the local scene he played a great part in the planning and foundation of a university for his adopted state. Baldwin drew up a bill that provided for the entire educational system of Georgia. He arranged for its funding, and in particular for that of a college. He was one of the original trustees of Franklin College and was responsible for its being modeled after Yale, though with less emphasis on theology. For a time Baldwin was titular president of the college, which became the University of Georgia. He served on its board until his death.

But despite his continued interest in the educational example of Yale and his service to members of his family back in Connecticut, once a Georgian, Abraham Baldwin was a complete convert to the southern view of most social and political questions and a dependable spokesman for southern attitudes and interests in offices he held. In Philadelphia, the most important of his eight speeches before the Great Convention concerned slavery. In it he described the right to own and acquire slaves as one of Georgia's "favorite prerogatives." He insisted that the question was of a local nature, mocked the theory of human equality by making reference to Hindu superstition, and concluded that the government could be strengthened with the authority of the states in their own spheres left intact. In that expectation he made common cause with the men of his birthplace, the members of the Connecticut delegation. Indeed, he actually sat with Connecticut during much of the Convention and reported on the proceedings to his friend, President Ezra Stiles of Yale. The view of the place of slavery in the republic entertained by Sherman, Ellsworth, and Johnson was moderated by the Puritan from Georgia, and they convinced him of the importance to the small states that they retain their equality with the other commonwealths in the Senate. Originally Baldwin had favored a division of the Senate based on property, but his northern friends persuaded him to change his vote. The result of this anomalous association of delegations was union.

After the Great Convention, Baldwin returned to the Congress. Once the Constitution had been ratified, he was elected by middle Georgia to sit ten years in the House of Representatives and thereafter to serve eight more as one of Georgia's U.S. senators. For a time in the Seventh Congress (1801–1802), he was president pro tem of the upper house. His life as a southerner was spent almost entirely in public duties. He was never a wealthy man; indeed, he scorned the schemes that made rich men of many a Federalist officeholder. He opposed the assumption of state debts, Jay's Treaty, and the Alien and Sedition Acts. He fought to repeal the Judiciary Act of 1801 and voted to convict Justice Chase on three of the articles of impeachment. With regularity he assailed attempts to present to Congress petitions against slavery and the slave trade. He disliked the tariff, disliked big spending, and backed the candidacy of Thomas Jefferson, since he felt the Virginian would as president support a restricted conception of the federal power. In his last years, Baldwin (with his colleague from Georgia,

Gen. James Jackson) became one of the South's most trusted figures—wise, moderate, accommodating, but firm. In 1802, it was he who, as the leader of a commission, resolved to general satisfaction the dispute over Georgia's western lands. It was he who avoided war along the southern frontier, and he who cried out, even in the last years of his life, the theme of his long stewardship—caution and restraint: "Hold the wagon back." (See Henry C. White, *Abraham Baldwin, One of the Founders of the Republic and Father of the University of Georgia* [Athens, Ga.: McGregor Press, 1926]; Charles C. Jones, Jr., *Biographical Sketches of the Delegates from Georgia to the Continental Congress* [Boston: Houghton Mifflin, 1891]; Franklin Bowditch Dexter, *Biographical Sketches of Graduates of Yale College, with Annals of the College History,* vol. 3 [New York: Henry Holt, 1903], pp. 432–434; Albert B. Saye, *New Viewpoints in Georgia History* [Athens: University of Georgia Press, 1943]; Kenneth Coleman, *The American Revolution in Georgia, 1763–1789* [Athens: University of Georgia Press, 1958], pp. 267–282; Franklin Bowditch Dexter, ed., *The Literary Diary of Ezra Stiles,* vol. 3 [New York: Charles Scribner's Sons, 1901], pp. 293–295; E. Merton Coulter, *Abraham Baldwin: Patriot, Educator, and Founding Father* [Arlington, Va.: Vandamere Press, 1987].)

# WILLIAM FEW

June 8, 1748–July 16, 1828
Soldier, farmer, lawyer, banker, and political leader of
Georgia during and after the American Revolution

*A genuine frontiersman. An exceedingly mild Federalist who supported the Constitution because Georgia, as an undeveloped state on the southern boundary of the nation, required external protection. A silent presence at the Great Convention, though frequent in his attendance and instrumental as a member of the Confederation Congress in the transmission of the Constitution for examination in the several states. Son of William and Mary Wheeler Few. Devout Methodist. Born in Maryland near Baltimore but raised, after his father's failure as a tobacco planter, in the North Carolina backcountry near Hillsborough. Only two years of formal schooling, but much practical training in clearing land and farming on his own or with his father's "servants." Both father and uncle involved in the Regulator movement, protesting abuse by the colonial government, which in 1771 resulted in the Battle of Alamance. James Few, his uncle, hanged as "outlaw" by Gov. William Tryon, family farm destroyed, and father forced to flee in order to avoid prosecution. William was left behind to complete his father's business, settle suits, sell land, and move, in 1776, to a home near Wrightsboro, Georgia.*

William Few rose rapidly to a position of leadership in the upper counties of Georgia as the movement toward American independence spread into that state. As a young man in North Carolina, he had read voraciously from whatever books he could find and had developed a particular interest in law and politics. Not only did he handle the complicated business affairs of his family, he also attended sessions of the court when he could. Once in Georgia, he won admittance to the bar and set up practice in Augusta. A vigorous patriot, a frontier Whig in the Regulator tradition, he was chosen lieutenant colonel of the local militia regiment of dragoons and, along with his brother Benjamin, served with distinction against British troops, Tories, and Indians loyal to the Crown during the years when most of Georgia was under English control. Few was elected to the Georgia provincial congress in 1776. During the Revolution, he served in the assembly in 1777 and 1779 and was at those times a member of the state executive council. Later, Few represented his state in the Congress (1780–1785) and at the same time continued to hold posts of importance at home, as Indian commissioner, surveyor general, and member of the legislature (1782–1784, 1786). By this time he had become a recognized spokesman of the Georgia frontier.

Few's votes in the Constitutional Convention reflected Georgia's interest in slavery, in debt retirement, and in the national defense. He missed five or six weeks of the debates because discussion of Indian depredations drew him to the Confederation Congress; but while present in Philadelphia, he generally supported the views of his associates in the Georgia delegation, and he was a signatory to the finished document. After returning home from the Philadelphia Convention and the Congress in New York, Few served in the Georgia ratifying convention, in the state's constitutional convention, and, once the federal Constitution was adopted, was sent by his state as one of its original U.S. senators (1789–1793). At the end of his abbreviated term in the Senate, he resumed his life in Georgia, got involved in the dispute over the Yazoo fraud (against the speculators), sat again in the state legislature, and in 1796 was appointed judge for the second judicial district of Georgia. Surprisingly, he resigned this post in 1799 and removed to New York, where he found the climate to be more salubrious and where he had made friends while representing Georgia under the Articles and as senator. Inverting the life pattern of his friend Abraham Baldwin, Few prospered in the North, where he served four terms in the New York Assembly (1802–1805), became state inspector of prisons (1802–1810), alderman of New York City (1813–1814), and U.S. commissioner of loans (1804–1816). From 1804 to 1814, he was director of the Bank of the Manhattan Company. He ended his career in the presidency of the City Bank (1814–1816). He died a wealthy man.

In his later years, Few retired from politics because of his distaste for the Federalist atmosphere of public life in his adopted state. He had lost his connection with that party not long after the approval of the Constitution and was indeed never an advocate of "energetic government"—as the high Federalists understood that doctrine. Few was a classic illustration of the self-made man, the American success story, though he brought a little of frontier Carolina with him as he rose to the summit. (See William W. Abbott, "The Structure of Politics in Georgia: 1782–1789," *William and Mary Quarterly* 14 [January 1957]: 47–65; Charles C. Jones, Jr., *Biographical Sketches of the Delegates from Georgia to the Continental Congress* [Boston: Houghton Mifflin, 1891], pp. 34–39; "Autobiography of Colonel William Few of Georgia," *Magazine of American History* 7 [November 1881]: 343–358; Albert B. Saye, *New Viewpoints in Georgia History* [Athens: University of Georgia Press, 1943]; Robert G. Ferris, ed., *Signers of the Constitution* [Washington, D.C.: National Park Service, 1976], pp. 161–162; Kenneth Coleman, *The American Revolution in Georgia, 1763–1789* [Athens: University of Georgia Press, 1958]; Margaret C. S. Christman, *The First Federal Congress, 1789-1791* [Washington, D.C.: Smithsonian, 1989], pp. 256–258; Judson A. Dewar, "William Few and Georgia: A Biographical Perspective on the State's History" [M.A. thesis, Georgia State College, 1968].)

# WILLIAM LEIGH PIERCE
1740–December 10, 1789
Soldier, merchant, and political figure in Georgia in
the years immediately following the Revolution

*Remembered today for his incisive literary sketches of colleagues in the Great Convention. One of the "military Federalists," convinced by the experiences of war (and by the complicated vulnerabilities of his adopted state) of the need for a stronger central government, one capable of defending the nation's frontiers. Identity of parents and place of birth unknown. Probably born in Virginia. Obviously well educated. Served throughout the Revolution as an officer in the Continental army. Aide-de-camp to Gen. John Sullivan and then to Gen. Nathanael Greene. Received the thanks of Congress and a sword for his valor under fire at the Battle of Eutaw Springs, September 8, 1781. Left service as a brevet major, and in 1783 went into trade in Savannah, becoming eventually the head of the house of William Pierce and Company. Married into a distinguished South Carolina family. Elected member of the Georgia House of Assembly in 1786. Chosen by that body as a delegate to the Confederation Congress for 1786– 1787. One of six Georgians appointed as representatives of their state in the Constitutional Convention, and one of four who actually attended.*

William Pierce was a bit late in his arrival in Philadelphia, and he left the Convention sometime in July to join William Few in the Confederation Congress, where they appealed for aid in dealing with the frontier and Indian problems of Georgia. But he was present in the company of the Framers long enough to give us an assessment of it by way of his prose-portraits, the best source concerning its members at that moment in their lives. During the deliberations of the Convention, Pierce spoke four times. Members of the lower house of the proposed Congress, he argued, should be elected by the people, and those of the upper house by the states. With this distinction he hoped to see the wealth and property in society protected from democratic excess and the people secured against abuses of authority. He wished to see the states surrender some, but not all, of their authority. He also advocated a three-year term for the proposed Senate.

In September of 1787, William Pierce and William Few cast the vote of Georgia in the Confederation Congress to convey the new Constitution to the states for ratification. It was Pierce who carried a copy of the instrument back to Savannah in the following week and arranged for its publication there. His support was influential in securing its approval in Georgia. Yet his life turned swiftly. While in Philadelphia, he could congratulate himself and write with pleasure, "I possess ambition, . . . and the flattering opinion . . . of my Friends." But he did not long survive the conclusion of his brief service on the great stage of national politics—in what he called "the wisest Council in the world." In 1789, he was honored by his comrades-in-arms by his election as vice-president of the Society of the Cincinnati in Georgia. But his business failed, and his health was frail. At his untimely death he left among his effects a manuscript since described as "Pierce's Reliques," including certain notes on the Convention and his famous sketches, which were first published almost forty years after their composition. (See Kenneth Coleman, *The American Revolution in Georgia, 1763–1789* [Athens: University of Georgia Press, 1958]; Charles C. Jones, Jr., *Biographical Sketches of the Delegates from Georgia to the Continental Congress* [Boston: Houghton Mifflin, 1891], pp. 155–159; Albert B. Saye, "Georgia Delegates to the Federal Convention of 1787: Who They Were and What They Did" [M.A. thesis, University of Georgia, 1935], and his *New Viewpoints in Georgia History* [Athens: University of Georgia Press, 1943].)

# WILLIAM HOUSTOUN

March 1757–1812
Lawyer, planter, and political representative of the aristocracy of Georgia

*A "nabob," and one of the great planters in the Convention. Rightly described by his colleague from Savannah, William Pierce, as "a gentleman of family."*

*Wealthy, at least in landed property, thanks to estates purchased in his name by the family and for the family of Houstoun from among properties amerced or confiscated in Georgia from Houstouns who had been loyal to George III. In Philadelphia, though not outspoken, a confident figure. Yet, since 1787, almost lost from the record of history. Youngest of the five sons of Sir Patrick Houstoun, fifth baronet Houstoun of Renfrewshire, Scotland (1698–February 5, 1762), who had immigrated to General Oglethorpe's fledgling colony as a young man, and Lady Priscilla Dunbar Houstoun (October 31, 1711–February 26, 1775). Born at Rose Dhu, his father's plantation on the Ogeechee River. Educated at home, in local schools, and, between 1776 and 1781, at the Inns of Court. Attentive to his connections in Great Britain, and no warm advocate of the Revolution. Yet, upon his return to America, not tainted by the stigma of loyalism. Therefore able to keep in the family the large holdings of his Tory brothers, Sir Patrick Houstoun (1742–1785), the sixth baronet, and Sir George Houstoun (October 19, 1744–June 9, 1795), the seventh baronet.*

William Houstoun was admitted to the bar by act of the Georgia General Assembly on August 3, 1782. He was elected in that year to represent Chatham County in the Georgia legislature. Soon after his first appearance in the House of Assembly (1783), he was chosen by it to be a delegate from his state to the Confederation Congress. Because of a delay in receiving his credentials, he did not serve that year at the national level. But he was reelected in 1784 and soon thereafter journeyed north to join William Gibbons in representing his state. Houstoun continued in this appointment until 1786 and acquired while in the Congress a reputation for capability and a fiery disposition.

The William Houstoun who sat from May 31 to July 26 of 1787 in the Great Convention is summarized in his letters home in which he refers to Georgia as "my country"; in his unreasoning fear that the other states might—in impatience with its failure to cooperate—decide to expel or abolish his own; and in an earlier episode, reported by a contemporary, when Houstoun appeared in Congress wearing his sword after a delegate from Rhode Island, James Manning, had, in Houstoun's opinion, "reflected upon" the southern states. For, in the words of a witness to this event, Houstoun was "quick to avenge any insinuation" against Georgia or the region to which it belonged. Yet Houstoun's reputation in the Congress was generally good. He was a member of the "Grand Committee," which first considered useful changes in the Articles of Confederation and, despite his sectional loyalties, always the advocate of a stronger government. Like most of the major figures in Georgia, he saw in the Constitution a security for the integrity and future development of his state, the exposed southern frontier of the nation. In Philadelphia, Houstoun voted the Federalist line on most issues, with the exception of the slave trade and other sectional questions. Indeed, he recommended a strong federal supervision over the drafting of state constitutions, lest there be disorders or disputes concerning the legitimate source of authority such as had plagued Georgia during the Revolution. During the Philadelphia sessions he spoke seven times but apparently left when William Few returned from the Congress in New York.

In 1788, he married the daughter of Nicholas Bayard III. In his remaining years, Houstoun was as much connected with the state of New York as with his birthplace. In 1790, he was admitted to practice before the Supreme Court. From time to time he returned to Georgia, but most of his obscure, very private life found him in the city of New York, where he died at the age of fifty-five. (See Edith Duncan Johnston, *The Houstouns of Georgia* [Athens: University of Georgia Press, 1950], pp. 317–342; Charles C. Jones, Jr., *Biographical Sketches of Delegates from Georgia to the Continental Congress* [Boston: Houghton Mifflin, 1891], pp. 118–119; Forrest McDonald, *We the People: The Economic Origins of the Constitution* [Chicago: University of Chicago Press, 1958], pp. 85–86; Albert B. Saye, "Georgia Delegates to the Federal Convention of 1787: Who They Were and What They Did" [M.A. thesis, University of Georgia, 1935]; W. Berrien Burroughs, "William Houstoun," in *Men of Mark in Georgia*, vol. 1, ed. William J. Northern [Atlanta: A. B. Caldwell, 1907], pp. 173–174.)

# INDEX

The names of the framers are omitted from this index because they are easily accessible in other ways; what is indexed are the events, ideas, institutions, people, and places of which these men were a part.